Use Case Modeling

The Addison-Wesley Object Technology Series

Grady Booch, Ivar Jacobson, and James Rumbaugh, Series Editors

For more information, check out the series web site at www.awprofessional.com/otseries.

The Component Software Series

Clemens Szyperski, Series Editor

For more information, check out the series web site at www.awprofessional.com/csseries.

Use Case Modeling

Kurt Bittner

Ian Spence

ADDISON–WESLEY

Boston • San Francisco • New York • Toronto • Montreal
London • Munich • Paris • Madrid
Capetown • Sydney • Tokyo • Singapore • Mexico City

The publisher offers discounts on this book when ordered in quantity for bulk purchases and special sales. For more information, please contact:

U.S. Corporate and Government Sales
(800) 382-3419
corpsales@pearsontechgroup.com

For sales outside of the U.S., please contact:

International Sales
(317) 581-3793
international@pearsontechgroup.com

Visit Addison-Wesley on the Web: informit.com/aw

Library of Congress Cataloging-in-Publication Data

Bittner, Kurt.
  Use case modeling / Kurt Bittner, Ian Spence.
    p. cm.
  Includes bibliographical references and index.
  ISBN 0-201-70913-9 (pbk. : alk. paper)
    1. System design. 2. Use cases (Systems engineering) I. Spence, Ian, 1961- II. Title.

QA76.9.S88 .B575 2003
004.2′1—dc21   2002074790

ISBN 0201709139

This product is printed digitally on demand.

Contents

Chapter 4   87

Finding Actors and Use Cases

Chapter 5   119

Getting Started with a Use-Case Modeling Workshop

Chapter 10   251

Here There Be Dragons

Chapter 11   277

Reviewing Use Cases

Foreword

Use cases have come a long way since I first proposed them in 1986. Their value and power were clearly revealed by Object-Oriented programming. Use cases both contributed to and benefited from the development of the Object-Oriented paradigm. Today, knowledge of use cases is critical to one's understanding and application of UML and other modern software processes, such as the Rational Unified Process (RUP).

When used effectively, use cases have proven particularly valuable as part of the requirements activities of the software process. They have vastly improved communication between development teams and stakeholders and have made the determination of requirements far easier and more precise.

Use cases are unique in their ability to help teams understand the value the system must provide for its stakeholders. Because use cases describe how users use the system and what the system does for those users, they provide a unique way to build consensus about what the system must do. Building consensus is essential to a project's success: If the stakeholders cannot agree on the value the system must deliver, it is unlikely that the project can be successful.

Because use cases help create this understanding, they naturally provide an excellent principle around which to structure project activities. Use cases play an important role for analysts, who work with the requirements of the system; developers, who apply use cases to design and develop the system; testers, who verify that the system delivers the value demanded by the stakeholders; technical writers, who document how the system is used; and user-experience professionals, who help to make the system easy to use. All these project team members must understand use cases in order to develop better solutions.

To date, there has been something missing from the literature of use-case modeling: a description of the practical, day-to-day details of identifying and describing use cases. This book provides those details, defining the use-case model and fleshing out use-case descriptions. It's a perfect extension and complement to my earlier works, finishing the story of how the use cases are identified and how they evolve.

Use Case Modeling builds on the basic concepts by leveraging the practical experience that Kurt and Ian have gained through their many years of work in various industries—working with development teams either as consultants or as team members themselves. They have nicely distilled that experience into this very practical and insightful work. For people new to the field, this book provides an excellent tutorial. For use-case veterans, it provides an excellent reference that can be called upon on a daily basis.

This is the very best book on use cases ever written. Read it to understand use-case ideas and to apply those ideas with common sense based on the kind of system you are building and the maturity of your team members.

—*Ivar Jacobson*
July 2002

Why Bother with Use Cases?

WHAT ARE "USE CASES" ALL ABOUT?

In a world where it seems we already have too much to do, and too many things to think about, it seems the last thing we need is something new that we have to learn. As Eric Sevareid observed, the chief cause of problems is solutions.

But use cases do solve a problem with requirements: with strict declarative requirements it's hard to describe steps and sequences of events. To see why, let's consider a simple example:

Example

Some requirements that must be satisfied by an automated teller system:

1. The system shall allow customers to withdraw cash from their accounts.

2. The system shall ensure that the customer's account is never overdrawn.

3. If the customer attempts to overdraw the account, the system will allow the account to be overdrawn, up to a specified amount, for a transaction fee.

4. If the customer is using an automated teller machine (ATM) that is owned by a financial institution other than the one to which the account belongs, an additional fee will be charged to the account.

Simple enough, you say. Or is it?

In what order should these things be done? Does it matter? If the ATM is not one that is owned by the customer's financial institution, should the ATM usage fee be charged before or after checking for overdraft? If the customer's account balance is less than the ATM usage fee, charging the ATM usage fee before checking for overdraft will automatically result in an overdraft charge being applied, even if the customer decides to cancel the transaction. Is this the right behavior? With only declarative requirements, which is all that many projects have, it's impossible to say.

Use cases, stated simply, allow description of sequences of events that, taken together, lead to a system doing something useful. As simple as this sounds, this is important. When confronted only with a *pile of requirements*, it's often impossible to make sense of what the authors of the requirements really wanted the system to do. In the preceding example, use cases reduce the ambiguity of the requirements by specifying exactly when and under what conditions certain behavior occurs; as such, the sequence of the behaviors can be regarded as a requirement. Use cases are particularly well suited to capturing these kind of requirements. Although this may sound simple, the fact is that conventional requirement capture approaches, with their emphasis on declarative requirements and "shall" statements, completely fail to capture the dynamics of the system's behavior. Use cases are a simple yet powerful way to express the behavior of the system in way that all stakeholders can easily understand.

But, like anything, use cases come with their own problems, and as useful as they are, they can be misapplied. The result is something that is as bad, if not worse, than the original problem. Therein lies the central theme of this book—how to utilize use cases effectively without creating a greater problem than the one you started with.

WHO SHOULD BE INTERESTED IN USE CASES?

The short answer to this question is "just about everyone," or at least everyone involved in some aspect of delivering a system that satisfies the needs of the customer. To be more specific about who should be interested in use cases, the following roles can benefit from the use-case technique of describing system behavior:

- **Customers**, who need to be sure that the system that is getting built is the one that they want
- **Managers**, who need to have an overall understanding of what the system will do in order to effectively plan and monitor the project
- **Analysts**, who need to describe and document what the system is going to do
- **Developers**, who need to understand what the system needs to do in order to develop it

- **Testers**, who need to know what the system is supposed to do so that they can verify that it does it
- **Technical writers**, who need to know what the system is supposed to so that they can describe it
- **User-experience designers**, who need to understand the users' goals and how they will use the system to achieve these goals.
- And anyone else who wants to better understand what needs to be built *before* it is actually constructed

HOW TO READ THIS BOOK

This book is fundamentally about creating use-case models and, more importantly, about writing detailed descriptions of use cases. To remain focused on this task, we have intentionally left out the parts of the project life cycle that use the use cases but are not directly involved in writing them. These areas include user-interface design, analysis, design, technical writing, testing, and project management. Other authors have covered a number of these areas adequately, and we felt that you, the reader, were best served if we focused narrowly on the use cases themselves. We hope you will agree.

This book is intended to be a ready reference for the practitioner, the person who is actually doing the work and grappling with the unique problems of working with use cases. It can certainly be read cover to cover, but the real intent behind the book is to provide you with something that can continue to add value after the first reading, providing you with a "mentor" at your fingertips. The topics presented in the book have arisen from working with countless project teams who grappled with the same issues facing you.

The book is divided into two parts. In Part I, Getting Started with Use-Case Modeling, we introduce the basics concepts of use-case modeling that you will need to understand in order to be effective using use cases. We conclude Part I with a description of an excellent way to get started with use cases: with a workshop.

- The first chapter, A Brief Introduction to Use-Case Modeling, provides practical background for people who are unfamiliar with use cases, or for people who have read other books and articles and still find themselves wrestling with the basic ideas. The purpose of the chapter is to provide a brief overview of the use-case approach without getting into a lot of formal details.
- The second chapter, Fundamentals of Use-Case Modeling, presents the foundations underlying the use-case modeling technique. The concepts presented here will provide the basis for the subsequent chapters in the book.

- The third chapter, Establishing the Vision, provides the essential tools for determining the business problem to be solved, for identifying the stakeholders in the solution, and for deciding what the system should do for those stakeholders to solve the business problem. This information is essential if we are to define the right solution when we develop our use-case model.

- The fourth chapter, Finding Actors and Use Cases, describes the process and subtleties of identifying the key elements of the use-case model. The purpose of this content is to help you through the sometimes-confusing task of getting started by providing a sound understanding of the basic concepts of actors and use cases.

- The fifth chapter, Getting Started with a Use-Case Modeling Workshop, describes the practicalities of getting started using use cases, including how to run a use-case workshop and how to deal with the practical details of starting to work with use cases.

In Part II, Writing and Reviewing Use-Case Descriptions, we explore the finer details of working with use cases, including the anatomy of a use case, how to write use-case descriptions (instead of the simple but incomplete descriptions presented in Part I), and what it means to work with use cases in practice. In these chapters, we explore in-depth how to write detailed use-case descriptions.

- The sixth chapter, The Life Cycle of a Use Case, describes the transitions that a use case undergoes as it evolves from concept to complete description. This chapter establishes context for the remaining chapters and places the content of Part I into a larger context.

- The seventh chapter, The Structure and Contents of a Use Case, describes the various constituent parts of a use case—the basic flow, preconditions, postconditions, and the alternate flows, as well as related topics.

- The eighth chapter, Writing Use-Case Descriptions: An Overview, describes the objectives and challenges related to writing detailed descriptions of use cases and presents strategies for successfully mastering this challenging task.

- The ninth chapter, Writing Use-Case Descriptions: Revisited, discusses the mechanics of how to go about writing use-case descriptions, how to handle details, and how to structure the descriptions for readability. This is done using an evolving example in which a variety of techniques are progressively and systematically applied to improve the quality of the use-case description.

- The tenth chapter, Here There Be Dragons, describes the problems that most teams encounter when using relationships between use cases (specifically the *include, extend,* and *generalization* relationships) and relationships between actors.
- The eleventh chapter, Reviewing Use Cases, describes how to organize and conduct reviews of the use-case model, including a summary of areas where particular focus is needed.

The final chapter, Chapter 12, Wrapping Up, touches on a number of topics related to how use cases are used in the larger context of the project, bringing our journey into the world of use cases to a close. In doing so, we provide the reader with a number of references to sources to consult for further information about how use cases are used in other disciplines.

ACKNOWLEDGMENTS

We have had the pleasure over the years to work with many colleagues and customers who have helped shape the views that are presented here. A full enumeration of all of these people would be impossible, but we find ourselves especially indebted to a number of our colleagues for contributing to our views on use cases. We are in great debt to Ivar Jacobson, who originated the concepts of use-case modeling and initially defined their role in the modern software development process, for his support and encouragement on this project. We are also indebted to our colleague Dean Leffingwell for his work defining the role of use cases and traditional requirements-management approaches. We would also like to thank Bryon Baker, Chris Littlejohns, Anthony Kesterton, Gary Evans, Laurent Mondamert, Peter Eeles, Brian Kerr, and Susan August for their insightful suggestions at various points in the long evolution of this book. Special thanks go to Douglas Bush and Ida Audeh for their assistance in helping us to write clearly and concisely. We would also like to thank the many technical consultants at Rational whose experiences and questions have helped to shape this book. Finally, we would like to thank the customers with whom we and these consultants have worked, since their experiences and questions have ultimately made us realize that this book has been sorely needed. To all these people goes a great share of the credit for this book; any flaws or shortcomings are exclusively our own.

Kurt Bittner and Ian Spence
April, 2002

PART I

GETTING STARTED WITH USE-CASE MODELING

As we discussed in the Introduction, use cases are a simple and powerful way to express the functional requirements, or behaviors, of a system. The following chapters describe the basic concepts behind use cases, their basic structure and format, and their contents. We conclude with a description of an excellent way to get started with use-case modeling: with a workshop.

The intent of these chapters is to gradually introduce you to the basic concepts by successively revealing more detail—much in the way that one peels an onion. The earlier chapters provide basic but important information upon which the later chapters build. As a result, nearly everyone who works with use cases in even a casual way will find the first few chapters useful, while those who write use cases will want to read Chapters 1–5 in their entirety.

The goal of Part I is to allow you to identify actors and use cases, give them brief descriptions, and to start outlining and describing the use cases. Part II provides more information on how to deal with the practicalities of writing use-case descriptions, structuring the use-case model, managing details in the use-case descriptions, and handling the daily complexities of working with use cases.

So without further preamble, let's get started.

Chapter 1

A Brief Introduction to Use-Case Modeling

The purpose of this chapter is to introduce use-case modeling and why you would want to use it. It provides a concise overview of the basic concepts employed in use-case modeling, describes how these concepts are related to more traditional requirements-capture techniques, and describes why use cases provide a superior way to capture and understand the behavior of a system. The intent is to provide people who may be unfamiliar with use-case modeling with a brief overview of the use-case approach without getting too embroiled in lots of detail. We will return to these concepts for a more in-depth look in Chapter 2, Fundamentals of Use-Case Modeling.

ACTORS AND USE CASES

The basic idea behind use-case modeling is quite simple: To get to the heart of what a system must do, you must first focus on who (or what) will use it, or be used by it. After you do this, look at what the system must do for those users in order to do something useful.

The use-case model includes the following components:

Actors represent the people or things that interact in some way with the system; by definition, they are outside the system. We focus on the actors to ensure that the system does something useful. Actors have a name and a short description, and they are associated with the use cases with which they interact.

Use cases represent the things of value that the system performs for its actors. Use cases are not functions or features, and they cannot be decomposed. Use cases have a name and a brief description. They also have detailed descriptions that are essentially stories about how the actors use the system to do something they consider important, and what the system does to satisfy these needs.

The set of all actors and use cases describing a system are known as the system's **use-case model**. And that's basically it. Well, not completely—otherwise there would not be much to fill a book. The subtleties of working with use cases come from writing the use-case descriptions.

USE-CASE DIAGRAMS

The actors and use cases can be depicted on use-case diagrams. Actors are represented by stick people and use cases by ellipses. Arrows (representing relationships) connect the actors and the use cases that interact. The arrowheads help to indicate the initiator of the interaction. Figure 1-1 shows some of the actors and use cases for a very simple telephone system. The purpose of the diagram is to summarize what the system will do. The diagram does not

Figure 1-1   A simple telephone system

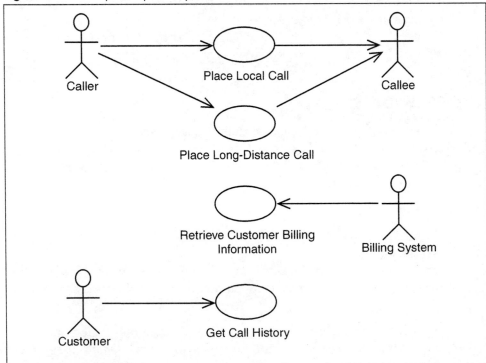

really describe the system—mistaking the use-case diagram for a complete use-case model is a common error many teams make. The diagram provides a summary, but the bulk of the description is held, as text, in documents associated with the use cases. These use-case descriptions provide the full story of what happens in the use case. So for every use case in the use-case model, there will be a document describing how the actors and the system collaborate to fulfill the goal represented by the use case. In this book, when we refer to a use case, we mean the totality of the use case, including its iconic representation, its relationships, and, most importantly, its detailed description.

And that's about it. Use cases help us focus on what is essential and ultimately create a system that does something useful. The description of what the system does is principally captured as text; the use-case diagram serves as an overview or a summary of the system's behavior.

THE RELATIONSHIP BETWEEN USE CASES AND REQUIREMENTS

Use cases are primarily a way to express a system's requirements, principally its behavioral ones. To understand what this means, we need to look at the broader context of requirements management. The purpose of requirements management is to establish and maintain agreement with the customers and other stakeholders on what the system should do. Often this agreement is recorded as some sort of requirements specification.

Types of Requirements

A requirement[1] describes a condition or capability to which a system must conform; it is either derived directly from stakeholder or user needs or stated in a contract, standard, specification, or other formally imposed document. Sometimes it is useful to express different kinds of requirements:

- **Needs:** Things that the stakeholders believe that the system needs to do; problems that they need to have solved. Needs, while important to understand, are so informal that we need other ways to express the requirements of the system.
- **Features:** Informal statements of capabilities of the system used often for marketing and product-positioning purposes, as a shorthand for a

---

[1] The Unified Modeling Language (UML), a standard for software descriptions provided by the Object Management Group (OMG—see www.omg.org/uml), describes a requirement as "a desired feature, property, or behavior of a system."

set of behaviors of the system. Although useful when discussing the system in casual settings, features are not very useful for defining the behavior of the system in precise enough terms to design, develop, or test the system.

The problem with features is that they are "all over the map"; they have no precise definition and/or consistent level of abstraction. They are useful, however, as a kind of shorthand for something that the system must do. The feature list for a particular release of one of our products included

- Discussion Groups, which allowed team members to discuss requirements and collaborate on their definition
- Multiselect Lists, which allowed users to select multiple values for the value of a requirements attribute

The main thing to note about this is that these two features are at wholly different levels of abstraction. The key thing about a feature is that it highlights some area of the functionality of the system that is important to the users of the system *at the moment*. The features for the next release of the system (the things we wanted to highlight) were completely different.

Since features cannot be used to define precisely the capabilities of a system, we need something else to capture the required capabilities of the system. This leads us to

- **Software Requirements:** Individual statements of conditions and capabilities to which the system must conform.

Each software requirement is the specification of an externally observable behavior of the system; for example, inputs to the system, outputs from the system, the functions of the system (the mapping of inputs to outputs and their various combinations), the attributes of the system, or attributes of the system environment. The software requirements specify the things that the software does on behalf of the user or another system. These are the detailed, unambiguous requirements that are specific enough to direct the implementation and testing of the system.

Software requirements specifications are expressed in various ways. One of the most common is to use declarative statements. Examples of software requirements for our simple telephone system could include the following:

- The response time between the completion of dialing and the ringing of the requested device shall be less than 0.5 seconds in 95 percent of all cases.

- Dialing and connection errors shall be reported to the user in the main language associated with the handset's country code.
- The system shall terminate the call when either the caller or the callee hangs up.

In their book *Managing Software Requirements: A Unified Approach*, Leffingwell and Widrig use the graphic presented in Figure 1-2 to illustrate the different requirement types and their relationship to the problem and solution domains. The separation of the problem domain from the solution domain indicates that the subject of the requirements specification is the solution rather than the problem. The needs represent our understanding of the needs of the users and other stakeholders who will be affected by our solution. These are the aspects of the problem to be directly addressed by the solution. The shape of the pyramid reflects the relative volumes of requirements: A few needs may give rise to a number of features, which are, in turn, defined by many more requirements. This relationship among the three kinds of requirements is expressed using traceability relationships. The traceability is bidirectional because a balance must be maintained between capturing the unconstrained stakeholder needs and requested features and the feasibility of producing a system that meets these desires.[2]

Figure 1-2 Requirement types and traceability

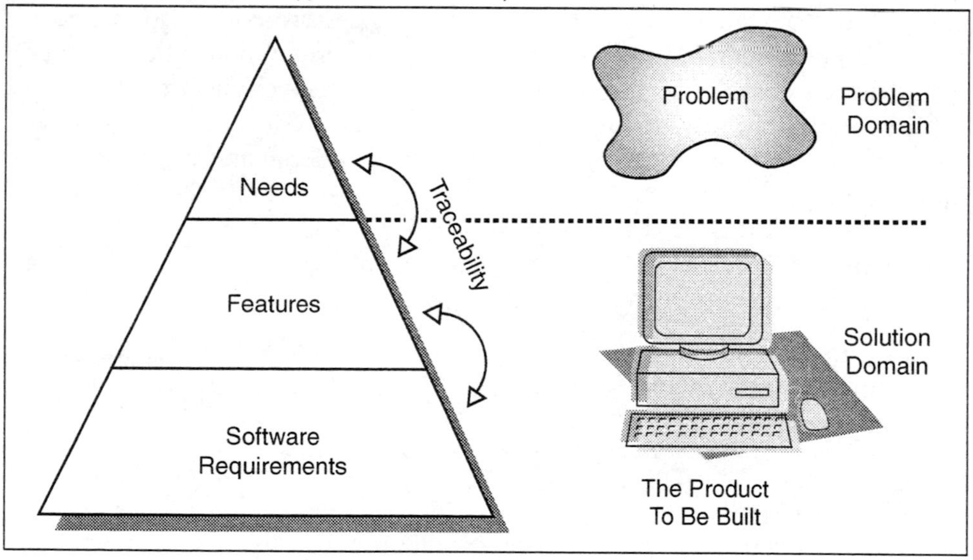

---

[2] The relationship between needs, features, and use cases will be presented in Chapter 3, Establishing the Vision.

While the needs informally characterize what stakeholders want from the system and the features provide an informal way of expressing what a system (or a release of a system) provides, software requirements express what the system must do. There is not a hierarchical decomposition of needs into features into requirements. Instead, these concepts are largely orthogonal, expressing different views of the system for different audiences. We present needs and features mainly to establish the context for the application of the use-case modeling approach; most of this book is about requirements expressed in the form of use cases.

Functional and Nonfunctional Requirements

Requirements are sometimes divided into two categories:

1. Functional requirements (things that define the required behavior of a system)
2. Nonfunctional requirements (other qualities or constraints to which the system must conform)

Functional requirements are those actions that a system must be able to perform, without taking physical constraints into consideration. The functional requirements specify the input and output behavior of a system. Nonfunctional requirements specify the other qualities that the system must have, such as those related to the usability, reliability, performance, and supportability of the system.[3] Many requirements are nonfunctional and describe only attributes of the system or attributes of the system's environment.

Even with the very small number of example requirements we have looked at so far we have seen examples of both functional and nonfunctional requirements.

Functional: The system shall terminate the call when either the caller or the callee hangs up.

Nonfunctional: The response time between the completion of dialing and the ringing of the requested device shall be less than 0.5 seconds in 95 percent of all cases.

---

[3] One way of remembering these requirements categories is the **FURPS+** model (see Grady, *Practical Software Metrics for Project Management and Process Improvement*, 1992, Prentice Hall), using the acronym FURPS to describe the major categories of requirements: **f**unctionality, **u**sability, **r**eliability, **p**erformance, and **s**upportability. The "+" in FURPS+ is a reminder that there are additional requirements to consider, such as design constraint, implementation, interface, and physical requirements.

We have looked at various concepts related to capturing, documenting, and understanding the requirements of the system, and we have examined the different levels and categories of requirements. So, let's have a look at how these concepts relate to use cases.

The Role of Use Cases

Use cases are a very powerful requirements-modeling technique. They provide us with a standard way of capturing, exploring, and documenting what a system should do (the requirements of the system). So, what level of requirements detail do use cases represent?

The use cases we have seen so far appear to have names that could be applied to the features of the system. We have a use case "Place Local Call," which sounds like a feature of the system: *People can place local calls using the system*. Even a cursory examination of our simple telephone system and a selection of its features demonstrate the difference between features and use cases and the nature of the relationship between them (Table 1-1). A number of things should be apparent here:

1. The names of use cases are active and expressed as goals of the actors: Place Local Call, Get Call History, and Retrieve Customer Billing Information. The features are more passive and expressed as capabilities of the system: allow the placing of local calls, provide a continuously up-to-date call history for all accounts, be available 24 hours a day, seven days a week.

2. The granularity of the features and the use cases are very different. Although the set of use cases can, on the face of it, appear to be a reasonable set of features, the reverse is not necessarily true: Not all features would make sensible use cases.

Table 1-1 Mapping Features to Use Cases

Feature	Use Case Affected
People can place local calls	Place Local Call
People can place long-distance calls	Place Long-Distance Call
The system finds the least-expensive routing for all long distance calls	Place Long-Distance Call
The system provides call history for all accounts	Get Call History Retrieve Customer Billing Information
The system is continuously available 24 hours a day, seven days a week	All Use Cases

3. As shown in the example by the "Place Long-Distance Call" use case and the "The system provides call history for all accounts" feature, there can be many features provided by a single use case, or a feature could be provided by more than one use case. Features are not use cases, and vice versa.

So, if use cases are not the equivalent of features, then what are they?

A feature is a kind of shorthand for a whole set of behaviors, but it doesn't describe those behaviors at all. Features may be useful when discussing the system at a high level, as one would in marketing literature, but they are not specific enough to really understand what the system does. That's where use cases come in—they are specific enough to allow us to understand the behavior of the system.

Whereas features represent capabilities of the system that help meet the actor's goals, use cases take a broader view by identifying the goals themselves and how the actor interacts with the system to accomplish those goals. The description of the way in which the actors and the system collaborate takes the form of a narrative or dialog between the parties involved. If we think about the content of this dialog, we see that it is going to involve describing three things:

1. The events raised by the actors and the system
2. The system's response to the events (its behavior)
3. The information exchanged between the actors and the system (the system's inputs and outputs)

In other words, a use case contains the description of a set of software requirements; the software requirements are presented in the form of a narrative rather than an itemized list (as is common when documenting software requirements in a declarative format).

A use case places the software requirements it contains into the context of a description of something that the user wants to achieve. The context provided by the use cases has many benefits when capturing, manipulating, verifying, and managing requirements. For this reason, use cases are our preferred mechanism for the capturing and documentation of software requirements.

Use Cases Place Software Requirements in Context

Given that the use cases themselves are containers for sets of related software requirements, how does a use-case model handle functional and nonfunctional requirements?

Use cases easily capture sets of functional requirements; they describe the behavior of the system as it interacts with its users and other systems to do something useful for its users. Use cases place the functional requirements into the context of a user actually doing something useful. Use cases can also be used to capture any nonfunctional requirements that are specific to a use case. For example, the following requirement can be attached to the Place Local Call use case:

> The response time between the completion of dialing and the ringing of the requested device should be less than 0.5 seconds in 95 percent of all cases, and in no case more than 1 second.

Nonfunctional requirements are best described using declarative requirements. These are then attached or traced to the use cases to which they apply.[4] Trying to describe nonfunctional requirements within the text of the use-case description is at best confusing; in some instances the results may be disastrous. Subsequent chapters deal more directly with this problem, as well as the problem of representing detail without becoming overwhelmed by it.

To sum up, all functional requirements can be captured as use cases, and many of the nonfunctional requirements can be associated with use cases.

There are two common misconceptions related to use cases that often cause people problems when they first start to use the technique:

- Use cases are just a way of capturing the functional requirements of a system and nothing else. The nonfunctional requirements are all captured somewhere else.
- Use cases are all that you need to capture the requirements of a system.

In fact, use cases capture a large, usually the largest, subset of the software requirements for the system. This relationship is shown in Figure 1-3. The use-case model itself is a vehicle for organizing the software requirements in an easy-to-manage way. It allows stakeholders, customers, users, and developers to understand the requirements and enables them to communicate about their needs in a consistent, nonredundant way. It also allows the developers to divide the requirements-capture work among themselves and then to use the results (primarily use cases) as input when analyzing, designing, implementing, and testing the system.

Use cases are very powerful because they place requirements in context by showing how the system provides value for its stakeholders while making

---

[4] For a thorough discussion of requirements-gathering techniques, including representing nonfunctional requirements and the relationship of those requirements to use cases, see Leffingwell and Widrig, *Managing Software Requirements: A Unified Approach*, 1999, Addison-Wesley.

Figure 1-3 Mapping use cases to the requirement types

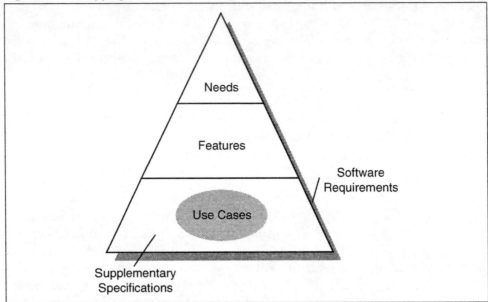

the requirements easier to understand. Use cases focus on the functionality of the system and require additional, more declarative requirements statements to provide a full software requirement specification.

We always expect the use-case model to be complemented by additional requirements documentation that contains functional and nonfunctional requirements or systemwide requirements that do not readily fit into the use-case model. These are captured in the supplementary specifications documentation and are often referred to as *Supplementary Specifications* (the Supplementary Specification is one of the standard Rational Unified Process requirements artifacts). We would be very suspicious of any project that used only use cases to document its requirements; it would suggest to us that a large set of the requirements of the system (predominantly the nonfunctional requirements) were missing or forgotten.

TO "USE CASE" OR NOT TO "USE CASE"

New techniques may solve old problems, but they often bring a whole set of new problems as well. Consider the automobile—we no longer have to worry much about feeding and cleaning up after carriage horses, but we have other things—mechanical failure, regular tune-ups, emissions tests—to worry about. Any time you adopt some new technique or technology, you should take a little time to consider why you are making the change to ensure that the change is worthwhile.

When Are Use Cases Useful?

Or to put it another way, "when does the use-case technique work when other techniques do not?"

Sometimes the hardest thing to visualize is how the system will work. We can have *excruciatingly* detailed requirements[5] and have almost no idea of what the system is supposed to do. The use-case descriptions give us a way of visualizing how the users and the system will interact so that everyone can see that the system will do something useful.

Because use cases focus on ways of using the system to do useful things, it is easier to ensure that we are building the right system. We can see how the system reacts when the user does something, or when some external event occurs, but most importantly we make sure that the system does something of value. The problem with so many systems is that they may satisfy many or most of their stated requirements but are still not really useful because they do not give the users what they want or need; they do not work the way that people want or expect them to work. Use cases help by allowing us to visualize what the system does and how to use it.

Use Cases Provide a Conceptual Model of the System

What use cases help us with is what Donald Norman, in *The Design of Everyday Things,* calls the *conceptual model.* This is the model that the stakeholders and users of the system have of the system itself. In other words, use cases help us form a mental model of how the system works, at a conceptual level.

To use a system, we must have a mental model of how it works; this mental model helps us to form strategies of how we can use the system to accomplish tasks. Without a mental model, we are unable to use the system effectively, and the simpler the mental model, the easier the system is to use. The electronic spreadsheet metaphor is powerful because it has a simple mental model—the paper-based spreadsheet. The word processor we are using to write this book has another simple mental model. The internal designs of electronic spreadsheet and word processor programs are nothing like the mental

---

[5] One system on which we worked had over 18,000 requirements. The development team was completely lost and had very little idea of what the system really needed to do. Applying use cases helped to straighten out the mess, resulting in a system with less than 30 use cases.

model a user has for them, but the mental model is nevertheless essential to using the programs effectively.

Use cases help us to explore, form, and refine the mental model of how the system will work. If the system is to be usable, it is essential that it have a simple mental model that is consistently applied throughout the design. The users and the builders of the system must share this mental model for the system to be useful. For simple systems, achieving a shared vision is not so difficult, but as the complexity of the requirements increases, the chances of it happening naturally decrease. When written correctly, use cases can become a catalyst for creating this shared mental model of the system.

Use Cases Describe How the System Is Used and What It Does for Its Stakeholders

Use cases are also very good at describing the interactions between the users of a system (either people or other systems) and the system itself. They capture what a user does to initiate some behavior in the system, and, in turn, what the system does to provide the required behavior. They clearly define the responsibilities of the system with regard to satisfying the goals of the users, and the responsibilities of the users with regard to supporting the system. They are excellent vehicles for envisioning the system and for coming to agreement with users and customers of the system on what the system must do. They help facilitate discussion and build common understanding among all the stakeholders of a system. For the development team, they provide a means to better understand the system behavior and to derive the design and other artifacts used to build the system.

Does Everything the System Does Have to Be Described in a Use Case?

Yes, and no.

In order to have a comprehensive overview of the behavior of the system, it is important that all of the use cases be identified and briefly described. What this means in practical terms is that you must understand who or what uses the system and what they expect to achieve by using the system. Failure to understand this will result in a system that does not meet the expectations of its stakeholders. Use cases provide us with a simple way to capture this.

On the other hand, not every use case needs to be fully described. In some cases, a brief outline of the flow of events of the use case will be sufficient for everyone to understand what needs to be done, and the description can stop there. In other cases, however, when the flow of events is complex and the flow of control branches in complicated ways, a full description will be essential to both build and test the system. So some parts of a system will be deeply described, and other parts will be described more superficially. The balance will vary depending on how dynamic the system to be built needs to be. Where there is a lot of interaction between the system and its actors (for example, an automatic teller machine), a detailed description will be useful, even necessary, to make sure we understand the behavior well enough to develop and test it. In cases where the interactions are few and/or very simple, a simple description supplemented with declarative requirements and user-interface prototypes may be sufficient. In all cases, however, we at least identify the use cases and briefly describe them.

Because use cases are descriptions of behavior, they need to be supplemented with nonfunctional requirements in order to present a complete picture of what the system must do. These nonfunctional requirements include system platform requirements, design constraints, performance requirements, and other requirements that cannot be expressed as sequences of actions that the system performs. Since these nonfunctional requirements augment or supplement the use cases, we call them *supplementary requirements*. Requirements-management tools can track and trace these requirements to their related use cases, enabling us to have a complete picture of the system.

These observations are explored in greater detail in subsequent chapters.

GENERAL PRINCIPLES OF USE-CASE MODELING

The intent of this book is to capture and present *best practices* derived from day-to-day exposure to the successes and failures of many, many project teams who have employed use cases as a way to capture requirements and understand the systems they are to build. Some of these best practices are fundamental and underlie everything that we have to say about use cases and their application.

Use Cases Do Not Exist in Isolation

The use cases, like the system that they describe, do not exist in isolation. To assess the effectiveness and applicability of a use-case model, we must first understand the environment in which the system will exist. To use use-case modeling techniques effectively, you must understand the economic, technological, political, and business environment into which the system will be introduced and how that environment will be changed by the new system. Many formal techniques can be used to develop and capture this understanding, such as business modeling and other more general requirements-management techniques.[6] This information can be developed alongside the use-case model itself, with the use-case model acting as a catalyst and facilitation device for its construction.

An understanding of the following factors complements and provides context for the use-case model:

- **The Stakeholder Community:** the set of people who are materially affected by the development of the system. The stakeholders also expect to get some value from the system.
- **The Users:** the set of people who will use the system, playing the roles defined by the actors. The users are one particular kind of stakeholder.
- **The Customer:** the ones who have commissioned the system (the folks who are paying for it). These people may have a set of goals and interests distinctly different from those of the users of the system.
- **The Various Stakeholder Requests:** requests and ideas for new functionality, which will be generated throughout the life of the system. These must be accepted and managed alongside the use-case model.
- **Constraints:** restrictions on the degree of freedom the developers have in providing a solution, imposed by requirements such as *the system must run on a handheld organizer*. Constraints such as this will mean that it would be pointless to describe a system that required a windowing, multitasking operating system (at least at the time of this book's writing). It is pointless to specify a solution that cannot be built.
- **The Underlying Problem to Be Solved:** it is important to always bear in mind the underlying problems that the system is intended to solve and ensure that all of the functionality provided by the system is directly contributing to the alleviation of these problems.
- **The Problem Domain:** a model must also be built to capture the terminology and facts about the problem domain addressed by the system. At the very minimum a glossary must be maintained to define the vocabulary used within the use-case descriptions.

It is a very common mistake to build the use-case model in isolation. If the stakeholders and users are not continuously involved in the production and validation of the model, it can quickly and easily become an expression of the assumptions and prejudices of the development team rather than the actual requirements of the system. If the constraints implied by the technological and business environments are ignored, then the solution described may be uneconomical or technically infeasible.

These issues, and how to handle them, are examined in Chapter 3, Establishing the Vision.

---

[6] A number of these techniques are explored in Chapter 3, Establishing the Vision.

Use Cases Are a Synthetic Rather Than an Analytic Technique

The problem with requirements is that we drown in them. There are innumerable things that the system must do, endless details that must be attended to, and from this massive wish list it's impossible to see the real system and how it will work. We may be able to build an infinite number of systems that would satisfy the requirements but not the people who must use the system. Requirements are also often ambiguous and sometimes conflicting; we need a way to sort through all this.

Some people treat use cases as an analytic technique, whereby functional requirements are understood, grouped, and then decomposed into little packages of functionality that they call a use case. This is classic analytic thinking at work: Take a big problem and break it down into smaller problems. This works in a lot of fields such as mathematics and engineering in which the problem is well understood but the solution is not. In developing systems, the problem is often not very well defined either. So taking an ill-defined problem and breaking it down into smaller pieces creates problems of its own, not the least of which is that we can't really see the original problem anymore. To build successful systems, we need a way to better understand the problem, to build up our understanding of the problem.

The term *analysis* means to break something down into its constituent elements, whereas *synthesis* means to build something up from its constituent parts. Use cases are fundamentally a synthetic technique, targeted at building shared understanding among the various stakeholders. The goal of writing a use case is to ensure that everyone has the same conceptual model (or mental picture) of what the system will do and how it will work. We build up this understanding from the raw materials of features, functional requirements, nonfunctional requirements, user interface prototypes, domain models, and the ideas in the heads of stakeholders. If we employ use cases in an analytic way, we lose their primary value—building shared understanding.

Rules of Thumb

Before we dive into the definitions of actors, use cases, and the other basic building blocks of a use-case model, five rules of thumb should be borne in mind throughout the evolution of any use-case model:

1. **Focus on Effective Communication.** The purpose of the use-case model is to facilitate communications.
2. **Pursue Simplicity.** The model should be as simple and straightforward as possible.
3. **Remember Your Stakeholders.** The audience for the model is the entire stakeholder community.

4. **Good Enough Is as Good as It Gets.** There is no such thing as perfection in use-case modeling.
5. **Write Things Down.** You will have to write down what the system is supposed to do in detail—there is no way to avoid this.

Not only are these five rules of thumb applicable to use-case modeling, they also provide a good foundation to adopt when writing documents about the nature and application of use cases. Their application has been fundamental in shaping the content and style of this book.

SUMMARY

Use cases are a simple and powerful technique for representing the behavior of a system. But for all their simplicity, they are easily misapplied. The basic ideas are quite simple:

- **Actors** are people or things that interact in some way with the system; by definition, they are outside the system. Actors have a name and a brief description.
- **Use cases** are stories about how the actors use the system to do something they consider important. Use cases are a technique for primarily expressing functional requirements, but they are not functions or features, and they cannot be decomposed. Use cases are particularly useful for describing the behavior of a system when that behavior consists of some sequence of events triggered by actions of the user (or some entity external to the system).

Use cases can be depicted in diagrams, but they are principally described in text. Too much focus on the diagrams often leads people down the path of *decomposition*. Remember that the use case must tell a story about how an actor achieves something significant with the system.

Finally, remember that use cases are used to build up our understanding of what the system should do. They are not used to analyze or break down the requirements into smaller parts; that is the job of analysis and design.

In subsequent chapters we will delve more deeply into the structure and contents of a use case, as well as discuss how use cases are discovered and how they are used. This chapter provided a basic introduction to the question of *what* use cases are and *why* they exist. After a little more background, we can take up the questions of *how* use cases are identified and described and *when* they are developed.

Chapter 2

Fundamentals of Use-Case Modeling

The preceding chapter presented a brief and relatively informal picture of use-case modeling and its goals. As with many techniques, there is a bit more to use-case modeling that needs to be understood before it can be successfully applied.

Use-case modeling is based on a formal technique. This is both a strength and a weakness. It is a strength because we can use the underlying formalisms to improve our precision and provide additional depth and rigor to our modeling activities. It is a weakness because it is easy to (mistakenly) assume that use-case modeling is limited to drawing diagrams and because the formality and terminology can be confusing to people who are new to use cases. The reality is that the formalism provides a framework for the creation of our models and the diagrams provide a nice overview of the system, but the real value of a use case is in the textual use-case descriptions. It is in the use-case descriptions that the majority of the model's content resides, and it is in the authoring of the use-case descriptions where most effort will be expended.

In this chapter we look at the formal definitions of the fundamental elements of the use-case model, consider the contents of the use-case descriptions, and describe the artifacts that are required in addition to a use-case model to form a complete software requirements specification. This chapter is structured as a reference guide to the basic components of a use-case model and provides the foundation for the subsequent chapters in the book. If you are familiar with the basic building blocks of use-case modeling and want to start writing your own use cases, you can skip to Chapter 3, Establishing the Vision, and come back to this chapter later.

THE USE-CASE MODEL

The use-case model is the set of all the use cases, actors, and use-case–actor associations used to describe a particular system. See Figure 2-1. The UML (Unified Modeling Language) defines a model as

> a semantically closed abstraction of a subject system

In other words, a model is a complete description of a system from a particular perspective. (Here, *complete* means self-contained; you don't need any additional information to understand the model.) In software development, as in many other fields, the models are simplifications of reality, created to enhance understanding of the system being built.

So, does the use-case model provide a complete description from a requirements perspective? No, it doesn't. To provide a complete requirements definition, the use-case model must be complemented by other requirements models and artifacts.[1] Use cases place requirements in context and often contain all of the functional requirements of a system. This is the relationship that drives the UML definition of a *use-case model*:

> A model that describes the functional requirements of a system or other classifier in terms of use cases[2]

The use-case model presents a system in terms of its usage. When treated formally, the use-case model describes all the possible ways of using the system. Use-case models can also be used less formally where the set of use cases illustrates the most significant ways of using a system rather than all possible ways of using the system.

Figure 2-1 Use-case model

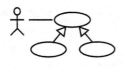 A use-case model is a model of a system defined in terms of use cases, actors, and the relationships between them.[*]

A use-case model can contain, and is often represented by, a set of use-case diagrams.

[*]Ivar Jacobson, et al. *Object Oriented Software Engineering: A Use-Case Driven Approach,* 1992, ACM Press, introduced all the fundamental concepts of use-case modeling: actors, use cases, use-case models, use-case instances and descriptions, and related concepts. We have based our work on these original concepts, and have focused on applying these concepts rather than introducing new concepts.

---

[1]These are described in the Supporting Artifacts section later.
[2]Although this book focuses on using use cases to describe systems, they can be used anywhere that there is a clear boundary.

THE BASIC BUILDING BLOCKS OF A USE-CASE MODEL

The basic building blocks of the use-case model are the actors, the use cases, the relationships between them, and the diagrams in which they appear. In this section we explore these concepts in more depth.

Actors

If we refer to our simple telephone system, the subtle distinction between the roles the users can play and the users themselves will become clear. See Figures 2-2 and 2-3.

In the system in Figure 2-2, we have three actors that define roles that will be adopted by the users of the system. Now obviously, several users can play the same role; in fact, the list of people that can take on the role "Caller" or "Callee" is almost unlimited. It is equally obvious that the same person can take on more than one role: In most cases the Customers (the people who actually pay the bills) would be very upset if they could not also be Callers or Callees.

A list of all the actors would be a list of all the different roles that people or other systems could play while interacting with the system. This is subtly different from a list of users, which would be a list of all the different people and other systems that are allowed to interact with the system. Like the term *user*, the term *actor*, is often taken to imply a person, especially given its stick-person representation, but few systems operate without interacting with

Figure 2-2 The graphical representation of an actor

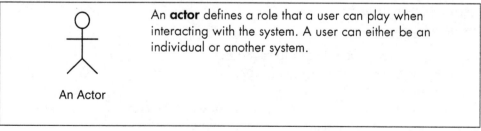

An **actor** defines a role that a user can play when interacting with the system. A user can either be an individual or another system.

An Actor

Figure 2-3 Human actors

Callee   Caller   Customer

other systems, and many systems interact only with other systems. In the example of the simple telephone system, actors also define roles to be taken by other systems. See Figure 2-4.

Just like the human users of a system, these other systems are beyond the control of the system being built and they impose certain requirements on what the system being built must do.

Now you may be thinking, "If the actors are either humans or systems why are they all represented by stick people?" The answer is that the role defined by the actor is not restricted to being only a human or a system. In Figure 2-3, an answering machine, a fax machine, or a computer could take the role of Callee. The telephone system will treat these in exactly the same way as it would a human Callee, and the Caller may not even be able to tell the difference. When defining actors, it is important to capture their characteristics and any constraints that these place on their interaction with the system rather than making assumptions about the form that the users playing the roles will take.

Actors According to the UML

The more formal UML definition of actor is

> A coherent set of roles that users of use cases play when interacting with these use cases

We prefer our more expansive, but compatible definition, as it is less self-referential, and, we hope, more approachable.

Actors in Summary

To sum up, actors:

- Can represent people or other systems
- Define the roles that users or other systems play while interacting with the system
- Are outside the system, and usually outside the control of the system
- Impose requirements on what the system being built must do

Figure 2-4 System actors

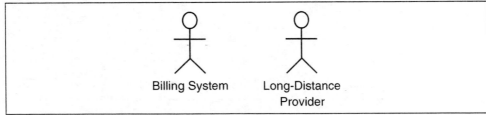

Billing System   Long-Distance Provider

Use Cases

Several concepts in this definition in Figure 2-5 are central to a thorough understanding of use cases:

A use case has a description. Use-case modeling provides much more than a simple visual representation of a system and its actors. Like an iceberg, the true extent of the use case is not immediately apparent; the ellipse is just an iconic placeholder for a description of how the system and its actors interact. A use case is mostly text that describes what the system does for a particular actor; the use-case diagram can be thought of as a visual aid to comprehension but does not tell the whole story.

The actor uses the system. When defining and describing use cases, remember that the system provides the use case and the actor starts the use case.

The use cases describe how the system provides value to one or more of the actors. Each use case delivers something of value to at least one of the actors. The concepts of actor goals and the delivery of value to the actors are fundamental to the successful discovery, definition, and application of use cases. The use cases should reflect the goals of the actors and enable, at least in part, their achievement.

For example:

- The actors use the system only if it enables them to do something that they want to do.
- The actors perform a use case only if doing so helps them achieve one of their goals. The physical manifestation of the goal is the value that the use case delivers to the actor.
- A concrete value can be put on the successful performance of a use case. Every use case should have an easily understandable and clearly identifiable value.

Figure 2-5 The graphical representation of a use case

A use case describes how an actor uses a system to achieve a goal and what the system does for the actor to achieve that goal. It tells the story of how the system and its actors collaborate to deliver something of value for at least one of the actors.

A Use Case

From a well-formed set of use cases you can immediately, and intuitively, identify the benefits that the system offers its actors, why the actors would want to use the system, and why you would want to buy or develop it.

Use Cases, According to the UML

The formal UML definition of a use case is

> A description of a set of sequences of actions, including variants, that a system performs that yields an observable result of value to a particular actor[3]

We prefer our less formal, and more expansive, expression—it's easier for people to understand, and therefore easier to apply. The UML definition focuses more on the form that the story described by the use case should take than the underlying purpose of use cases.

Too often, when presented with this kind of formal definition, people get hung up on the meaning of the specific phrases it contains, phrases like *sequences of actions*. The original meaning with respect to a use case was more informal and simply referred to some sequence of steps that occurred together or not at all. The story metaphor works better for most people; it is simpler and gets to the real essence of the use case—providing a coherent picture of how the system is used and what it does.

The Use-Case Description Is a Kind of Story

The use-case description tells a story of how a system and its actors collaborate to achieve a specific goal. It is a step-by-step description of a particular way of using a system. The structure of a use case is essentially narrative in nature. The story it tells is of how the system and its actors work together to achieve something of significance to the actors involved. This collaboration takes the form of a dialog between the system and its actors, with all the parties contributing to the completion of the use case.

Just like a story, every use case should have a clear beginning (how the actor starts the use case), middle (how the system and actors work together), and end (how the use case is concluded). The use case starts when an actor does something, causing the system to do something in response. This dialog continues (at least) until the system has done something useful for at least one of the actors. The use case is *not* a complete description of all possible ways that some task is performed, nor does it in any way say anything about how the system is designed or implemented. It's just a story, although sometimes a

---

[3] Booch, *The Unified Modeling Language User Guide*, 1999, Addison-Wesley, p. 468.

very detailed one. As the term suggests, use cases describe typical ways (or *cases*) of using the system.

Each use case expresses a goal of the actors involved and describes a task that the system, with the assistance of the appropriate actors, will perform. You can get an idea of a use case's goal simply by observing its name and associations. In the example of our simple telephone system, the use cases clearly represent the goals of a Caller. See Figure 2-6. When treated formally, the collected set of a system's use cases constitute all the possible ways of using the system.

Use Cases in Summary

To sum up, use cases:

- Are started by an actor
- Are provided by the system
- Can involve more than one actor
- Describe how a system and its actors collaborate to fulfill at least one of the actors' goals
- Provide a coherent picture of how the system will be used and what it does

Connecting Actors and Use Cases

The system and its actors interact by sending signals or messages to one another. To indicate such interactions, we use a communicate association between the use case where the interaction occurs and the actors involved in the interaction. See Figure 2-7. A use case has at most one communicate association to a specific actor, and an actor has at most one communicate association to a specific use case, no matter how many interactions there are. The

Figure 2-6 The goals of the Caller

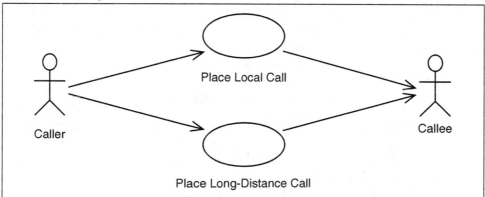

Figure 2-7 The graphical representations of a communicate association

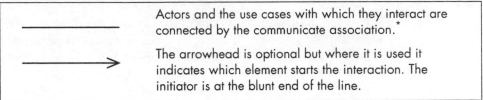

——————————————	Actors and the use cases with which they interact are connected by the communicate association.[*]
——————————————>	The arrowhead is optional but where it is used it indicates which element starts the interaction. The initiator is at the blunt end of the line.

[*]There are other associations between actors, and between use cases, that we will discuss later in Chapter 10, Here There Be Dragons. While getting started with use cases, the *communicate* association is all that we will need to be concerned about.

complete network of such associations provides a static picture of the communication between the system and its environment.

This view is essential to the understanding of the use-case model. To fully understand the role defined by an actor, you must know in which use cases the actor is involved. To fully understand the scope of a use case, you must know the actors with which it communicates. This is shown by communicate associations between the actors and the use cases.

Actors communicate with the system for many reasons, including:

- To start a use case. Use cases are always started by actors.
- To ask for some data stored in the system, which the use case then presents to the actor.
- To change the data stored in the system by means of a dialog with the system.
- To report that something special has happened in the system's surroundings that the system should be aware of.

One actor initiates a use case. However, after the use case has started, the use case can communicate with several actors. Communicate associations are added between the use case and the supporting actors to show the actors with which the use case communicates.

The communicate association is sometimes mistakenly regarded as representing *data flow*. It does not. The communicate association represents a dialog between the actor and the system, a kind of communication channel over which data flows in both directions during the dialogue.

Use cases communicate with actors for many reasons, including:

- If something special has taken place in the system, an actor might need to be informed.
- A use case may need to ask an actor for help in making a decision needed to achieve a goal.
- A use case may delegate responsibility to an actor.

It is common, but not always true, that the use case waits for an answer when it has sent a signal to an actor. This time period may be a microsecond, a minute, a day, a year, or any length of time. The details of the communication between the actors and the use case is explicitly described in the use case.

In the simple phone system example, we can see quite clearly how the communication association works. When placing a local call, the Caller communicates with the system to set up the call (by lifting the handset and dialing the number), and the system communicates with the Callee (ringing the Callee's telephone). The communication is bidirectional, with the telephone system relaying information back to the Caller, thereby enabling the Caller and Callee to communicate directly as soon as the call is established. See Figure 2-8.

In Figure 2-8 which actors start which use cases? From the diagram, it's not possible to say. By adding arrowheads (optional in the UML), we add clarity to the diagram. See Figure 2-9.

Figure 2-8 Communicate associations without arrowheads

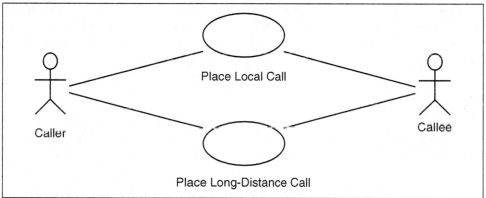

Figure 2-9 Communicate associations with arrowheads

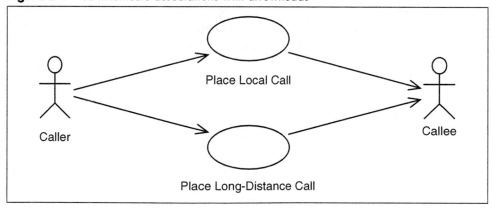

The use of the arrowheads allows us to clearly see who starts the interaction. As shown by Figures 2-8 and 2-9, the diagrams are far more communicative when the arrowheads are included, especially when you consider that no meaning is attached to the positioning of the actors on the diagram.

To sum up:

- The communicate association shows which actors are involved in which use cases.
- Arrowheads indicate which party initiates the interaction; this provides a visual indication of which actor starts the use case.

Use-Case Diagrams

The use cases, actors, and their associations can be shown on use-case diagrams, such as Figure 2-10. On this diagram, we see an actor called "Customer" and a use case called "Get Call History." The direction of the arrow shows that the Customer initiates the communication.

A use-case diagram provides a view of a use-case model. Many use-case diagrams can be used to view and provide different perspectives on a single use-case model. A use-case diagram may contain only actors, only use cases, or any combination of the two. Commonly used use-case diagrams include the following:

- An overview diagram showing all the use cases and actors
- Actor summary diagrams showing a set of conceptually related actors
- Actor perspective diagrams showing all the use cases involving an actor
- Use-case summary diagrams showing a set of conceptually related use cases
- Use-case perspective diagrams illustrating how a use case relates to its actors and other user cases

The diagrams are used to convey who the actors are, what the use cases are, and how they are related. The diagrams are just views into the underlying use-case model; they should not be confused with the use-case model itself.

Figure 2-10 A simple use-case diagram

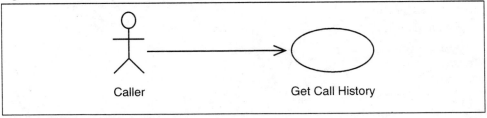

Caller   Get Call History

Brief Descriptions

Each actor and each use case must have a brief description, no more than a few sentences long, that states what it is and why it exists. For example, our simple phone system model generates the following descriptions:

A **Caller** is any person or external device that uses the system to make a phone call.

A **Customer** is the person, or authorized representative of the organization, that pays the bills. The Customer is the owner of the account with the telecom's provider. The Customer is identified by an account number.

The use case **Get Call History** provides the **Customer** with the ability to access the details of all of the calls that have been charged to the account. This call history is made available in both text and audio formats.

The purpose of these brief descriptions is to make sure we know what we are talking about, or more important, to make sure that we all agree on the purpose of and the value provided by the use cases. Without a brief description of the actors, we may *think* we agree on who or what the actors represent when in fact we may have slightly different conceptions. Without a brief description of the use cases, we may not agree on the purpose of the use case, or worse yet, we may think we agree when we do not. In many senses, the diagrams alone are incomplete. Without more explanation, they are ambiguous at best. This is never truer than when a team spends several hours filling white boards and flip charts with use-case diagrams of actors and use cases, forgetting to record the brief descriptions that flow naturally during the brainstorming process. Days later, the diagrams can become a source of confusion if no one remembers whether the use case "Manage Orders" includes order fulfillment or not. Recording brief descriptions prevents this.

The brief descriptions should be at least a sentence or two long, but no more than a short paragraph; anything longer is probably overkill. Keep the descriptions simple and direct. If you cannot come up with a simple and direct description of the actor or use case, then you should reconsider whether you need it—if you can't define it you may not have a clear idea of what you are trying to achieve. This is always a good first sanity check of the actors and use cases chosen by the modelers. There's a different vehicle for the more complete description—the use-case description itself.

Use-Case Descriptions

Use cases are much more than just a named ellipse and a brief description. For each use case there will also be a use-case description where the full story of the use case is told.

The use-case descriptions provide the substance of the use-case model, and they are the basis for most of the use-case modeling work. The graphical representations we have seen so far are useful in positioning and scoping the system to be built, but they only provide a very general overview of what it will do—they represent merely the tip of the use-case modeling iceberg. More than 90% of the use-case model lies beneath the surface, in the textual use-case descriptions themselves.

Ever since Ivar Jacobson first popularized use cases,[4] the industry has seen many different approaches to the writing of use case descriptions. Each approach recommends a different writing style and level of detail and content. Alistair Cockburn has described 18 different styles of use-case description that he has seen in use on projects.[5] One of these styles is the one proposed by Jacobson in his book and subsequently adopted by the Rational Unified Process. We have found it to be the most effective, and so it is the one we present here.

The use-case description is where the details of the use case, sometimes referred to as the *use-case properties*, are defined. The UML defines many properties for a use case. Here we concentrate on the key properties of the use case: the flow of events, preconditions, and postconditions. It is important that you have an understanding of the principles behind these key use-case properties before you start attempting to identify your system's use cases. This will help you to find an appropriate set of use cases for your system. We explore the full set of use-case properties in Chapter 7, The Structure and Contents of a Use Case.

The Flow of Events

The most important part of the use-case description is the Flow of Events. This is the section where the story is told. Although the flow of events is only considered a single use-case property by the UML, it has a well-defined and significant structure.

THE FLOW OF EVENTS AS A MAP OF THE TERRITORY

The flow of events provides the description of how the system and actors collaborate to deliver the value promised by the use case, including all the things

---

[4] See Jacobson, et al., *Object-Oriented Software Engineering: A Use-Case Driven Approach*, 1992, ACM Press.
[5] See A. Cockburn, "Goals and Use Cases," *Journal of Object-Oriented Programming*, 10(5), Sept., 1997.

that can prevent the value from being achieved. It acts as a map of the territory for people interested in what the system will do. Unlike a pictorial map, or flowchart, it does not merge all of the paths together into a single picture. The storylike nature of the use case leads to a much more narrative format where the normal route is described first, followed by a description of alternative routes. The use-case descriptions focus on describing each path individually as a unique flow of events.

The approach taken is the one that people use when providing directions to others:

Instructions to Get to Kurt's Party

Turn right out of the car park. Carry straight on down the main road for five miles until you reach the crossroads. Take the first right and then the second left. The house is the third on the left. Don't forget to bring something to drink.

If the main road is busy, you can turn off by the pub and follow the winding country lane, but normally this will take a lot longer.

If you need to get some alcohol on the way, there is a wine shop in the shopping center opposite the pub. If the wine shop is shut then the pub will do carry outs. If you can't get any alcohol at all then just come anyway.

First the expected, successful route is described, followed by the alternative routes and variations on the normal route. This is exactly the way that use-case descriptions are structured. There is a bit more formality in the way that the text is formatted and the actor and system interactions are described, but the basic principle is the same. First the expected flow of events is described, and then the alternatives and exceptions are detailed. The normal, expected route is called the *basic flow*. All the other routes, regardless of whether they end in success or failure, are called *alternative flows*.

We will now start to look at how an actual use-case description is constructed. The focus here is on how the flow of events is structured and how the different kinds of flow are related to each other. To this end, the descriptions are kept at the outline level—we will look at how to complete the use-case descriptions in Chapter 8, Writing Use-Case Descriptions: An Overview, and Chapter 9, Writing Use-Case Descriptions: Revisited. The example we will use is the Place Local Call use case from the Simple Telephone System example.

THE BASIC FLOW

The basic flow is the description of the normal, expected path through the use case (sometimes referred to as the *happy day scenario*). This is the path taken by most of the users most of the time. The basic flow for the Place Local Call use case could look like this:

Use Case—Place Local Call

Basic Flow

The use case starts when the Caller lifts the receiver.

The Caller enters the number to be called.

The system connects the Caller's phone to the requested device.

The call is made.

The connection is terminated.

The details of the call are recorded.

The use case ends.

Remember that this is just an outline, not the full use-case description. The assumption behind the basic flow is that it will successfully enable the actor to achieve the goal.

ALTERNATIVE FLOWS—OPTIONAL BEHAVIOR AND VARIATIONS ON A THEME

Because of the circumstances that may prevail at the time the use case is being performed, other, less common elements of behavior may be required to extend the flow of events.

If the basic flow represents the normal route to success, the alternative flows can be considered as detours. Some of these occur at the actor's discretion, perhaps providing an easier or more scenic route. Others occur at the system's discretion, perhaps enforcing a higher degree of security, exploiting the system's knowledge of the user's preferences, or handling special cases. For example, the variant and optional behavior in the Place Local Call use case could include the following alternative flows:

No Answer

If the Callee does not answer, the Caller replaces the handset and use case ends.

Line Busy

If the Callee's line is in use, the system rings the *busy* tone. The Caller then replaces the handset and the use case ends.

Note: the descriptive text is included for explanatory purposes only and is not supposed to represent how the alternative flows of events themselves would be written.

When you consider all of the possible optional and variant behavior that could be defined for a system, it is easy to become overwhelmed with the available possibilities and forget to focus on the system's core, essential behavior. One of the benefits of the flow of events' structure is that all of this information is kept independent of the use case's basic flow. The basic flow defines the core behavior; the alternative flows complement this. Some of these are essential to the success of the system, but many are extraneous "bells and whistles" and wish-list materials. The structure of the flow of events allows us to address each flow on its own merits and maintain our focus on the system's essential behavior.

ALTERNATIVE FLOWS—EXCEPTIONS/ERROR CONDITIONS

The most common kinds of alternative flows are those that describe the errors that can occur and how they should be handled.

In our experience 60 to 80 percent of all software is written to handle exception and error conditions. Use cases are no exception to this rule; it is very common for 60 to 80 percent of the text in the use-case descriptions to describe what errors can occur, when they can occur, and how they are handled. For example, in the Place Local Call use case, the exceptional and error handling behavior could include the following alternative flows:

Number Dialed Not Known

The system cannot identify a receiving device from the number dialed.

Number Is Engaged

The receiving device is already involved in a call.

The Signal Is Lost

The carrier / signal is lost during the call.

When you start to consider all the things that could go wrong at each step in the basic flow, you quickly generate a long list of error-related alternative flows. This is one of the reasons that the use-case descriptions adopt the additive structure described here. This allows the basic flow to be kept simple and avoids swamping it with descriptions of all the exceptions that can occur. This structure also helps you write the use cases; plan the project; and scope, test, analyze, design, and implement the system.

SUBFLOWS

As a use case becomes more detailed, the text of the individual flow of events can become unwieldy and overlong. This is true for even the simplest systems. Generally, as a flow of events grows in size, it naturally falls into a series of smaller, self-contained subsections, each with its own clearly identifiable purpose. For example, the Place Local Call use case includes the sentence:

> The system connects the Caller's phone to the requested device.

This requires elaboration into a set of individual actions and responses:

> The system analyzes the digits of the entered number and determines the network address of Callee.
>
> The system determines whether a connection can be established between Caller and Callee.
>
> The system establishes the connection.
>
> The system rings Callee's phone.

This expansion can lead to the thread of the flow becoming lost in the details. In cases like this, the individual sections of the flow can be broken out into self-contained sections of text called *subflows*. These are given their own title and are presented as a miniflow of events.

Subflow—Connect Caller and Callee

> The system analyzes the digits of the entered number and determines the network address of Callee.
>
> The system determines whether a connection can be established between Caller and Callee.
>
> The system establishes the connection.
>
> The system rings Callee's phone.

They are then included in the original flow of events by their title:

> The Caller enters the number to be called.
>
> Perform connect Caller and Callee.
>
> The system maintains the connection until either the Caller or the Callee terminates the call.

This name of the subflow could be entered into the electronic format as a hyperlink or in a different text style. What is important is that you can see that this is a placeholder and not the actual text from the flow of events.

Remember that the key to writing effective use cases is to focus on communication. It is only worth splitting up the flow of events into subflows if they make the use case itself easier to read.

THE RELATIONSHIP BETWEEN THE VARIOUS FLOWS

Another side effect of developing the use-case descriptions is that the identified alternatives and subflows will start to have alternatives, exceptions, and subflows of their own. This can even be seen in the simple example, "Instructions to Get to Kurt's Party": ". . . If the wine shop is shut then the pub will do carry outs" or ". . . If you can't get any alcohol at all then just come anyway." One of the powerful things about the way that use cases are structured is that we are always dealing with the same, simple constructs. As we saw in the preceding example, defining subflows is very easy. A section of the flow of events is extracted and given a separate section and a heading. It can then be included in any other flow of events in the use case by simply placing its title in the text and providing a pointer to it. Defining alternative flows is also very simple. We just have to define when and where these flows may occur, what the alternative flow of events is, and where the original flow of events is resumed if the use case is not explicitly ended by the alternative flow. When writing basic and alternative flows, it is important that the basic flow of events is written independently of the alternative and that it has no knowledge of the alternative flows; it must make complete sense without reference to the alternatives. The alternative flow knows the details of when and where it is applicable as opposed to the original flow. It *inserts* itself into the basic flow when a particular condition is true. See Figure 2-11.

If the subflow or alternative flow is being applied to another subflow or alternative flow, then the rules are the same except that the original flow of events is no longer the basic flow. Figure 2-11 illustrates the typical structure of a flow of events.

We shall look at these relationships in more detail in Chapter 7, The Structure and Contents of a Use Case.

The Size and Complexity of a Use-Case Description
Or "how long is a piece of string?"[6]

Typically, use-case descriptions are 5 to 15 pages long. We have seen some as short as half a page and others as long as 30 pages. The key thing to

---

[6] Answer: It should be as long as necessary to accomplish the task at hand.

Figure 2-11 The typical structure of the flow of events. The straight arrow represents the basic flow of events, and the curves represent alternative paths in relation to the basic flow. Some alternative paths return to the basic flow of events, whereas others end the use case.

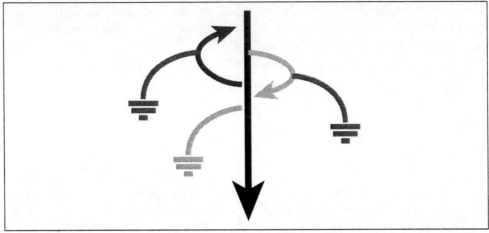

remember is that each use-case description has to be long enough to clearly tell its story. It has to explain the basic and alternative flows in a form that satisfies all of the stakeholders. For a very simple, data-capture use case with few or no alternatives, this can be a few sentences long, and in other cases—say for a complex interaction involving many actors with many alternatives—this will require a lot of text. Even in a use case as simple as one describing how to withdraw cash from an automatic teller machine, we have seen as many as 22 alternative flows identified. If the alternatives and exceptions themselves have lots of alternatives and exceptions, this will again lead to longer use-case descriptions.

Use-case descriptions should be as long as it takes to tell the full story. As we shall see in Chapter 10, Here There Be Dragons, there are various techniques we can use to help to manage the textual descriptions of the use cases. However, these techniques do not really change the underlying size and complexity of the use-case model, they just move text from one use case to another and should be used sparingly, if at all.

We have met some who might say that detailed use cases are unnecessary. To this complaint we would respond "is the behavior required?" If the system must do the things described, then you'll have to capture the requirements at some point, and a use case offers a number of advantages over other means of description.

Preconditions

To elaborate on our map analogy a little more, we can see that the description provided by the flow of events is of no use unless you are at the correct starting point. The Instructions to Kurt's Party are of little or no use to you unless you are either in the car park or know how to get there.

In the use-case model, this starting point is represented by the states of the actor(s) and the system at the time the use case is to be started. This statement is known as a *precondition*. For example, the Place Local Call use case could be given the following precondition:

The Caller's device has a connection to the system, i.e., the carrier signal is there.

Preconditions are not a description of the event, or trigger, that starts the use case, but rather a statement of the conditions under which the use case is applicable. The precondition is necessary for the use case to be started but is not sufficient to start the use case. The use case must still be started by an actor but can only be started when the precondition is true. In the example, the precondition clearly states that no local calls can be made when there is no carrier signal available.

Postconditions

In addition to using preconditions to clarify when the use case is available, it is often very useful to also specify the state of the system when the use case ends. This is done by the use of postconditions.

A postcondition for a use case should be true regardless of which alternative flows were executed; it should not be true only for the basic flow. If something could fail, you would cover that in the postcondition by describing the states in which the system can be when the use case is completed. For example, the Place Local Call use case could be given the following postcondition:

The connection between the Caller and Callee has been terminated and all call details have been recorded.

This may seem trivial, but we know that as alternative flows are added to the use case, they can often lead to the system being left in unacceptable states. For example, one of our colleagues was once phoned by a friend who was using a prototype next-generation mobile phone. Unfortunately, the new system didn't allow the termination of the connection from the Callee's phone. When the initial call was over and the prototype phone was returned to its owner's pocket, the call button was accidentally pressed and the phone redialed our colleague's number. He answered the call and hung up when nobody replied to his greeting. This should have ended the call, and, by implication, the use case, but unfortunately it did not terminate the connection between the two phones. He was able to repeatedly pick up the phone receiver and listen to events at his friend's house, such as the playing of music, and so on. The end result was that our colleague's phone was left in an unusable state for the next few days as a consequence of receiving a call from a badly behaved system.

The clear definition of the use case's postcondition can go a long way toward alleviating this kind of problem, because it provides a clear statement of the responsibilities of each use case and defines the state the system must be left in when the flow of events completes.

Preconditions and postconditions can be powerful tools when initially defining and scoping the use cases. You first define when the use case is applicable, using a precondition, and what the use case is supposed to achieve, using a postcondition. You can then describe how to reach the postcondition from the precondition by writing the flow of events. See Figure 2-12.

Figure 2-12 A precondition is the state of the system and its surroundings that is required before the use case can be started. A postcondition is the state the system can be in after the use case has ended.

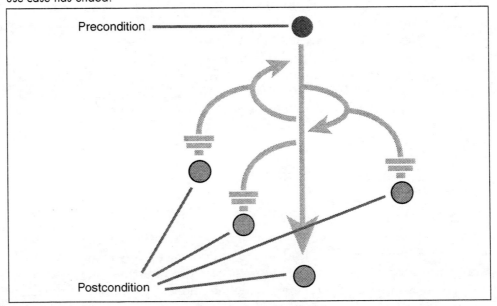

Care should be taken when using pre- and postconditions: Only use them if the use-case audience perceives this as adding value. We introduce them here to illustrate that use cases don't have to start from square one all the time. We revisit preconditions and postconditions in more detail in Chapter 7, The Structure and Contents of a Use Case.

Use-Case Descriptions in Summary

To sum up:

- Ninety percent of the use-case model is beneath the surface shown by the use-case diagrams; the diagrams themselves are merely overviews of system behavior.
- The most important part of a use case is the detailed description.
- The most important part of the use-case description is the flow of events.
- The flow of events has a well-defined structure based around the concepts of the basic and alternative flows.
- The basic flow describes the normal way of achieving the goals of the use case.
- Alternative flows extend the basic flow to cater to variants and exceptions.
- Subflows can be used to make a complex flow of events easier to read.
- Use cases do not have to start from square one but can make assumptions about the state of the system at the time that they start.
- Preconditions and postconditions can be used to clarify the scope of a use case and document any assumptions the use-case author has made about the state of the system.

SUPPORTING ARTIFACTS

We have alluded repeatedly to the insufficiency of use cases alone to fully specify a system's requirements. As we observed in Chapter 1, additional requirements-related documentation is needed to provide a full software requirements specification. In this section, we take a brief look at these supporting artifacts, their format, and the role they play.

The Glossary and/or the Domain Model

A model that describes the essential concepts of the problem domain and environment to be addressed is required to support all use-case modeling endeavors. If we do not have a good set of shared definitions related to the problem to be solved, then we do not have a firm foundation for the construction of our use cases. This model usually takes one of three forms:

1. **A simple, textual glossary**

   The problem domain is described by a simple set of textual definitions and is presented as a traditional glossary of terms. The glossary in Appendix C illustrates the format and level of detail that are usually used.

2. **A formal domain model**

   An in-depth model is required and so a UML domain model is produced.[7] This visual model of the objects in the problem domain is more formal than the glossary. A domain model is particularly important if there are complex relationships among the problem domain objects. These become much clearer if they are shown visually.

   A class diagram or similar technique is used to represent the domain model. In this case, the domain model replaces the textual glossary entirely and contains all of the definitions required to understand the use cases and their supporting documentation.

3. **A textual glossary with illustrative domain model(s)**

   You may build a domain model to complement and further visualize the terms in the glossary. In this case, the domain model is only a partial representation of the glossary, containing only the visualization of a subset of the more complicated concepts.

The important thing to remember is that the purpose and role of these different representations is the same: to define the important terms used in the project. Whatever its format, the focus of the model is on capturing the common vocabulary to be used in all textual descriptions of the system, especially those terms and concepts used in the use-case and actor descriptions.

In general, we use the term *glossary* to refer to this model.[8] The term *domain model* refers to the optional, more formal, UML representation of the glossary. Whatever its format, this model is the project's conceptual model of the world and represents the project team's understanding of the problem domain. Project members use the glossary primarily to understand

---

[7] The domain model is a subset of the "Business Object Model," as described in Jacobson et al., *The Object Advantage*. If a Business Object Model does not exist, some business modeling may need to be undertaken to understand the business and its processes. The alternative is to "guess" at the business objects, which may be acceptable for very simple business processes but which will be inadequate for more complex business processes.

[8] Various other terms are used for what is essentially a model of the world where the system will be deployed. The name adopted is often driven by the source and method used to produce the model. We have seen it referred to as the *essential model*, the *business object model*, the *conceptual model*, the *business information model*, and the *high-level logical data model*. When considered in relationship to the use-case model, all of these models play the role of the glossary in that they define the terminology to be used when describing the system's interaction with the world.

terms that are specific to the project. However, it is important to many other activities:

- **Understanding the Context of the Project.** Stakeholders use the glossary to understand the problem domain as well as the terminology used in the project and its documentation.
- **Creating Use Cases and Other Requirements Documentation.** Analysts use the glossary to capture the terms that are specific to the problem being solved, to clearly define business rules, and to ensure that requirement specifications make correct and consistent use of the terms. As we shall see in Chapter 8, Writing Use-Case Descriptions: An Overview, the glossary is one of the most effective tools we have to help us manage detail and complexity when writing use-case descriptions.
- **Designing the Resulting System.** Developers use the glossary to understand each other's work and make use of the terminology when designing and implementing the system.
- **Producing the User Documentation.** Course developers and technical writers use the glossary to construct training material and documentation using recognized terminology.

To find common terms in the problem domain, consider the terms used by the stakeholders and the development team's general knowledge of the system to be built. Focus on terms that describe the following:

- The concepts and objects used in the organization's daily work or in the system's expected operating environment. In many cases, a list of concepts of this kind already exists in the form of an organizational or industry glossary.

Example

In the simple telephone system, conversation is about, among other things, local calls, long-distance calls, virtual circuits, connections, customers, tariffs, accounts, bills, and payment methods.

- Real-world objects of which the system needs to be aware. These objects occur naturally and include such things as a person, car, dog, bottle, aircraft, passenger, reservation, or letter.

Example

In the simple telephone system, we may also need to consider real-world concepts such as the working week, bank holidays, and postal codes, which have an existence and definitions outside the world of telephone systems.

- Events of which the system needs to be aware. An *event* is a point in time or an incident that the system must be aware of, such as a meeting or an error.

Example

> A natural event in the simple telephone system is the billing date. For each customer the system should "remember" the billing date, the calls that have been made, the tariff that should be applied, and the preferred method of payment.

Each term is typically described as a noun, with a definition. Terms should be in the singular ("bill" and "account," not "bills" and "accounts"). All interested parties should agree on definitions for the terms. Each term should be given a clear and concise definition and be used consistently throughout the use-case model. It is important to remember that, from a use-case modeling perspective, the only terms that require definition are those used in the use-case and actor descriptions. This relationship helps us to constrain any domain modeling that we undertake to the definitions required to define the solution to the problem at hand.

Remember, each glossary term should be used somewhere in the actor or use-case descriptions. If it isn't, it may imply that an actor or use case is missing or that the existing use cases are not complete. It is more likely, though, that the term is not included because it is not needed. In that case, you should remove it from the glossary.

The glossary may also be used to capture the terminology of the process and techniques used when discussing how the software is to be developed (for example, the definitions of *actor* and *use case*). Although useful to the project, these terms are not essential to the well-being of the use-case model.

In projects that do not include business modeling or formal domain modeling, the glossary is the only artifact used to capture the business domain of the project. If you are building your use-case model in an environment where comprehensive business modeling has already been undertaken, then all of the terms required should already have been captured. If the level of detail required to support the use-case model is not there, then you must either update the business models to include it or develop a complementary glossary to complete the documentation of the problem domain.

Conceptually, there should be only one glossary for the system. This artifact is important to all stakeholders, especially when they need to understand or use terms that are specific to the project or the problem domain. It defines the common vocabulary to be used in all the textual descriptions of the system, especially in the use-case descriptions, and its use simplifies description production and comprehension. It also helps to avoid misunderstandings among the stakeholders about the use and meaning of terms. Regardless of its format, it must be easily accessible to all the project's stakeholders.

The production and maintenance of a comprehensive glossary is essential to any successful large-scale use-case modeling exercise. Only the most trivial of systems can be described without the production of an effective and widely used glossary. For most projects, we recommend capturing the glossary as a set of textual definitions, with additional, partial UML domain models to add rigor where required. The glossary should also be augmented with examples and illustrations where these help to clarify and illuminate the terms adopted. The situation to avoid is the one where the same concept is defined both in the glossary and in a domain model. When this occurs, problems ensue because it is inevitable that the two different definitions will diverge.

The role of the glossary in the production of good use-case descriptions is one of the major concepts addressed in Chapter 9, Writing Use-Case Descriptions: Revisited.

Supplementary Specifications

Not all of a system's requirements fit nicely in the use-case descriptions of the system. Many requirements apply to many use cases and do not benefit from being forced into the narrative structure of the use-case descriptions. In the Rational Unified Process there is a special artifact for capturing these requirements: the Supplementary Specification. The requirements captured in these artifacts are referred to as *supplementary requirements*.

The supplementary requirements capture the system requirements that are not readily captured in the use cases of the use-case model. Such requirements include

- Legal and regulatory requirements

Example

The customer must be of legal age to purchase alcohol (for our party).

- Application development standards

Example

The system must be developed in accordance with the Rational Unified Process.

- The quality attributes of the system to be built, including usability, reliability, performance, and supportability requirements

Example

The system must be available at least 90 percent of the time.

- The constraints placed on the design and implementation of the system, such as operating systems, environments, compatibility requirements, programming languages, and other design constraints

Example

The system must be written in Java.

- Other requirements that don't fit naturally into the use cases

Example

Whenever the system is idle for more than 20 seconds during a customer session, the system shall sound the warning beep for 30 seconds. If the customer interaction is not resumed within this time period, then the system shall retain the card and terminate the transaction.

The term *supplementary* often makes people think that these requirements are not as important as those captured in the use cases and in many cases, people assume that they don't need to have them at all. This is a major mistake; many projects have failed because project members have forgotten to focus on some of the major supplementary specifications. In many cases, the supplementary specifications form the major part of a system's critical success criteria.

For example, one of us was once called in to try to turn around a project that was having difficulties passing the most basic user-acceptance tests. The target market for this particular system was a large customer with 300 to 500 simultaneous users. On entry into the user-acceptance test, the system would only support eight simultaneous users. One of the major supplementary specifications, and success criteria, for the project had been completely ignored by the developers, who instead had focused all of their efforts on the system's user interface. As the testing progressed and other problem areas came to light, it became apparent that the developers had failed to investigate any of the requirements beyond the scope of the most basic flow of events. Not surprisingly, the system was never deployed.

As this example illustrates, the supplementary specifications are particularly good at focusing on and capturing the nonfunctional requirements of the system. This makes them a perfect complement to the use cases, which are generally more functional in nature. The difference is not purely between the functional and nonfunctional requirements. Use cases are often the best place to capture many of the nonfunctional requirements, especially those that apply only within the context of a single use case. The supplementary specification is often the best place to capture many of the functional requirements, especially those that are global in nature or do not vary from one use case to the next.

The correct way to think of the relationship between the use cases and the supplementary specifications is one of balance. See Figure 2-13. The balance will vary depending on how dynamic the system to be built needs to be. Where there is a lot of interaction between the system and its actors (for example, an automatic teller machine), the majority of the requirements will be captured in the use cases, with just a few global, nonfunctional requirements captured in the supplementary specifications. In other cases where the amount of interaction is small (for example, a compiler), the majority of the requirements will be captured in the supplementary specification, with a just a few use cases illustrating the goals of, and the interaction with, the user.

If the focus is purely on the use cases, then the overall quality objectives of the system are often ignored. If the focus is purely on the supplementary specifications then the real objectives of the system, in terms of the facilities it offers the users, are often overlooked. In our experience, all systems benefit

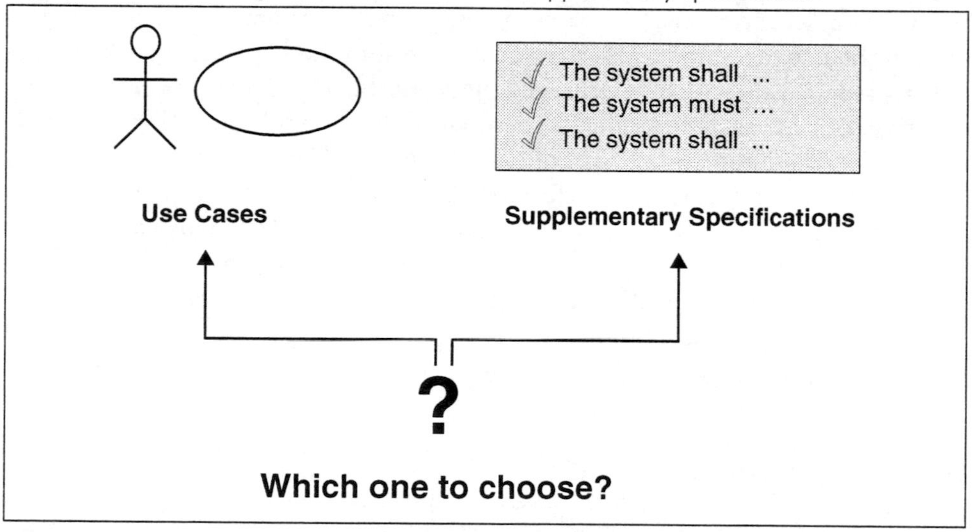

Figure 2-13 Choosing between use cases and supplementary specifications

from being considered from both perspectives and producing both a use-case model and a set of supplementary specifications. The trick is to keep the two in balance and not be lured into focusing all the project's time and effort into one form of specification to the detriment of the other (and usually the project as a whole).

Declarative and Special Requirements

The concept of supplementary requirements maintained outside the use-case model and special requirements, which can be maintained inside the use-case descriptions themselves, are often confused.[9] Special requirements are additional requirements that complement, and only make sense in the context of, individual use cases. They are sometimes captured in their own section within the use-case description, but we prefer to capture them alongside the other supplementary specifications and trace them to the use cases.

The most common form for capturing the supplementary and special requirements is in the form of traditional, declarative requirement statements. These generally take the form of statements indicating what the system shall or must do. For example, the simple telephone system could be given the following supplementary specifications:

There shall be no more than 10 percent signal loss on all communications.

It shall take no longer than 0.1 seconds to make a connection.

Just as a balance must be struck between the requirements that are captured in the use cases and those that are captured in the supplementary specification, balance also must be achieved between those that are captured in the narrative, conversational format of the flow of events and those that are captured in the more traditional declarative format. Care must be taken to choose the right tools for the job. For those adopting use-case techniques, a good grounding in other requirements specification techniques is always an advantage. These techniques will help when deciding where and how extensively to use use cases. Remember all these techniques are purely a means to an end and not an end in themselves.

---

[9] The UML defines a use-case property "special requirements" as "a textual description that collects all requirements, such as nonfunctional requirements, on the use case, that are not considered in the use-case model, but that need to be taken care of during design or implementation."

There are many techniques available for the elicitation and documentation of these requirements. In subsequent chapters we discuss how these requirements are related to use cases and provide some further hints and tips on how to document them. Here, our focus is on how to create and write good use cases rather than the broader, more general topic of requirements management.[10]

SUMMARY

In this chapter we have looked at the definition and role of the basic building blocks of a use-case model. You should now have a better understanding of actors, use cases, the communicate associations, and the use-case diagrams on which they appear and realize that most of the value of the use cases, and consequently the effort required to produce a use-case model, is in the use-case descriptions themselves.

There is more to the components of a use-case model than the elements visible on the use-case diagrams. As well as the visible elements of the use-case model—the actors, use cases, and their associations—a good understanding of the key properties of the use case is also required.

The most important property of a use case is the flow of events. This is where the story is told. Within the flow of events there are three kinds of flows:

1. The basic flow, the most important part of the flow of events, which describes the normal way of achieving the use-case's goal.
2. Alternative flows, which extend the basic flow to allow for variants and exceptions.
3. Subflows (subsections of the other flows), which are extracted to make the original flows easier to read. These are self-contained, titled mini-flows that are included in the original flows by reference to their title.

This structure is important because it allows us to elaborate on all of the variant, optional, and error-handling behavior without losing focus on the essential behavior required of the system.

To be effective, the use-case model must be supported by other requirements-related artifacts:

---

[10] For more detail on how to capture and document the supplementary and special requirements, we recommend Leffingwell and Widrig, *Managing Software Requirements,* 2000, Addison-Wesley.

- The glossary or problem domain model, which is a model of the concepts inherent in the problem domain to be addressed. This is essential to any successful, large-scale use-case modeling exercise.
- Supplementary specifications, an artifact capturing those requirements that do not readily fit into the use-case model. A balance must be maintained between the mainly functional, narrative-driven requirements captured by the use case's flow of events and the declarative, mainly nonfunctional requirements captured in the supplementary specification and the special requirements.

Use-case modeling is based on a formal technique. Like any modeling technique, it is important to understand what the technique is telling you, but it is also important not to overinterpret its application and let the process degenerate into pointless discussions about whether the perfect set of use cases has been attained. Just as a class diagram of a software system can tell you something about the major elements and their relationships but next to nothing about the behavior of the system, a use-case diagram tells you about the relationships between the actors and use cases but very little about what the system does. For that we have to dig into the details.

Chapter 3

Establishing the Vision

Too many project teams dive into the details of the use-case model before they have established a stakeholder community, a shared vision, the real need for the product, or the constraints under which it is to be built. Proceeding with use-case modeling without this kind of foundation often causes immense problems. Some projects are completed before the team realizes that the system produced doesn't meet any of the stakeholders' real needs. Other project teams find it impossible to produce a stable use-case model or even to agree on one at all.

To avoid these kinds of problems, it is essential that the team:

- Establish a good understanding of the stakeholder community
- Demonstrate an understanding of the problem to be solved
- Capture the real needs of the stakeholders and the system features required to fulfill them
- Ensure that the views of the stakeholder community are actively and appropriately represented throughout the project

In this chapter we look at strategies that will help you in these activities and the positive effect that this will have on the quality of the use-case model you produce.

In Chapter 1, we briefly introduced the concept of the requirements pyramid, as shown in Figure 3-1, to clarify the role, purpose, and context of use cases. In this chapter we look more closely at the other elements of the requirements pyramid, discuss how they can be captured, and describe how they affect the construction and detailing of use-case models.

Figure 3-1   The requirements pyramid: Our map of the territory

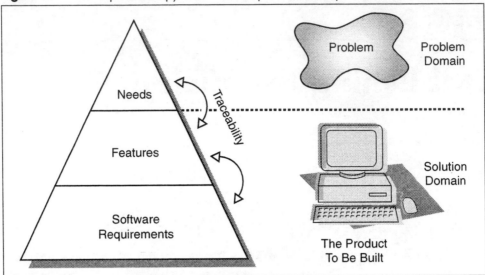

INTRODUCING STAKEHOLDERS AND USERS

Before you start any use-case modeling or other requirements-management activity, you must understand the project's stakeholder community and how it will be involved in the project. You must understand the stakeholder community in order to tackle the following tasks:

- Establishing an understanding of the problems the project should be addressing. This is very hard to do without first identifying who is affected.
- Preparing for a requirements workshop. If a workshop is to be run to identify the system's actors and use cases, then the coordinator needs to know who to invite and which aspects of the business the invitees represent.
- Identifying the sources of the system's requirements. Requirements come from many sources, including, but not limited to, customers, partners, users, and domain experts. Understanding these sources of requirements will allow the project team to decide how best to elicit information from them.

To deliver an effective solution, one that will be wholeheartedly accepted by the stakeholder community, you must have a clear understanding of the stakeholders and their particular needs. It is also important that the people asked to become involved in the project understand the role that they are expected to play and the responsibilities that they are expected to fulfill.

In this section we will look at:

- The definition of a stakeholder
- Why stakeholders are important
- The role of stakeholders in the project
- Why it is necessary to explicitly identify users, stakeholders, and actors.
- How to identify and involve the stakeholders in the project
- The relationships among stakeholders, users, actors, and use cases

What Are Stakeholders?

A stakeholder is

> An individual who is materially affected by the outcome of the system or the project(s) producing the system.[1]

Using this definition, some obvious stakeholders spring to mind:

- The users of the system. If the users are not materially affected by the outcome of the system, they won't use it and the system itself will be a failure.
- The development team. If these people are not materially affected by the outcome of their project and the system that it produces, there is probably something amiss with the commissioning organization's reward structure.

The full set of stakeholders will actually be larger than this. For example, the people who suffer from the problem being addressed are also stakeholders, regardless of the kind of solution chosen.

The decision to develop a system will often affect a great many other people. For example, the decision to invest in a new system involves the investors themselves in the success of the system; the decision by the development team to use third-party software in their solution will involve the suppliers as additional stakeholders. Although these people may not be directly affected

---

[1] This definition is a combination of the definitions of stakeholder from the RUP (the stakeholder role is defined as anyone who is materially affected by the outcome of the project) and Leffingwell and Widrig, 1999 (a stakeholder is an individual who is materially affected by the outcome of the system). This new definition reflects the fact that the stakeholder community comprises both the individuals directly affected by the system and those that are indirectly affected by the system by their involvement in the project.

by the original problem, they are affected by the outcome of the project. Figure 3-2 sums up the relationship between the stakeholders and the problem and its solution.

There can be millions of stakeholders for even the smallest project. Consider for a moment the simple telephone system discussed in the first two chapters. Everyone who uses, or potentially could use, the system is a stakeholder. If you take into account all those who could be materially affected by the outcome of the system, the stakeholder community must also include

- The company's customers: the people who will be paying the bills
- Other telephone companies: the suppliers of the other telephone systems involved in making long-distance calls
- The other companies' customers and users

And so on.... It is obviously impossible to identify all of these people as individuals and involve them all in a project. However, it is entirely possible (not to mention good practice) to put in place a mechanism to allow us to understand the views of all the different types of stakeholder and to ensure that they are all represented in the project's requirements and decision-making process.

Identifying Stakeholder Types

The first step to understanding the stakeholder community is to identify the types of stakeholder affected by the system.

Figure 3-2 The stakeholder community is made up of those people that suffer from the problem and/or are materially affected by the outcome of the solution.

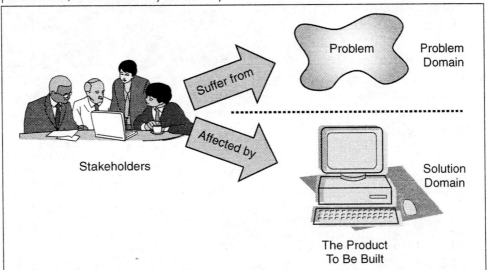

Stakeholder Type: The classification of a set of stakeholders sharing the same characteristics and relationships with the system and/or the project that produces the system.

In the phone system example, users, customers, customer support representatives, technical support staff, developers, marketers, other telephone companies, and the customers of other companies are all candidate stakeholder types for the project producing the simple telephone system.

Stakeholders typically fall into the following categories:

- **Users:** The most obvious types of stakeholder are the actual users of the system. These are the people who will be taking on the roles defined by the actors in the use-case model.
- **Sponsors:** The business managers, financiers, shareholders, champions, department heads, sellers, marketers, steering committee members, and other people who are investing in the production of the system. These stakeholders are only indirect users of the system or are affected only by the business outcomes that the system influences. Many are economic buyers for or internal champions of the system.
- **Developers:** Project managers, system maintainers, testers, support staff, designers, coders, technical writers, production staff, and any other types of developer involved in the production and support of the system.
- **Authorities:** Experts in a particular aspect of the problem or solution domain. These include legislative authorities, standards organizations, organizational governance departments, external and internal regulatory bodies, domain experts, and technology experts.
- **Customers:** The people and/or organizations who will actually be purchasing the final system. These can include the buyers, evaluators, accountants, and agents acting on behalf of the purchasing organizations.

The actual list of stakeholder types for a project will be more concrete than this; it will identify specific user types, agencies, and organizational units. The key thing is to ensure that all those affected by the outcome of the system are considered. When identifying the stakeholder types, focus on understanding how they are affected by the project and the system it will produce.

Identifying Stakeholder Representatives and Stakeholder Roles

The next step is to define a set of stakeholder roles within the project that enable the views of all the stakeholder types to be represented. Appropriate people can then be recruited to fulfill these roles. The objective is to recruit a set of *stakeholder representatives* to be directly involved in the project.

> **Stakeholder Representative:** A member of the stakeholder community directly involved in the steering, shaping, and scoping of the project. A stakeholder representative represents one or more stakeholder types.

Before you can recruit an appropriate set of stakeholder representatives, you must define how these representatives will participate in your project.

> **Stakeholder Role:** The classification of a set of stakeholder representatives who share the same roles and responsibilities with respect to the project.

The definition of the stakeholder roles allows the stakeholder representatives to understand the commitment they are making to the project, the responsibilities that they are taking on, the level of involvement they will be required to provide, and who they are representing. When identifying the stakeholder roles, you are interested in understanding how they will interact with the project as well as which subset of the stakeholder types they represent. It is important to ensure that each type of stakeholder is represented and that their representation is at a level that reflects both the importance of the stakeholders to the project and the capabilities, and availability, of the representatives.

Some methodologies go so far as to explicitly define a set of stakeholder roles to complement the more commonly defined developer roles. For example, the Dynamic System Development Method (DSDM)[2] explicitly defines the following stakeholder roles as essential to any user interface-intensive project:

- **Ambassador User:** Responsible for bringing knowledge of the user community into the project team and disseminating information from the team back to the rest of the users. The ambassador users act as the major source of requirements to the project.
- **Advisor User:** Responsible for representing users not covered by the ambassador users. Typically part of a panel of staff that attends workshop-style demonstrations of prototypes. Outside prearranged events, the Advisor Users channel their information and feedback through the Ambassador Users.
- **Visionary:** Responsible for ensuring that the right decisions are made with respect to system scope and that the original business objectives of the project are met.
- **Executive Sponsor:** Responsible for project funding. Executive sponsors are the ultimate decisionmakers in the business area.

---

[2] The Dynamic Systems Development Method is a rapid application development method for constructing use interface-intensive systems popular in the United Kingdom.

That stakeholders play four critical roles further underscores the importance of achieving the correct level of stakeholder involvement in modern software development practices. (By way of contrast, only two developer roles have been defined: Senior Developer and Developer.[3])

It is impossible to define a useful, universally applicable set of stakeholder roles. These generic roles will inevitably be too abstract to be useful as anything more than a checklist (that is, how many user types does each ambassador user represent and how exactly do you involve them in the project?). We recommend that you instead perform a formal analysis of the stakeholder types and define a specific set of concrete stakeholder roles. This significantly increases the chances that you will secure a sufficient and appropriate level of stakeholder representation and involvement in the project. (Remember that for a large-scale project there could be many millions of stakeholders, far too many to directly involve in the development project.)

In most projects, the term *stakeholder* is used to indicate the set of stakeholder representatives directly involved in the project. Little thought is given to the broader stakeholder community and to the fair representation of their views. Because stakeholder representatives can play a much more significant role than they are sometimes given credit for, it is well worth your effort to ensure that they understand both their responsibilities to the project and to the people they represent.

The practicalities of defining stakeholder types and stakeholder roles are covered in the section Involving Stakeholders and Users in Your Project later in this chapter. This section also explains how to recruit stakeholder representatives and suggests ways to involve them throughout the project.

The Role of Stakeholders and Stakeholder Representatives

Stakeholders and stakeholder representatives own the problem and are affected by the proposed solution. They are also the primary source of requirements. Figure 3-3 illustrates this relationship. The problem itself being fairly intangible, it is the stakeholder representatives that bridge the gap between the problem and the specification of the proposed solution. The requirements documentation itself is a formal articulation of the stakeholders' goals and acts as their surrogate on the project when the stakeholder representatives themselves are not available. Figure 3-4 sums up the relationships between the stakeholders, the system, and the requirements documentation.

---

[3] These roles are presented for illustrative purposes only and are not intended to reflect the full set of roles defined by the DSDM.

Figure 3-3 The stakeholders are the primary source of requirements.

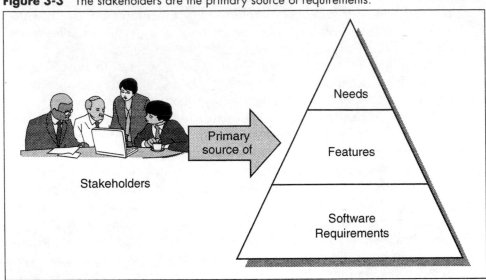

Figure 3-4 The requirements act as the representation of the stakeholders' goals.

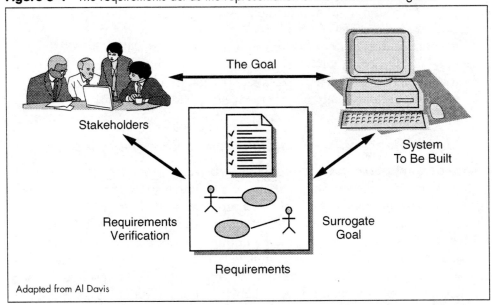

Consider which stakeholder types will be the sources of the requirements when defining stakeholder roles and appointing stakeholder representatives. All stakeholder types must be represented, but it is important to focus attention where it will receive the best return. For example, shareholders are a type of stakeholder, but they will not provide many, or any, requirements to the project. Although their interests should certainly be considered and represented, the project team should focus on addressing the requirements of the more direct stakeholders, such as users and developers. The makeup of the set of stakeholder representatives should reflect the relative importance of the stakeholder types as requirements sources.

The stakeholder representatives who will act as the primary source of requirements information must be directly involved in the project and have a clear understanding of the role that they are expected to play. Many projects run into trouble because the stakeholder representatives are not actively engaged in the project and do not provide feedback when it is needed. Stakeholder representatives' indifference may manifest itself by their unavailability when eliciting project requirements, not making time to review and sign off on project deliverables, not committing themselves for the full lifetime of the project, or just plain forgetting why they are involved in the first place. The quality of the final result is often directly derived from the quality of the participation of the stakeholders.

To combat this, clearly define the stakeholder roles and ensure that stakeholder representatives understand their roles and their responsibilities in representing different stakeholder communities. The role of stakeholder representative includes but is not limited to the following:

- Faithfully representing the views and needs of the section of the broader stakeholder community they represent
- Taking an active role in the project
- Participating in requirements and other project reviews
- Participating in the assessment and verification of the product produced
- Attending workshops and meetings
- Doing independent research
- Championing the project to the stakeholders they represent

There are many ways of involving the stakeholder representatives in the project. If you are developing an information system to be used internally within your company, you may include people with user experience and business domain expertise in your development team. Very often you will start the discussions with the business needs and corresponding processes rather than with the system requirements. Alternatively, if you are developing a product to be sold to a marketplace, you may make extensive use of your marketing people and tools such as questionnaires and surveys to better understand the needs of customers in that market.

Each and every project requires focused stakeholder involvement. For all projects:

- Active stakeholder involvement is imperative.
- A collaborative and cooperative approach involving all the stakeholders is essential.[4]

Remember: The stakeholders own the problem and are the source of the project's requirements. If the system is not a success with the stakeholders, then it is not a success, period.

Users: A Very Important Class of Stakeholder

We now focus on one important type of stakeholder: system users. Users will play most of the roles defined by the system's actors, and their requirements help to shape the use-case model. Every user is a stakeholder, because he or she will be *materially affected by the outcome of the system*, but not all the stakeholders are necessarily users.

In Chapter 2 we discussed the difference between users and actors. Even in our simple telephone system the difference between the users and the actors is quite clear. The actors define roles, whereas the same user could play many roles. In some cases the caller (the person making the phone call) will be the customer (the payer of the bills). In some cases (if reversing of charges is supported) the person being called could be the customer.

To fully understand the user environment and provide context for the actor definitions, you must undertake a detailed analysis of the various types of users.

> **User Type:** The classification of a set of users with similar skill sets and other characteristics who share the same roles and responsibilities within the system's environment.[5]

A User Type is a fine-grained definition of a particular stakeholder type. Having a full profile of each user type is essential so that you can understand their skill set, attitude, language, and other characteristics. When dealing with the more abstract concept of actors, it is very easy to forget that actual users may have varying skill levels and capabilities.

---

[4] These are variations of two of the nine principles that drive the Dynamic Systems Development Methodology.

[5] If RUP-style business modeling is being undertaken, then the user types are the subset of the business workers and business actors that directly interact with the system.

Some user types[6] for the simple telephone system example are

- **Technology Adopters**—Many of the potential users are technology adopters interested in exploiting the full set of facilities provided by the system, especially text and e-mail capabilities.
  - *Characteristics:* High-volume users of the system. Technology adopters currently make up 40 percent of the company's customer base. They are typically young and highly influenced by trends, fashion, and marketing.
  - *Competencies:* Technically literate, happy to learn complex operating procedures to set up and use their systems. Have e-mail accounts and other on-line facilities.
  - *Success Criteria:* Reliability, range of functionality, and low cost of additional facilities.
  - *Actors:* Caller, Callee, and Customer.
- **Standard Users**—A large subset of the existing user community having no interest in exploiting the technical capabilities of the telephone network and requiring a simple system that functions in the same way as traditional telephone systems.
  - *Characteristics:* Low-volume users of the system. Standard users currently make up 60 percent of the company's customer base. They are typically older and resistant to trends, fashion, and marketing.
  - *Competencies:* Would like to use the more technical features of the system but are frustrated by having to learn complex operating procedures to set up and use their systems.
  - *Success Criteria:* Reliability, ease of use for traditional features, no increase in cost for, or imposition of, additional facilities.
  - *Actors:* Caller, Callee, and Customer.
- **Messaging Devices**—Fax machines, voice-mail systems, answering machines, and other devices capable of sending and receiving telephone communications.
  - *Characteristics:* Over 50 percent of the current customer base connect secondary devices to their systems to send and receive messages.
  - *Competencies:* Limited capabilities to respond to messages from the system. Negotiate messaging protocols etc. with each other.
  - *Success Criteria:* High speed, high bandwidth, low noise connections.
  - *Actors:* Caller, Callee.

---

[6] This is not intended to be the full user list but an illustrative sample. Other user types include those related to the support and maintenance of the system. These are not required for the purpose of this illustration.

All of these user types play the roles defined by the Caller and Callee actors but they have different characteristics and capabilities. They also have different success criteria and requirements for the system being built. This will impact on the contents and structure of the use-case model and the other requirements documentation. If these variations in emphasis are not considered during the use-case modeling, then the system produced may end up satisfying only a very small segment of the target customers.

As one of the most important types of stakeholder, active users are essential to most projects. The amount of user involvement required is variable; one user may be a full-time *user ambassador* permanently assigned to the project, another may be a member of a user panel, and yet another may simply submit ideas and feedback by questionnaire. When defining the stakeholder roles, you should take into consideration the amount of user involvement necessary to support the project, the style of user involvement most suited to the project and the users, the availability of the users to the project, and the level of commitment the users have to the project.

In most cases, it will be impossible to involve all of the users. What is essential is that the set of stakeholder representatives includes user representatives and that for each type of user there is clearly defined representation. Users must understand how they are represented in the project, and user representatives must understand their responsibilities toward the users they represent.

For the project developing the simple telephone system, the stakeholder roles have the following responsibilities for representing the users:

- **Marketer**—The marketing team representative to the project; also represents the interests of the marketing and sales departments as well as the users. The marketer is available to attend workshops and reviews related to the system's requirements.
  - *Users Represented:* Technology Adopters, Standard Users.
- **Ambassador User**—A member of the customer support team has been seconded to the project to provide full-time user representation; responsible for representing all the users of the system, including the organization's support and operational teams. The ambassador user is key member of the project's requirements team, creating requirements documentation as well as attending workshops and reviews.
  - *Users Represented:* Technology Adopters, Standard Users, Messaging Devices, plus the company's internal users (as yet undefined).
- **Support Working Group Member**—A working group has also been set up to represent the support and operational staff affected by the

new system. This is chaired by the Ambassador User and meets once a month to discuss the requirements and progress of the new system.
  – *Users Represented:* The company's internal users (as yet undefined).
- **Focus Group Member**—Various focus groups are set up and run by the Marketer to explore requirements issues with representative groups of target and existing customers. These are formed on an as-needed basis and facilitated by the Marketer and the Ambassador User.
  – *Users Represented:* Technology Adopters, Standard Users.

Stakeholders and Use-Case Modeling

An understanding of the stakeholders and their particular needs is essential to developing an effective use-case model. In many cases, the system has indirect (or secondary) goals that are not directly related to satisfying the needs of the actors (and by implication, the users). Other stakeholders may have a vested interest in the outcome of a particular use case. This is often the case when management reports must be generated or management information captured but none of the managers is directly involved in the use case. "What are the actor's goals? Where is the value to the actor?" ask the use-case modelers. In these cases, the user, playing the role of the actor, is often a more junior employee whose only real goal is to do a job, which is a valid goal for a use case to support and can certainly be considered of value to the actor.

The set of stakeholders who supply the requirements for the use case is not restricted to those who represent the users involved in the use case (that is, play the role specified by the actors). If you want to know the amount of management information that must be captured, you should talk to the managers who will be using the information and not the operators who will be producing the reports. Understanding these indirect relationships can be of great help when viewing the use-case model, because the goals of the broader stakeholder community can often be contrary to those of the actor involved. For example, the stakeholders may require additional security checks or impose limits and restrictions on what the actor is allowed to achieve.

The most effective way to work with stakeholders is to directly involve the stakeholder representatives in the development and review of the use cases themselves. Figure 3-5 illustrates the relationship between the stakeholder representatives and the actors and use cases. As we explain throughout the book, use-case modeling is a synthetic rather than analytic

Figure 3-5 The relationships between stakeholders and actors and stakeholders and use cases

technique. If you do not involve the correct stakeholder representatives in the creation and validation of the use-case model, then the model itself will be worthless. Identifying and involving the correct set of stakeholder representatives is the essential foundation of any successful use-case modeling activity.

We have often been subcontracted to facilitate workshops or provide training to software engineers who have been charged with producing a use-case model to express the requirements of the system they are about to build. One thing soon becomes clear: Given a challenge, these highly talented people will rise to the occasion and produce a solution. No matter how little experience they have of the problem to be addressed or the domain in which it occurs, they will produce a use-case model and by the end of its development believe that it is an accurate reflection of the actual requirements. In reality, the use-case model produced will be a fiction, reflecting the technical objectives of the developers rather than the business needs of the stakeholders. Unless the people involved in creating the use-case model have excellent domain experience and communicate thoroughly with the other stakeholders, the model produced will not capture the real requirements.

Knowledgeable stakeholder representatives must be involved in all of the use-case modeling activities throughout the life cycle of the project if the project is to be a success. To facilitate this involvement, it helps to trace the stakeholder roles to the areas of the use-case model where their input is most useful. Table 3-1 shows the relationship between the stakeholder roles and the use cases for the simple telephone system example.

Table 3-1 Relating Stakeholder Roles to Use Cases for the Simple Telephone System

Stakeholder Role	Use Case
Ambassador User	Place Local Call Place Long-Distance Call Get Call History Get Billing Information
Marketer	Place Local Call Place Long-Distance Call Get Call History
Support Working Group	Get Billing Information

INVOLVING STAKEHOLDERS AND USERS IN YOUR PROJECT

The following steps can be applied iteratively to establish an appropriate level of stakeholder involvement in your use-case modeling activities.

Step 1: Identify Stakeholder and User Types

Because the number of actual stakeholders can be very large, you should first identify the various types of stakeholder that must be involved in the project. Model the stakeholder community by defining discrete types of stakeholders: The set of types is determined by the problem domain, user environment, development organization, and so on. Depending on the domain expertise of the development team, identifying the stakeholder types may be easy or hard. A good start is to ask decisionmakers, potential users, and other interested parties the following questions:

- Who will be affected by the success or failure of the new solution?
- Who are the users of the system?
- Who is the economic buyer for the system?
- Who is the sponsor of the development?
- Who else will be affected by the outputs that the system produces?
- Who will evaluate and sign off on the system when it is delivered and deployed?
- Are there any other internal or external users of the system whose needs must be addressed?
- Are there any regulatory bodies or standards organizations to which the system must comply?
- Who will develop the system?
- Who will install and maintain the new system?

- Who will support and supply training for the new system?
- Who will test and certify the new system?
- Who will sell and market the new system?
- Is there anyone else?
- Okay, is there anyone else?

Stakeholder Type information

When defining the stakeholder types, be sure to capture the following information:

- **Name:** Name the stakeholder type.
- **Brief Description:** Briefly describe what the stakeholder type represents with respect to the system or the project. Typically, users take on the role of one or more system actors.
- **Stakeholder Representative:** Summarize how the stakeholders will be represented within the project. This is typically done by referencing the applicable stakeholder representative role or roles.

For stakeholder types that are also user types, the following information is also worth capturing:

- **Characteristics:** User types may be characterized in terms of their physical environment, social environment, numbers, and other general characteristics such as gender, age, and cultural background.
- **Competencies:** Describe the skills that users need to perform their job, as well as any other relevant information about the user type that is not mentioned elsewhere. This can include their level of domain knowledge, business qualifications, level of computer experience, and other applications that they use.

A more detailed definition of the stakeholder and user types may be required if the stakeholder or user community is particularly complex. In these cases, full stakeholder and user descriptions can be produced. Examples of such descriptions are provided in the Vision documents included in the case study and template appendices.

Step 2: Identify and Recruit the Stakeholder Representatives

After the stakeholders in the project have been identified, it is time to start recruiting the stakeholder representatives who will actively participate in the project. Of particular interest are those who will be directly involved in the use-case modeling activities. Before you approach any individuals to become stakeholder representatives, you should attempt to define exactly what their roles and responsibilities toward the project will be as well as which part of the stakeholder community they will represent. You do this by defining a set of stakeholder roles and relating these to the stakeholder types that they explicitly represent.

Stakeholder Role information

When defining stakeholder roles, be sure to capture the following information:

- **Name:** Name the stakeholder role.
- **Brief Description:** Briefly describe the stakeholder role and what it represents with respect to the development project. Typically, the role is to represent one or more stakeholder or user types, some aspect of the development organization, or certain types of customer or some other affected area of the business.
- **Responsibilities:** Summarize the role's key responsibilities with regard to the project and the system being developed. Capture the value the role will be adding to the project team. For example, responsibilities could include ensuring that the system will be maintainable, ensuring that there will be a market demand for the product's features, monitoring the project's progress, approving funding, and so forth.
- **Involvement:** Briefly describe how they will be involved. For example, a permanent user ambassador will undertake use-case modeling and other requirements activities, attend requirements workshops during the inception phase, and serve as a member of the change control board.

Again, sometimes a more detailed definition of the stakeholder role is required if the stakeholder community is particularly complex or stakeholder involvement is particularly difficult to achieve. In such cases, a full stakeholder role description can be produced. Examples of such descriptions are provided in the Vision documents included in the case study and template appendices.

The set of stakeholder roles and their relative importance will evolve over time. Certain stakeholder roles may be more important during the production of the first release of the product than the later releases. For example, the initial version of a product may be aimed at only certain user types that have the characteristics of the early adopter, whereas later versions may be geared toward less technologically advanced types of users.[7]

---

[7] See *Crossing the Chasm: Marketing and Selling Technology Products to Mainstream Customers* by Geoffrey A. Moore, 1991, HarperCollins, for the definitive text on early adopters and other forms of customers. This highlights the reasons why the analysts must understand their stakeholders if they want their product to be successful.

When setting up the initial set of stakeholder representatives, look for users, partners, customers, domain experts, and industry analysts who can represent your stakeholders. Determine which individuals you would work with to collect information, taking into consideration their knowledge, communication skills, availability, and "importance." These individuals will make good stakeholder representatives for the project—the set of stakeholder representatives form, in effect, an "extended project team." In general, the best approach is to have a small (2–5) group of people that can stay for the duration of the project. Also, the more people there are in your extended team, the more time it will take to manage them and make sure that you use their time effectively. Often these people will not work full-time on the project—they typically participate in one or more use-case modeling and requirements-gathering workshops in the early phases of the project, and later on they participate in review sessions.

Many companies have problems establishing effective communication between the business and IT communities. Very often it is difficult for software development projects to get any time from the appropriate business people; there is usually something more important to do than worry about a system that doesn't even exist yet. Recruiting the right stakeholder representatives to participate in the project is therefore extremely important. Potential stakeholder representatives should understand the commitment required of them to provide not only the initial requirements for the solution but also ongoing guidance and review of progress. Larger projects will require full-time user and business representatives. If you cannot find stakeholders willing to make such commitments, then you probably should question the commitment of the organization to the project. In companies where this happens, there are usually patterns of two sequential projects: one to develop the wrong system, followed by another to develop the right system.

Depending on the proximity and commitment of the stakeholder community to the project, identifying the stakeholder representatives may be easy or hard. Often, this simply involves formalizing the commitment the user and business representatives are making to the project.

The following questions can help you define the stakeholder roles:

- Is every stakeholder type represented?
- Is every affected business unit and department represented?
- Who will evaluate and sign off on the requirements specification?
- Who will attend the use-case modeling and other requirements workshops?
- Who will supply the domain knowledge required to develop a successful solution?

- Who will be involved in any market research undertaken to justify and validate the product?
- Which stakeholder types are the most important?
- Who is the target audience for the release of the product under development?

The stakeholder representatives that represent the users are only one subset of the stakeholder representatives. It is important to recognize that the set of stakeholder representatives must be broader than those drawn directly from the user community. A good way to ensure that all the stakeholders are covered by the set of stakeholder representatives is to check that every stakeholder type is represented by at least one stakeholder role and that there is at least one stakeholder representative fulfilling each stakeholder role.

Step 3: Involve the Stakeholder Representatives in the Project

Various techniques can be used to involve the stakeholder representatives in the project. They include (but are not limited to) the following:

- **Interviews:** Interviews are among the most useful techniques for involving stakeholders in a project. If you have a good understanding of the stakeholder's role, you can keep the interview focused on the issues at hand.
- **Questionnaires:** Questionnaires are a very useful technique, particularly when a large number of stakeholder representatives is involved. Questionnaires have to be designed, and the audience targeted, with great care.
- **Focus Groups:** A focus group allows you to sample sets of stakeholder representatives to get their perspective on what the system must do. Focus groups tend to be used to gather specific feedback on specific topics.
- **Advisory Boards:** An advisory board is a kind of standing focus group. It provides a way to gather stakeholder perspectives without the overhead of establishing a focus group. The disadvantage compared to a focus group is that the composition of the advisory board can't be varied according to topic.
- **Workshops:** Workshops can be a very useful way to capture requirements, build teams, and develop their understanding of the system. They should be well planned with a defined agenda that is sent to participants beforehand along with any background reading material.
- **Reviews:** Reviews are formal or informal meetings organized with the specific intent to review something, whether a document or a prototype.

- **Role Playing:** This is a facilitation technique that is typically used in conjunction with workshops to elicit specific information or feedback.

The choice of technique is very closely coupled to the definitions of the stakeholder roles and the availability of actual individuals to take on the responsibilities defined by the roles. There is no point in deciding that a project will have full-time ambassador users attending weekly requirements workshops if there are no experienced users in a position to take on this level of commitment. This is why the three steps should be applied iteratively and the level of stakeholder representative involvement constantly monitored. In our experience, paying attention to the stakeholder community and continuously involving them, in the project in appropriate ways significantly increases the chances of project success.

The technique most closely associated with the creation of use-case models is the workshop. These can, of course, be used to investigate many other aspects of a project, for example, to brainstorm the characteristics of the target customer, or to develop a vision statement. Chapter 5, Getting Started with a Use-Case Modeling Workshop, explicitly addresses how workshops can be used to kick-start the use-case modeling process.

To successfully build use-case models, you must have sufficient stakeholder representation in the creation and validation of the models, and stakeholder representatives must focus on satisfying the real needs of the broader stakeholder community.

CREATING A SHARED VISION

After the initial set of stakeholder representatives has been assembled to work on the project, the first thing to do is to create a vision of the system that they can all share. To be effective, this vision must provide a shared understanding of the problem to be solved and unify the various stakeholder perspectives. If there is no shared vision, then it will be very difficult to:

- Actively involve the stakeholder representatives in the project
- Assess whether real progress is being made
- Manage the project scope
- Validate the decisions made in the day-to-day running of the project
- Bring new developers or stakeholder representatives into the project
- Have effective communication among the stakeholders

To be able to achieve a truly collaborative and cooperative working environment, it is essential that everyone involved in the project share the same vision of the project and the system to be built.

In this section we will look at:

- Identifying the underlying problem to be solved
- Capturing the stakeholders' needs
- Providing a high-level requirements specification
- Providing a product overview
- How these elements complement the use-case model

Analyze the Problem

Before you dive into the specification and production of your solution, it is always a good idea to take a step back and consider the problems that you expect your solution to solve and the opportunities it will exploit. This will enable you to ensure that all of the functionality provided by the system is directly contributing to the alleviation of these problems and the success of the product. It will also help you to validate that you have the correct stakeholders involved in the project.

A problem can be defined as the difference between things as perceived and things as desired (Gause and Weinberg, 1989) or as a question or matter to be worked out (*Collins Modern English Dictionary*). Both of these definitions emphasize that there are many ways to solve a problem, not all of which require the production of a solution. In many cases, changing the customers' perception of what they have now or changing their perception of what they want is sufficient to resolve the problem. If a difference does not exist between what you perceive you have and what you want to have, then you don't have a problem.

If you want to satisfy customers' real needs, you must understand what problem they are trying to solve. You want to avoid hearing a "Yes . . . but . . ." when you deliver the final product (for example, "Yes, it meets the requirements, but it does not solve my problem."). Also, if you want to avoid extra work, it pays to focus on the real problem and to focus on the part of the problem that you actually need to solve. Solving the wrong part of the problem means you may have to go back and redo much of your work.

The best way to capture the problem is to construct a problem statement. This is a solution-neutral summary of the stakeholders' shared understanding of the problem to be solved. It includes an assessment of the problem's impact and the benefits to be gained by its solution. It can be captured using the simple template shown in Table 3-2. The beauty of the problem statement is its ability, as illustrated by Figure 3-6, to represent the tip of the requirements pyramid while simply and succinctly summarizing the problem to be solved. Understanding the problem is the first step in understanding the requirements. The stakeholders often describe the problem in terms of their own

Table 3-2 Problem Statement Template

The problem of	[describe the problem]
Affects	[the stakeholders affected by the problem]
The impact of which is	[what is the impact of the problem?]
A successful solution would	[list some key benefits of a successful solution]

Figure 3-6 The problem statement represents the tip of the requirements pyramid.

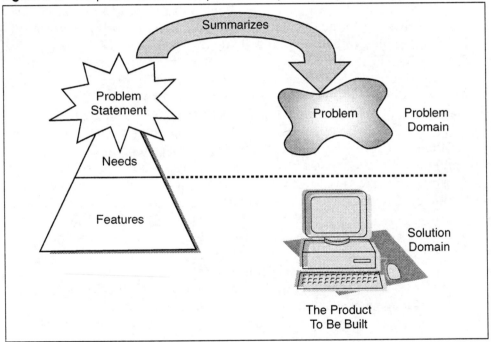

needs, but each need should reflect an aspect of the same underlying problem. All projects embarking on use-case modeling should take time to produce at least a simple problem statement.

Often, the stakeholders have different perspectives on the problem (these are represented by the different stakeholder needs; see the next section), but it is very important that they reach agreement on a shared problem at some shared level of abstraction. If they cannot agree on a simple problem statement, then they are unlikely to agree on the scope or suitability of any proposed solution. Sometimes, achieving a shared definition of the problem can be very difficult, yet it's essential to understand why stakeholders want to do something new. There are many ways to build up this understanding. Our favorite is to perform some root-cause analysis using fishbone diagrams and then apply the Pareto principle to help in leveling the root causes.[8]

Remember: After a team of people starts use-case modeling, it is very easy for them to forget the problems that the system is intended to address and to start inventing new use cases. It is very easy for their interest in applying a modeling technique, such as use cases, to totally override the original purpose that led to the adoption of the technique. You should always remember that use-case modeling is a means to an end and not an end in itself.

Table 3-3 shows an example of a problem statement for a customer support system. Note that in the problem statement, the subject is the stakeholder, "I need to . . . ;" in the corresponding requirements, the subject is the system "The system provides . . . ." The goal of this problem analysis is to make sure that all parties involved agree on what the problem to be solved is. To this end, it is important to consider the business aspects of the problem as well as technical ones. Without checks and balances, many development teams will immediately dive into the technical details of their proposed solution without even considering the business aspects of the problem the solution is intended to solve. It is essential that the project team have a good understanding of the business opportunity being met by the product and the market forces that motivate the product decisions. This will require the development of additional business-focused documentation (for example, a business case and supporting business model) to complement the problem analysis summarized by the problem statement.

Table 3-3   The Problem Statement for a Customer Support System

The problem of	untimely and improper resolution of customer service issues
Affects	our customers, customer support representatives, and service technicians,
The impact of which is	customer dissatisfaction, perceived lack of quality, unhappy employees, and loss of revenue.
A successful solution would	provide real-time access to a troubleshooting database by support representatives and facilitate dispatch of service technicians, in a timely manner, only to those locations that genuinely need their assistance.

---

[8] Leffingwell and Widrig, 2000.

Understand the Key Stakeholder and User Needs

Effectively solving any complex problem involves satisfying the needs of a diverse group of stakeholders. Typically, stakeholders will have different perspectives on the problem and different needs that must be addressed by the solution. These can be acknowledged and tracked by explicitly capturing and documenting the needs of each stakeholder type.

We'll define a stakeholder need as

> A reflection of the business, personal or operational problem (or opportunity) that must be addressed to justify consideration, purchase, or use of a new system.[9]

Figure 3-7 uses the requirements pyramid to illustrate the relationship between the needs and the problem statement. Capturing stakeholder needs allows us to understand how and to what extent the different aspects of the problem affect different types of stakeholders. This complements, and provides a deeper understanding of, the shared problem statement. You can think of stakeholder needs as an expression of the true "business requirements" of the system. They will provide an insight into the root causes of the overall shared problem and define a set of solution-independent requirement statements that, if met, will solve the underlying business problem.

Figure 3-7 Needs reflect the problem from an individual stakeholder perspective.

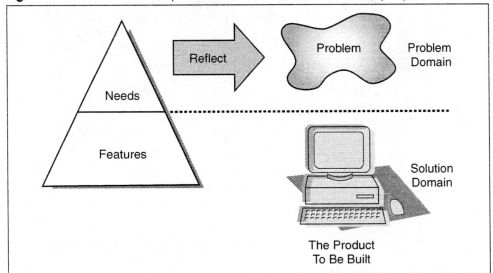

---

[9] Leffingwell and Widrig, 2000.

The description of each stakeholder need should include the reasons behind the need and clearly indicate why it is important to the affected stakeholders. The needs should be written in a solution-independent fashion and address the root causes of the problem only. Attempting to address more than the root causes will encourage the solution developers to produce solutions to problems that do not exist. For each stakeholder need it is also useful to understand

- The relative importance the stakeholders and users place on satisfying each need.
- Which stakeholders perceive the need
- How this aspect of the problem is currently addressed. State the current business situation. By specifying the current state you will better be able to understand the impact of the use cases you will write.
- What solutions the stakeholders would like to see. Specify the desired business situation.
- How success will be measured. All requirements should have some measurable success criteria. If you are unable to measure the success, you will never be able to determine whether you have reached your desired state. When changing something as large as a business, it may be that the success criteria cannot be measured for some time.

The documentation of the stakeholder needs does not describe

- The stakeholders' specific requests (which are captured in separate stakeholder request artifacts).
- The stakeholders' specific requirements. High-level requirements are captured as features, and the detailed requirements are captured in the use-case model and Supplementary Specifications.

The stakeholder needs to provide the background and justification for why the requirements are needed. A typical system will have only a handful of needs, usually somewhere between 10 and 15. For example, the set of needs for the simple telephone system includes

Easy to Use: The system shall be easy to use by both technology adopters and technophobes enabling all users to simply and effectively use both the standard and advanced features of the system.

Provide Up-to-Date Status Information: The system shall provide real-time information to all users related to the duration and costs of calls.

Extensible: The system shall be extensible, allowing the introduction of new services and facilities without disruption to the level of customer service supplied.

Elicitation activities may involve using techniques such as interviews, brainstorming, conceptual prototyping, questionnaires, and competitive analysis. The result of the elicitation is a list of requests and needs that are described textually and that have been given priority relative to one another.

We recommend the use of the MoSCoW rules[10] when prioritizing stakeholder needs. MoSCoW is derived from the first letters of the following prioritizing criteria:

Must have (Mo)
Should have (S)
Could have (Co)
Want to have but will not have this time round (W)

For most practitioners, the "W" actually stands for "Won't have." Ranking and cumulative voting techniques are used to identify the needs that **must** be solved as opposed to those that the stakeholders would like addressed. The use cases defined for the system can then be explicitly traced back to the stakeholder needs that they address. This allows a more objective assessment of the benefit provided by each use case and ensures that each use case is actually helping to address actual stakeholder needs.

Describe the Features and Other High-Level Product Requirements

To complement the use-case model and provide a high-level view of the system, it is very useful to create a high-level requirements view of the product to be built. This view is provided by the product feature set and, where required, other high-level product requirement definitions.

More on Features

Features are the high-level capabilities (services or qualities) of the system that are necessary to deliver benefits to the users and that help to fulfill the stakeholder and user needs. The feature set provides a summary of the advertised benefits of the product to be built. Figure 3-8 illustrates the relationship among the needs, the features, and the system to be built.

---

[10] The MoSCoW rules are a method for prioritizing requirements used quite widely in the United Kingdom especially by followers of the Dynamic System Development Method (DSDM). In *The Dynamic System Development Method*, Jennifer Stapleton introduces the MoSCoW rules thus:

> You will not find the MoSCoW rules in the DSDM Manual, but they have been adopted by many organizations using DSDM as an excellent way of managing the relative priorities of requirements in a RAD project. They are the brainchild of Dai Clegg of Oracle UK, who was one of the early participants in the DSDM Consortium.

Figure 3-8 The features fulfill the needs and summarize the product to be built.

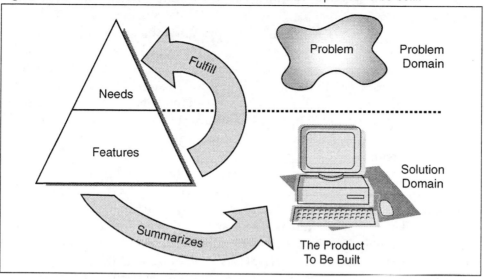

Features can be functional or nonfunctional. Many features describe externally accessible services that typically require a series of inputs to achieve the desired result. For example, a feature of a problem-tracking system might be the ability to provide trending reports. Other features describe the externally visible qualities that the system will possess. For example, another feature of the problem-tracking system might be the quality of the data used to produce the trending reports. Because features are used to summarize the capabilities and qualities of the product to be built, they must be accessible to all the members of the project team and all the stakeholders. The level of detail must be general enough for everyone to understand. However, enough detail must be available to provide team members with the information they need to shape, validate, and manage the use-case model and Supplementary Specifications.

The problem with defining features is that they are often "all over the map"; they have no precise definition and cannot be used to really drive the development or testing of the system. Although generally high level in nature, there is no defined level of abstraction to which a feature must conform. They just represent some area of the functionality of the system that, *at this time*, is important to the users of the system. Because they represent the things that are important *at this time*, there will always be a list of features for every release and these feature lists will be different each time.

Another side effect to the immediacy of the features is that there is no need for them to provide a complete definition of the system. They represent the advertised benefits, the hot aspects, of the latest release of the system rather than a summary of its entire functionality. In this way, they complement the use-case model, which, in terms of the set of use cases, presents an overview of the system's entire functionality and often shows no changes from release to release.

The immediate and informal nature of features makes them a very powerful tool when working with the stakeholders and customers in defining what they want from a system's releases. When asked, stakeholders will be able to quickly come up with a list of the top 10 features they would like to see added to the system; in contrast, they will often struggle to identify any new use cases that are required.

Features provide the fundamental basis for product definition and scope management. To effectively manage application complexity, the capabilities of the system should be sufficiently abstract so that no more than 25 to 99 features describe the system. Each feature will be manifested in greater detail in the use-case model or the Supplementary Specifications. The combination of features and use cases provides a very powerful mechanism for managing the scope of the system, keeping all of the stakeholders involved and informed about the progress of the system and ensuring that a complete requirements specification is produced in an easily accessible and manageable form. Individually, neither features nor use cases provide such a manageable or complete solution.

DOCUMENTING FEATURES

When documenting features:

- Include a description of functionality and any relevant usability issues that must be addressed.
- Avoid design. Keep feature descriptions at a general level. Focus on required capabilities and why (not how) they should be implemented.
- Assign each feature a unique identifier for easy reference and tracking.

In addition to system functionality, also consider the nonfunctional qualities required of the system, such as performance, usability, robustness, fault tolerance, scalability, licensing, installation, and documentation (user manuals, on-line help, labeling, and packaging).

The features of the system may be categorized and presented in many ways. For elicitation and verification, it is best to present the features by functional area and type. For scope management and publication purposes, it is best to group the features by target release, sorted in order of priority so that it is easy to distinguish between those that are in-scope and those that have been deferred. Again, as with the needs, we recommend the use of the MoSCoW rules to prioritize the feature set. Table 3-4 shows the prioritization of some of the features of the simple telephone system.

Table 3-4 Example Features for the Simple Telephone System

Identifier	Description	Priority
FEAT1	The system shall allow the caller to place local calls.	Must
FEAT2	The system shall allow the caller to place long-distance calls.	Must
FEAT3	The system shall select the cheapest routing for all long-distance calls.	Should
FEAT4	The system shall provide a continuously up-to-date call history for all accounts.	Must
FEAT5	The system shall be continuously available 24 hours a day, seven days a week.	Should

Other Product Requirements

Other high-level requirements may not be as readily captured as features of the product. These include any constraints placed on the development of the product and any requirements the planned product will place on its operating environment. These other product requirements should be documented separately from the features and clearly identified as either constraints or operational requirements to prevent team members from confusing them with the actual requirements of the product.

CONSTRAINTS

No matter how technology independent the requirements-gathering and the software development processes are, some constraints[11] are inevitably placed on the possible solution. Constraints are not related to fulfilling the stakeholders' needs; they are restrictions imposed on the project by external forces. Although constraints arise from the stakeholder community, they are not directly related to the problem to be solved. Figure 3-9 illustrates how the stakeholders impose constraints on the project and system to be built.

Many different kinds of constraint may be imposed on a project. These include

- **Business and Economic:** Cost and pricing, availability, marketing, and licensing issues

---

[11] A constraint is formally defined as "a restriction on the degree of freedom we have in providing a solution" (Leffingwell and Widrig, 2000).

Figure 3-9 The relationship between the constraints imposed by the stakeholders and the project and the system it is producing

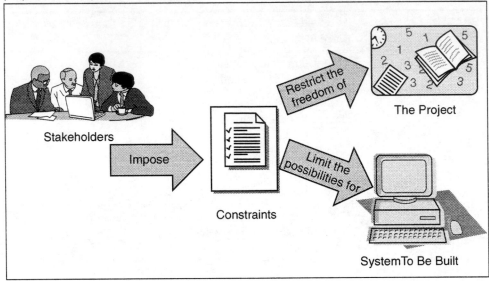

- **Environmental:** External standards and regulations that are imposed on the development project
- **Technical:** The technologies that the project is forced to adopt or the processes that the project has to follow (such as a requirement that the system be developed using J2EE)
- **System:** Compatibility with existing systems and operating environments
- **Schedule and Resources:** Dates the project has been committed to or limitations on the resources that the project must use

Stakeholders may impose constraints for a variety of reasons:

- **Politics:** Constraints may be placed on the project by the relationships among the stakeholders rather than the technical or business forces shaping the project.
- **Organizational Policies:** Organizational policies may be in place that constrain the way that the product can be developed. A company may have made a policy decision to move toward specific techniques, methodologies, standards, or languages.
- **Strategic Directions:** Strategic directions may be in place that constrain the project to use specific technologies and suppliers (such as a corporate decision to outsource all coding or to host all applications on a specific application server).
- **Organizational Culture:** The culture of the organization may itself constrain the project by limiting the way that the project must address the

problem. (There is a limit to the amount of change that people can cope with at any one time, and this could prevent a project from adopting its preferred technologies and methods.)

The constraints must be kept in mind when you create and assess the use-case model. Constraints imposed on the system will limit the freedom of the solution and therefore must be reflected in the style, scope, and structure of the use-case model. Understanding the constraints imposed on the system can be particularly useful when selecting the appropriate set of actors and use cases required to describe the system. This is discussed in more detail in Chapter 4, Finding Actors and Use Cases.

Most constraints are low-level design constraints arising from designers' choice of technology and method. These are captured as part of the Supplementary Specification alongside the nonfunctional software requirements. Here we are talking about identifying the much smaller set of high-level constraints: those that will fundamentally impact on the scope and direction chosen for the project. These are documented in the Vision document alongside the stakeholder needs and the product features.

Constraints can limit your ability to successfully provide a solution. Sometimes an apparently simple constraint can introduce tremendous complexity when it is examined. As a result, constraints must be constantly evaluated to determine how and where they will apply. Constraints may also influence your selection of stakeholder representatives, the manner in which those representatives are involved, and your choice of elicitation techniques. For example, a system that has a number of budgetary and financial performance constraints requires greater involvement of project accountants and financial analysts than one without financial constraints.

When documenting a constraint, you should also capture the source of the constraint and the rationale behind it. Because the constraints are unrelated to the problem being solved, they should be documented and tracked separately from the requirements.

OPERATING REQUIREMENTS

In some cases the product to be produced results in requirements being placed on the operating environment in which it will be deployed. These are not requirements to be fulfilled by the solution, but requirements that must be met by the operating environment if the solution is to be successfully deployed. These requirements may include:

- **System Requirements:** Any system requirements necessary to support the application. These can include the supported host operating systems and network platforms, configurations, memory, peripherals, companion software, and performance.

- **Operating Environment Requirements:** For hardware-based systems, operational issues can include temperature, shock, humidity, and radiation. For software applications, environmental factors can include usage conditions, user environment, resource availability, maintenance issues, and error handling and recovery.

These should be documented in the same way as the system's constraints, with attention paid to the source and rationale that led to their specification.

Provide an Overview of the Product

The features and other product requirements are not sufficient to provide a complete high-level view of the system. You also need to document the benefits, assumptions, dependencies (including interfaces to other applications and system configurations), and alternatives to the development of the product.

Product Position Statement

Every system is (or should be) built for at least one good reason. Like any good enterprise, the system requires a good "mission statement" or reason for being. You should be able to state in clear terms what the system does and why it does it. The description need not be long—in fact, the more succinct the better—but it should be put in writing.

Think of traveling in an elevator with the president of the company. Suppose the president asks what you are working on right now. You need a short answer that conveys the real value of the system being built. Most projects that find themselves in difficulties do so because, at least in part, no one really knows what is being built and why. The product position statement is a vehicle for communicating a brief definition of the system to all stakeholders.

The template shown in Table 3-5 can be used to express the product positioning statement, a key element of the vision.[12] This format reminds people about all of the things that must be considered when establishing a vision for the system. A description of the system is important because it gives everyone a common high-level understanding of what the system does. Anyone associated with the project should be able to briefly describe what the system does in simple terms. Being able to do so creates a foundation for common understanding that pays dividends as the project progresses.

Let's consider an automated teller system. What does it do? One might tend to give details in a description, such as how the user's identity is authenticated and how funds are allocated. These are important details, but they do

---

[12] This format is taken from Moore, 1991.

Table 3-5 Product Position Statement Template

For	(target customer)
Who	(statement of the need or opportunity)
For	(target customer)
Who	(statement of the need or opportunity)
The	**(product name)** is a (product category)
That	(statement of key benefit, that is, compelling reason to buy)
Unlike	(primary competitive alternative)
Our product	(statement of primary differentiation)

not belong in the basic description. Think like a venture capitalist: What is the system going to do for someone? What's the value? An example product position statement for the automated teller machine is presented in Table 3-6.

This description isn't fancy or complicated; it simply conveys the essence of what the system does. It should state what problem the system principally solves, who it principally serves, and what value it provides. When writing the description, try to describe the system as you would to someone who is unfamiliar with it and the problem it solves and try to convey the value it will deliver. If you cannot describe the system in very simple terms, you probably do not have a very clear idea of what the system will do.

Note that this description does not try to capture even a fraction of the requirements, and it should not. Is it important that the ATM prints a receipt?

Table 3-6 The Product Position Statement for an Automated Teller Machine (ATM)

For	Current account-holding customers
Who	Require instant access to their account details and the funds they contain
The	**Super ATM** is an automated teller machine
That	Provides the ability to perform simple bank transactions (such as withdrawing or depositing funds, or transferring funds between accounts)
Unlike	Accessing funds and details over the branch counter
Our product	Is available 24 hours a day and does not require the assistance of a bank teller

Not at this point. What about security? Not in the brief description. What about other kinds of transactions that might be handled? No need to describe them all here. We merely want to capture the essence of what the system does so that everyone will be clear about it.

Completing the Product Overview

To provide a complete overview of the product, you may also need to summarize other aspects of the product not directly captured by the high-level requirements. Typically, it is worth documenting:

- **Summary of Capabilities:** Summarize the capabilities that the system offers to its users. Presenting a brief overview of the use-case model will summarize the functionality offered by the system.
- **Customer Benefits:** Summarize the benefits that the product offers to its customers and which features provide the benefit. This may just be a matrix relating the stakeholder needs to the features.
- **Assumptions and Dependencies:** List any assumptions that have been made that if changed, will alter the vision established for the system. Also list any dependencies the product has on other products or the target environment.
- **Alternatives and Competition:** List any alternatives that the stakeholders perceive as available, including a description of their strengths and weaknesses, to allow comparison with the solution being proposed.

It is important to provide the stakeholders with these additional perspectives on the product, because they demonstrate that the product is not being considered in isolation from its target business and operational environments.

BRINGING IT ALL TOGETHER: THE VISION DOCUMENT

The Vision document is the Rational Unified Process artifact that captures all of the requirements information that we have been discussing in this chapter. As with all requirements documentation, its primary purpose is communication.

You write a Vision document to give the reader an overall understanding of the system to be developed by providing a self-contained overview of the system to be built and the motivations behind building it. To this end, it often contains extracts and summaries of other related artifacts, such as the business case and associated business models. It may also contain extracts from the system use-case model where this helps to provide a succinct and accessible overview of the system to be built.

The purpose of the Vision document is to capture the focus, stakeholder needs, goals and objectives, target markets, user environments, target platforms, and features of the product to be built. It communicates the fundamental "whys and whats" related to the project, and it is a gauge against which all future decisions should be validated.

The Vision document is the primary means of communication between the management, marketing, and project teams. It is read by all of the project stakeholders, including general managers, funding authorities, use-case modelers, and developers. It provides

- A high-level (sometimes contractual) basis for the more detailed technical requirements
- Input to the project-approval process (and therefore it is intimately related to the business case)
- A vehicle for eliciting initial customer feedback
- A means to establish the scope and priority of the product features

It is a document that gets "all parties working from the same book."

Because the Vision document is used and reviewed by a wide variety of involved personnel, the level of detail must be general enough for everyone to understand. However, enough detail must be available to provide the team with the information it needs to create a use-case model and supplementary specification.

The document contains the following sections:

- **Positioning:** This section summarizes the business case for the product and the problem or opportunity that the product is intended to address. Typically, the following areas should be addressed:
  - **The Business Opportunity:** A summary of business opportunity being met by the product
  - **The Problem Statement:** A solution-neutral summary of the problem being solved focusing on the impact of the problem and the benefits required of any successful solution
  - **Market Demographics:** A summary of the market forces that drive the product decisions.
  - **User Environment:** The user environment where the product could be applied.
- **Stakeholders and Users:** This section describes the stakeholders in, and users of, the product. The stakeholder roles and stakeholder types are defined in the project's Vision document—the actual stakeholder representatives are identified as part of the project plan just like any other resources involved in the project.

- **Key Stakeholder and User Needs:** This section describes the key needs that the stakeholders and users perceive the product should address. It does not describe their specific requests or their specific requirements, because these are captured in a separate stakeholder requests artifact. Instead, it provides the background and justification for why the requirements are needed.
- **Product Overview:** This section provides a high-level view of the capabilities, assumptions, dependencies (including interfaces to other applications and system configurations), and alternatives to the development of the product.
- **Features:** This section lists the features of the product. Features are the high-level capabilities (services or qualities) of the system that are necessary to deliver benefits to the users and satisfy the stakeholder and user needs. This is the most important, and consequently usually the longest, section of the Vision document.
- **Other Product Requirements:** This section lists any other high-level requirements that cannot readily be captured as product features. These include any constraints placed on the development of the product and any requirements the planned product places on its operating environment.

In many cases, a lot more work is put into uncovering the business opportunity and understanding the market demographics related to the proposed product than is reflected in the Vision document. This work is usually captured in-depth in business cases, business models, and market research documents. These documents are then summarized in the Vision document to ensure that they are reflected in the ongoing evolution of the products specification.

We recommend that the Vision document be treated primarily as a report and that the stakeholder types, user types, stakeholder roles, needs, features, and other product requirements be managed using a requirements management tool. If the list of features is to be generated, it is recommended that they be presented in two sections:

- In-Scope features
- Deferred features

DO YOU REALLY NEED TO DO ALL OF THIS?

You are probably thinking that this all sounds like an awful lot of work, and you probably want to get started on the actual use-case modeling without producing reams and reams of additional documentation.

Well, projects are typically in one of four states when the use-case modeling activities are scheduled to commence:

1. A formal Vision document has been produced.
2. The information has already been captured but not consolidated into a single Vision document.
3. There is a shared vision, but it has not been documented.
4. There is no vision.

If your project is in one of the first two states, and the information is available to all the stakeholder representatives, then you are in a position to proceed at full speed with the construction and completion of the use-case model. If your project is in one of the last two states, then you should be very careful not to spend too much effort on the detailed use-case modeling activities. This does not mean that use-case modeling cannot be started—it simply means that any modeling you do must be undertaken in conjunction with other activities aimed at establishing a documented vision for the product. In fact, in many cases, undertaking some initial use-case modeling can act as a driver and facilitation device for the construction of the vision itself.

Our recommendation would be to always produce a Vision document for every project and to relate the information it contains to the use-case model to provide focus, context, and direction to the use-case modeling activities. Formally relating the two sets of information also provides excellent validation of their contents and quality. If there is sufficient domain knowledge and agreement between the stakeholder representatives, then producing and reviewing the Vision document can be done very quickly. If there isn't, then there is no point in undertaking detailed use-case modeling; the resulting specifications would be ultimately worthless as they would not be a reflection of the product's true requirements.

SUMMARY

Before embarking on any use-case modeling activities it is essential to establish a firm foundation upon which to build. The foundation has two dimensions, which must be evolved in parallel with one another:

1. An understanding of the stakeholder and user community
2. The establishment of a shared vision for the product

Understanding the stakeholder community is essential as the stakeholders are the primary source of requirements. The following are the key to understanding the stakeholder community:

- **Stakeholder Types:** Definitions of all of the different types of stakeholder affected by the project and the product it produces.
- **User Types:** Definitions of characteristics and capabilities of the users of the system. The users are the people and things that will take on the roles defined by the actors in the use-case model.

For the use-case modeling activities to be successful, the stakeholders and users will need to be actively involved in them. The stakeholders and users directly involved in the project are known as stakeholder representatives. To ensure that the stakeholder representatives understand their commitment to the project, it is worthwhile to clearly define the "stakeholder roles" that they will be adopting. The stakeholder roles serve as a contract between the stakeholder representatives and the project, reflecting the responsibilities and expectations of both sides.

To establish a shared vision for the project, the following are essential:

- **The Problem Statement:** A solution-neutral summary of the problem being solved, focusing on the impact of the problem and the benefits required of any successful solution.
- **Stakeholder Needs:** The true "business requirements" of the stakeholders presented in a solution-neutral manner. These are the aspects of the problem that affect the individual stakeholders.
- **Features, Constraints, and Other High-Level Product Requirements:** A high-level definition of the system to be developed. These complement and provide a context for the use-case model and enable effective scope management.
- **Product Overview:** A summary of the other aspects of the product not directly captured by the high-level requirements.

The Vision document can be used to capture all of this information in a form that is accessible to all the stakeholders of the project.

The vision does not have to be complete before use-case modeling activities start; in fact, undertaking some initial use-case modeling can act as a driver and facilitation device for the construction of the vision itself, but if the vision is not established alongside the use-case model, then there is a strong possibility that it will not be a true reflection of the real requirements.

Chapter 4

Finding Actors and Use Cases

Identifying the actors of a system and the use cases in which they play a role sounds like a simple task—until you try to do it. To do it right, you have to have a good understanding of the system itself, yet in most cases you are developing use cases precisely because you are trying to get a better understanding of the system. Actors, as you will recall from Chapter 2, represent anything outside the system that uses the system to do something, so in order to identify the actors you have to decide what is inside the system and what is outside the system. This is sometimes harder to achieve than it sounds.

Let's illustrate this point with an example. If we consider an automated teller machine (ATM) system, it seems fairly obvious that the Bank Customer is an actor, but what about the Bank System itself?

Over a period of many years we have used this example as a teaching exercise, and invariably some students identify the Bank System as an actor because they view the Bank System and the ATM system as different entities. Other students argue that there is one *big* system that encompasses both the automated teller system and the back-end processing at the bank or financial institution.

Which view is correct? In reality, the Bank System *is* an actor to the automated teller system, but only because the system evolved this way. It is possible for there to be *one* large, all-encompassing system, but then this system would be very complex indeed. So the determination of who or what the actors represent depends on what the system is supposed to do for those actors. With this sort of circular definition, it is no wonder that people have trouble finding actors and use cases.

In this chapter we explore how to define the boundaries and purpose of the system, how to use this information to define the actors for the system, and how to use the actor definitions to find the system's use cases.

FINDING ACTORS

The key to finding actors is to decide where the system ends. Find the system boundary, and everything beyond that that interacts with the system is an actor. See Figure 4-1.

The easiest actors to find are those that represent people, because in the early stages it is almost impossible to confuse a person with a system. It is no accident that actors are represented diagrammatically as stick figures. To find the actors for a system, start by looking at the people who will use the system and then generalize to identify the roles they play. These are the actors.

Start by Identifying the Primary Actors

Start by thinking of the users that will really use the system—the subset of the users for whom the system provides value. Ignore for the moment those users who simply service the system. The real users are the ones without whom the system itself would be pointless and unnecessary. These should have already been identified as part of the system's vision.

Figure 4-1 When finding actors it often helps to treat the system as a single amorphous blob; a diagram on a white board or flip chart can help. The "blob" at the center of the diagram represents the system. These diagrams are sometimes called *context diagrams*.

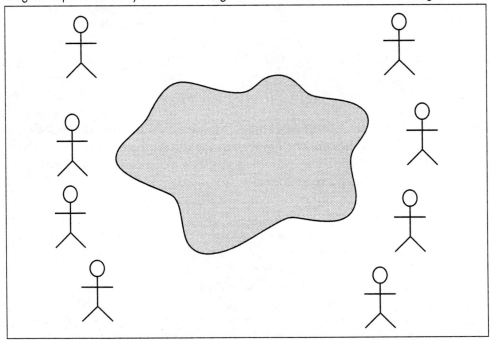

How should you represent the actors in a use-case model? We have already discussed the definition of user types as a fundamental part of establishing the vision for the system. We now need to start to define the relationship between these user types and the system to be built. The first step is to define the roles that these users will adopt with respect to the system—these system-related roles are modeled as actors. For each of the user types identified, ensure that there is at least one actor defined to address their needs of the system. The actors that represent the roles adopted by the key users are the primary actors. They are the first actors to be identified and agreed upon when you are finding the actors for a system.

Initially, it may seem that a trivial, one-to-one mapping between the user types and the system's actors is all that is required, but as we shall see, the relationship is generally more complex than this. Take, for example, the simple telephone system where we had the user types and actors defined as shown in Table 4-1. Remember use types are defined by their competencies and capabilities, whereas actors are defined by their goals and relationship with the system.

Work from the Specific to the General

Most of us do better at finding the specific and have more trouble with the general. Some of the longest brainstorming sessions in which we have participated have dragged on because the participants were trying to be so general that they could cover every possible case with the fewest number of actors. (In fact, one group got so general that it defined only one actor—the Performer.) There is a time for abstraction, but not usually while brainstorming. Working from the specific to the general is always easier. When you identify a few people who play the same actor role, the actor is nearly always obvious; working the other way around is almost always harder.

Once you have identified an actor, it must be named. A good starting point for this is to identify the role the user plays while interacting with the

Table 4-1 The User Types from the Simple Telephone System Example and the Actors Whose Roles They Adopt

User Types	Actors
Technology Adopter	Caller, Callee, Customer
Standard User	Caller, Callee, Customer
Messaging Devices	Caller, Callee

system. Don't get preoccupied with finding perfect actor names, especially early in the process; find an acceptable working name and refine it later if or when you need to. (In fact, there is no such thing as "perfect" in use-case modeling—remember that "good enough" is often more than sufficient to accomplish your objectives. Knowing when to "quit" is often a big part of success.)

If you have trouble dealing with all of these different levels of abstraction involving user types and actors, then start by being even more specific and think of some of the actual individuals who will use the system. Then think of how you can categorize them as both user types and actors. It is often a good habit to keep a few individuals (two or three) in mind and make sure that the actors you identify cover their needs.

Don't Forget the Supporting Actors

The primary actors are the ones for whom the system is built; they are the ones to whom the system provides sufficient economic value to warrant its construction. It is both necessary and correct that we should concentrate our efforts primarily on these actors and the users that will take on these roles. There are typically, however, other sets of actors essential to the successful operation of the system that are often forgotten. These are the actors that support the use cases provided by the system and those that support the system itself.

Nearly every use case requires information to be provided, or decisions to be made, by actors other than the one that started the use case. As the scope of a use case starts to emerge, other supporting actors will often be required for the system to be able to achieve its goal and deliver the value to the actor that initiated it. For example, additional information may be required that the system does not have. This can lead to the identification of additional actors as the source of this information. In other cases, a decision may be required that cannot be made by the system and the initiating actor alone. For example, in a banking system loans of over a specified amount may need to be approved by a senior member of staff as well as by the system.

Nearly every system requires some actor to start the system and to shut it down, and many systems require some sort of routine maintenance (ensuring that the system's data is backed up, for example). If the system must provide special behavior to support these actors, their use cases must be identified. Conversely, if standard utilities are used to back up the system, for example, there is no need to specify the actor or the use case unless these utilities are used in unique ways or are extended in some way. When you are identifying actors, make sure that the requirements related to supporting the system and its use cases are represented in some way by the actors.

Consider All Existing Requirements Information

Don't isolate the use-case modeling activities from the other requirements-related project activities; it is very rare that use-case modeling starts from a completely blank page. As discussed in Chapter 3, we would expect there to be some sort of Vision document in place containing information about the stakeholders, users, their key needs, the features required of the system, and the constraints placed upon the project. This is all useful information to consider when finding the actors and use cases of a system.

When finding actors the following relationships should be considered:

- **User Types to Actors:** Are there actors defined to cover all of the identified user types?
- **Stakeholders to Actors:** Are there enough actors to represent the interactions required by all the stakeholders?
- **Stakeholder Roles to Actors:** Do you know which stakeholder representatives will be validating decisions made about each actor definition?

You should also consider the impact of the defined features and constraints by revisiting the features and considering who is interested in a certain requirement or area of functionality. By asking yourself, "Who is interested in this capability," you may find additional actors and possibly stakeholders. Constraints may also give clues to the existence of yet-unidentified actors by defining things outside the system with which the system must interact. For example, there may be a constraint that mandates that the new system will integrate with an existing system to obtain all of its customer-related information.

Remember That Actors Are Not Always People

Some people see the iconic, stick-figure representation of the actor and assume that the actor must be a person. They assume that use cases are a technique for describing human–machine interactions, and in doing so they miss one of the main benefits of using use cases. In fact, they may be missing the most important purpose of use cases.

An actor represents anything that is outside the system that exchanges information with the system. This certainly includes people, and for many systems, people are the most important external users of the system. But for many other systems—including command and control systems, switching systems, and sensor-monitoring systems—the actors are primarily other systems, devices, or sensors.

Example

> Consider a simple fire detection system that monitors a series of fire detection sensors for signs of fire, and when one is detected it rings an alarm, sets off a set of sprinklers, and notifies the local fire department. Identifying the main use case, *Detect Fire*, is simple enough, but without human users the actors are hard to determine. A little analysis identifies the following actors: the *sprinkler control*, the *fire detector*, and the *fire department*.

Although this example may seem oversimplified, use cases evolved in an environment in which there was a great deal of internal processing and interaction with other systems and not a great deal of "human" interaction relative to the total amount of processing that occured—in telecommunication switching systems. It is a credit to the power and simplicity of the approach that use cases also work very well for systems that have a great deal of human interaction. In both cases, the systems must respond in very specific ways when certain events occur. In the case of highly technical systems in which there is not a great deal of user interaction, the technical complexity of these systems often obscures the real purpose for which the system is being built. Use cases help to solve this problem by focusing on what the system does in response to external events in order to provide the desired results.

As a result, use cases tend to be even more important for systems that have no significant user interface—they are often the only way that the stakeholders of the system can understand what the system does. When a system has a well-defined user interface and easily identified users, it is often easy to get good feedback on whether the system does what its users expect. With technical systems that exist deep within telecommunication networks or are embedded in devices, however, the "user" is often another system. Visualizing what happens in these systems is much more difficult, and use cases can play an important role in helping to define the desired and expected behavior under various circumstances.

Use cases are not just a user-centered design technique[1]; they are also essential for systems that effectively have no user. Don't let the actor icon fool you[2]—actors aren't just people.

---

[1] Larry Constantine is a great proponent of the use of use cases for user-centered design. Use cases are certainly useful for these purposes, but that is not their only function.

[2] In fact, UML allows the icon for any element (including the actor) to be changed. If project team members are confused by the stick-person representation of the actor, just substitute a more representative icon when the actor you are referring to is actually a system.

Focus on the System Boundary

Considering actors that are other systems forces you to confront the boundary of the system you are creating. What does your system do, and where does it end? If you consider only the human actors, you often end up with a system that includes other systems—and this really makes it difficult to figure out what your system is supposed to do. Representing other systems as actors helps to define what your system will and will not do—the boundary of the system. If you rely on some other system to do something, that other system is an actor to your system; if another system requests information from your system, it is also an actor to your system. Treating *everything* outside your system as an actor simplifies your problem—you need only focus on what your system must do for its actors.

To illustrate the effect of not being able to establish the system boundary on the scope of the system, consider once again the ATM. Nearly everyone identifies the bank customer as an actor, and many people identify an operator who services the ATM as an actor, but not everyone recognizes the banking network or some central bank system as an actor. This oversight leads to ambiguity about what the ATM does and what it does not do—is the ATM responsible for determining whether the customer has sufficient funds on hand, or is the banking network? If you cannot rapidly decide on the system boundary, you may eventually find that you are not focusing on what is necessary.

Identify the Information Sources

When considering the system boundary, focus on where the system will get the information and resources it requires to achieve its goals. Understanding the information exchanged between the actors and the system is fundamental to effectively determining the system boundary. The need for information is not limited to the passive querying of data from other systems, but may also involve real-time interaction with users to make decisions or authorize actions. The system is dependent on the behavior of the actors as well as the data that they can provide.

One easy way to determine whether behavior is inside or outside the system is to consider the location of information required to support the behavior. Does the system have the information it requires to handle some event that is generated by one of its actors? If it does not, typically some actor (perhaps not yet identified) must provide it. Assessing the information needs of the system can often uncover actors that would otherwise go unrecognized. You should also consider who would be interested in the information captured by the system. It may itself be an information source for other systems or users. This can again lead to the identification of additional actors.

Don't Preempt the Design

Sometimes it is difficult to tell if another system is really an actor or just part of the system's assembly. Often, we are faced with systems that could either be treated as actors or as devices. The choice of representation depends on a couple of factors. If the system is required to communicate with some other system, and the communication is something that affects the flow of events, then the system is an actor. If communication with the other system is simply a means by which the designer provides the required functionality, and the designer can choose how, when, or if the other system is used, then the other system is not an actor and should be omitted from the use-case model.

Examples

In an ATM system, the *banking system* is an actor because the ATM is required to contact the banking system to determine the identity of the user, to check balances, and to complete transactions. The designer of the system has no freedom as to how, when, and if the banking system is contacted—if the banking system is not available, the use case must end.

In the case of a Web-based geographic information system (GIS) that displays maps showing the location of certain tracked assets, the designers of the system may choose to use another Internet provider to provide the maps, or they may develop their own maps; it's up to them based on technical and economic factors. In this case, the fact that the maps are provided by another system is a mere convenience and does not affect the basic behavior of the GIS.

This last example illustrates why we don't consider the operating system, database, or other utilities as actors. Although we certainly make use of their capabilities, we are not required by the system to use them in specific ways at specific times. Things that are the designer's choice should not be represented in the use cases. Stated another way, anything that *must* be done a certain way should be documented in the use cases; anything that's purely up to the designers and developers should be left out. Put yet another way, *constraints* on the solution (such as *"the system shall run on the XXX operating system"*) should be recorded, but not in the use cases. The best way to handle constraints is to identify them, record them, and trace them to use cases that must satisfy the constraints. This allows us to make sure that nothing is forgotten while ensuring that the constraints do not get in the way of understanding the real behavior of the use case. One way to address this problem is to ask yourself: "Do I have control over the behavior of the other system?" If not, it is typically because the other system is developed and managed by another group and is wholly separate from your system. A rule of thumb for actors: "If you can't control it, it's an actor."

Whatever decisions are made about the appropriate set of actors for the system, the use-case modelers must never preempt the designers and try to use the use-case model to design the system.

Don't Confuse the Actors with the Devices They Use

Devices are typically mechanisms that actors use to communicate with the system, but they are not actors themselves. We are writing this book on a computer, but the keyboard is not the user of the word processing program—we are. If we were to say that the actor for the word processing system is the keyboard, we would lose track of the real goal of the system: to help us to write a book. There is more to this than simply entering keystrokes.

Sometimes it's harder to see this. In a fire detection system, what do we call the actor that first notifies the system that there is a fire? Because the system uses devices called sensors to report unusual increases in temperature, you might consider the sensor to be an actor. In fact, the fire is the actor, but we tend not to think of a fire as an animate thing. Even in an automated system, however, events can be reported manually—someone can ring the fire alarm. In this case, it's very easy to see that the fire alarm switch is not the actor; the actor is the person who pulls the switch. This points us to a more satisfactory solution: From the standpoint of the system, an automated sensor that signals a fire and a manual switch that signals a fire are identical, and both would trigger the same response by the system. We could use the same actor for both cases—an actor called Fire Detector—and (ideally) the same use case for both ways of reporting a fire. If the use cases (in other words, the requirements) are different for manual versus automated reporting, we could simply modify the names slightly, introducing the actors Manual Fire Detector and Automated Fire Detector.

Other devices, such as disk drives, tape drives, or communication equipment (including printers), have no place in the use-case model. Although they are important to the design of the system, introducing them as actors obscures the real purpose of the system. The purpose of devices is to support some required behavior of the system, and the requirement to use a particular device may impose certain constraints on the implementation of the system, but devices do not define the requirements of the system. The system may even be required to run on a particular device, such as a handheld computer, but this requirement does not define what the system must do for its actors. The focus must remain on system definition.

The printer-as-actor issue deserves a little more discussion. Often, systems must produce a printed report of information that it contains. Teams often want to show the printer as an actor that then forwards the report to the *real* actor. This isn't needed and it gets in the way. Just as the computer display or keyboard is not an actor, the printer is not an actor, either; it is just a mechanism for conveying information. The use case describes the compilation of the information and makes note that the report is printed, but for the purpose of the use case, we need to focus on what the system does to collect and format the information, not on how it is delivered. Besides, most systems allow information to be reviewed on a screen and then printed if the user wants a hard copy, so printing is really just an option in the use-case description.

This raises an important point—use cases are not an all-encompassing requirements technique, and you cannot represent *all* the requirements of a system with use cases. Use-case descriptions are a great way to approach the difficult task of describing the behavior of a system. Remember: Use cases are stories about how someone or something uses the system to accomplish something useful. Don't feel that you need to somehow account for all requirements in the use cases, and don't turn use cases into a design technique.

When You Can't Find the Actors, Start with the Use Cases

Sometimes the use cases for the system are obvious, but the actors involved are difficult to identify. This issue is often encountered when the system has so-called "batch" processing that runs unattended, typically overnight (if such a thing exists anymore in the round-the-clock world of some systems). The initial approach most teams take is to identify an actor called the *System Clock* to start the job. This is an awful lot like a device, and sometimes causes problems; at the very least it doesn't seem like the other actors in the system.

The way out of this dilemma is to consider that someone manages when these jobs should be started and stopped and that the system may support other use cases to allow this person to manage these jobs. For this reason, an actor with a name like Job Scheduler is a better choice. The specific mechanisms used to start and stop jobs in the system will vary, perhaps using the system clock or some other mechanism, but clearly something causes these jobs to start. The use of Job Scheduler may also remind us that we need a way to say when these jobs start, and we need a log of job status so that we can know that they were completed successfully.[3]

---

[3] These use cases typically need not be fully developed; job-entry management software has been around for a long time and is often a component of the operating system itself, as in the case of *cron* on UNIX systems or RJE facilities on OS/390 environments. It's a good idea, however, to identify the required behavior by identifying the actors and the use cases and briefly describing both. You may even need to describe the required behavior a bit to make sure that the requirements are satisfied by the native OS capabilities. If not, you will have to further develop the use cases to evaluate alternatives if you plan to buy the capabilities. If the required functionality cannot be purchased, you will have to build it, which means that the use cases must be described in detail.

Compare this case with the fire detector in our earlier example. It was easy to comprehend that the fire detector was an actor, so what is so special about time? The answer is "nothing." Both the fire detector and the job scheduler monitor external things, and when some particular event occurs, they cause something to happen inside the system. Sometimes it is more understandable to others to have actors with names that represent significant time events. For example, the system that controls the tidal barrier in London (a very large flood-defense system) may have to respond to high and low tide times. It may therefore be appropriate to use High Tide and Low Tide as the actors rather than the more abstract label Job Scheduler.

Focus First on the Familiar

Teams often get distracted by the esoteric, focusing on the novel and unusual rather than the basic functionality of the system. In the example of the fire detection system, the greatest amount of discussion typically focuses on the sensors, whereas the recipients of the information that there is a fire (the fire department, the people in the building, and systems that control fire suppression devices) are given short shrift.

In this case, the better strategy is to focus first on finding the *human* actors and then to look for the more obvious system actors. The esoteric cases are important, but not to the exclusion of the bulk of the behavior of the system. Consider the esoteric only after you have established a firm understanding of what the system will do. In the case of the fire detection system, recognizing that there is something that will report a fire (it could be a person activating an alarm) and calling this actor the Fire Detector is sufficient for the use-case model; the actual mechanisms that are used to detect or report a fire can be handled much later.

Evolve the Set of Actors Alongside the Set of Use Cases

Although many textbooks and guidelines (including this one) present the finding of actors as separate from the finding of use cases, in reality the two activities go hand in hand and are usually undertaken simultaneously and iteratively. Once an initial set of use cases has been identified to support the primary actors, many other actors will be identified that are required to support the use cases. These additional actors are required to support the use case by:

- Supplying information required by the system to successfully complete the use case
- Making decisions that the system is unable to make on its own

- Receiving updates and notification of the progress made by the system while undertaking the use case

It is very difficult to find these actors at the outset of the modeling activities before the use cases themselves have been identified and outlined. Instead, the use-case model will evolve and become more detailed as more and more of the actors and use cases they require are outlined and explored. Typically, the modeling will start by identifying the primary actors and the use cases required to support their goals and needs. These use cases are then looked at in more detail, leading to the identification of more actors that are required to support these use cases. This, in turn, leads to considering whether these supporting actors themselves require more use cases to satisfy their needs and so on.

Do not expect to find all of the actors for a system on the first pass, especially if this pass is not considering the detail of all of the use cases required to support these actors.

DOCUMENTING ACTORS

Once the actors have been identified, they will need to be officially named and documented.

How to Name Actors

The first thing you have to do when you find actors is to name them. When you name an actor, make sure that the name describes the role that the actor plays in relation to the system. Consider the other actors in the system and ensure that there is sufficient distinction between the actors to justify the creation of the new actor. If you are having difficulty reaching agreement on the name, list the alternative proposals and assess them for similarity. Also list the responsibilities of the actor with respect to the system. Sometimes a good name emerges naturally from the actor's responsibilities.

Good actor names are descriptive of their responsibilities. They describe the role the actor plays in relation to the system. An example of a good actor name would be ATM Operator for the person that keeps the ATM stocked with cash and paper, keeping the ATM in good working order. A poor actor name for this person would be Repair Person, because the actor's role goes quite a bit beyond simply repairing the machine.

A trap to avoid, however, is to simply restate the name of the use case in the form of an actor name. As an example, if we have a use case Withdraw Cash it would seem silly to have an actor Cash Withdrawer (instead of Bank Customer), but it is not uncommon to see such examples as an actor named Order

Shipper that interacts with a use case called Ship Orders. In this example, the actor name is not simply a reflection of the name of the use case. The actor name is probably adequate (see the next section for an explanation), but the use case name is probably wrong—orders result from a customer buying something, and it's that end-to-end experience that provides the real value. A better solution would be to have a use case called Order Goods that is started by a Customer and communicates to the order shipper to deliver the goods to the customer.

Don't Confuse Actors with Organizational Roles or Job Titles

Make a special effort to ensure that the actor name does not resemble some job title in the organization; if there is a similarity, change the name to make it clear that the actor is a role adopted with respect to the system and not a job title. Job titles are much more likely to be reflected in the set of user types than in the set of actors. Often, it is hard to find actor names that don't sound like job titles. If you are developing a system to manage the delivery of packages, you might naturally identify an actor you call Shipping Clerk. The only problem with this is that there is probably a person in the organization that has that job title. And so starts a good deal of confusion and misery.

In the use-case model, actors are really roles that a person (or system) plays when using the system. So the person with the job title Shipping Clerk also plays the role described by the actor Shipping Clerk. This is confusing, to be sure—no matter how hard we try, it's almost impossible to keep from equating the actor with the job title. The best thing to do, if possible, is to avoid the problem entirely: Use a different name for the actor.

In our package delivery system, we could sidestep the problem by choosing a slightly different, more role-based name for the actor, such as Package Shipper. The different name emphasizes how the actor uses the system versus the responsibilities of the person playing the actor role. In this case, Package Shipper is actually a better name for an actor. When we look at the role carefully, we find that many different people may ship packages, not just a shipping clerk. Package Shipper is a more general name anyway, and it avoids the confusion of job title with actor name.

Sometimes it's not so easy to differentiate between the role and the job title. Consider a use case used by a Project Manager to plan a project. It's not easy to think of another name for the actor other than Project Manager. We could try Project Planner, and this may be acceptable to the readers of the use case. But most people are conditioned to think of the project manager as the one who plans the project, so the natural tendency is to drift back toward an actor name that is the same as the job title of the person who plays the actor role. The real problem is that job titles have evolved out of the roles that people play. We can only come up with a finite number of names for these roles, so often actor names will sound very much like job titles. That's to be expected, but just remember that they are two different things, and similar names cause confusion. Strive to be clear about the differences and anticipate the potential confusion.

Example

In one company, which sold software development tools, there were sales teams that addressed certain vertical sectors. Each sector had a *Sales Administrator.* In reality, the Sales Administrator had multiple responsibilities, including maintaining team diaries, processing orders, handling customer queries, allocating temporary licenses, processing expenses, and so on.

Imagine if we were developing a system to support the day-to-day working of the team. We might come up with a partial use-case model like the one shown in Figure 4-2.

Using actors to represent job titles, or user types, rather than roles can cause problems for the long-term usage and stability of the use-case model as it ties the actors to the current organizational structure. Organizations, and the positions within them, change over time, but the underlying roles and responsibilities that people take on within the organization are often relatively stable. By using the actors to model the roles rather than the job titles, we end up with a system that is far more resilient over time.

A more role-based model is depicted in Figure 4-3. This figure more adequately expresses the underlying roles that the Sales Administrator is adopting when using the system and is far less brittle and inflexible. If the responsibilities of the Sales Administrator change within the business, the use-case model of the supporting system will still be correct.

Don't Overgeneralize

A problem related to the actor-name-as-job-title problem just described is overgeneralization of both actors and use cases. More than one team has followed this path to its illogical end, and it led them to having a single actor for the whole system: the "Performer" (or "User"). This actor was arrived at by taking to an extreme the admonition to use general role names and not specific job titles. The reasoning was that anyone using the system was "performing" some task and depending on the task's result. Taking generalization to an extreme obscures the roles that people play when they use the system. In the case of the system with the single "Performer" actor, the teams had lost sight of a critical fact: Different people use the system for different purposes. Even the same people will play different roles as they use the system to accomplish different things.

Figure 4-2 Using job titles in the use-case model

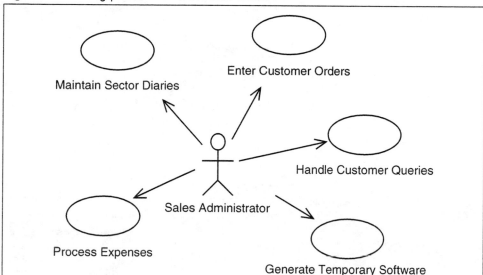

When you feel that an actor may be too general, ask yourself whether the actor name describes a distinct role that people play when they use the system. When you name the actor, make sure that the actor is not simply a reflection of the use case (for example, deriving the actor Inventory Manager from the use case *Manage Inventory*). Although there is syntactically nothing wrong with naming actors this way, it will certainly reduce the communication capabilities of the model itself. It can also lead to lost opportunities for the simplification of the use-case model that, typically, only become clear when you consider the full set of responsibilities allocated to each actor.

When defining the actors, don't worry about relationships between actors (such as generalization); simply capture the people or things that will use the system. Overgeneralization of use cases is a different matter and is discussed in Chapter 10, Here There Be Dragons.

Give Every Actor a Brief Description

Be sure to write a short description for each actor. When the time comes to determine what the actor needs from the system, a few sentences that capture the actor's role and responsibilities will help simplify discussions. The brief description should consist of no more than a few sentences that describe the role the actor plays with respect to the system. This last part is important—if the brief description starts sounding like a job description, you're headed in the wrong direction. The brief description should capture the responsibilities

Figure 4-3 Using roles instead of job titles as actor names

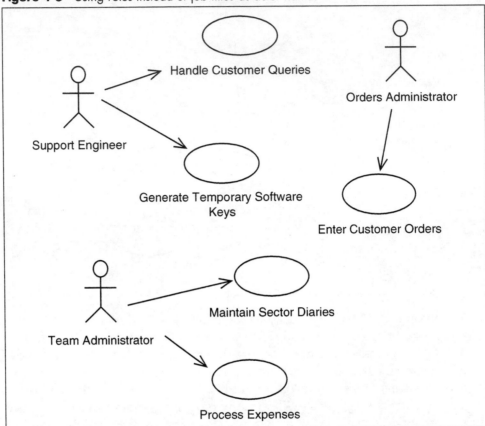

that the actor has with respect to the system, and it should state the goals the actor expects to achieve by using the system.

Example

Brief description for the actor Bank Customer in an ATM system

The Bank Customer conducts transactions at the ATM. He or she may withdraw funds, check account balances, deposit funds, and transfer amounts between accounts. A Bank Customer is created when a person opens an account at an affiliated financial institution.

Characterize the Actors

The characteristics of an actor might influence how the system is developed, and in particular how an optimally usable user interface is visually shaped. The actor characteristics include

- The actor's scope of responsibility.
- The physical environment in which the actor will be using the system. Deviations from the ideal case (where the user sits in a silent office, with no distractions) might affect the use of such things as sound, the choice of font, and the appropriate use of input device combinations (for example, keyboard, touch screen, mouse, and hot keys.)
- The number and type of users represented by this actor. This is a relevant factor when determining the significance of the actor and the significance of the parts of the system that the actor uses.
- The frequency with which the actor will use the system. This frequency will determine how much the actor can be expected to remember between sessions.

In most cases, a rough estimate of the number of users and frequency of use will suffice. A difference between 30 and 40 will not affect how the system is shaped, but a difference between 3 and 30 might.

Other actor characteristics can be derived directly from the user types by considering the following issues:

- The typical user's level of domain knowledge. This will help determine how much domain-specific help is needed and how much domain-specific terminology should be used in the user interface.
- The typical user's level of general computer experience. This will help determine how appropriate sophisticated versus simplistic interaction techniques are in the user interface.
- Other applications that the user uses. Borrowing concepts from these applications will shorten the users' learning time and decrease their memory load because they are already familiar with these concepts.
- General characteristics of the users, such as level of expertise (education), social implications (language), and age. These characteristics can influence details of the user interface, such as font and language.

Trace the Actors to the User Types, Stakeholders, and Stakeholder Roles

It is important to record the relationship between the actors and the user types, stakeholders, and stakeholder roles identified in the Vision document. Tracing the actors to the user types will help to capture and identify the actor's characteristics. Tracing the actors to the stakeholders and stakeholder roles will enable the correct members of the stakeholder community to be consulted during the production, evolution, and validation of the use-case model. This traceability also provides a measure of the completeness of the model itself. If there are user types that are not traced to at least one actor, then either they are not users of the system or there are still more actors to be identified. If there are actors that do not trace to at least one user type, then either these actors are superfluous or there are still more user types to be identified.

FINDING USE CASES

If the actors are things outside the system that interact with the system, the use cases are the things that the actors do with the system to accomplish something they need to do. A use case fulfills some goal of at least one of its actors, and it describes how actors interact with the system and the how the system responds to the actor's actions to fulfill these goals. Describing these interactions between actor and system serves several purposes:

- It forces us to focus on the value the system provides to its stakeholders rather than on developing arbitrary features that may not satisfy some actor goal.
- It forces us to confront the usability of the system by focusing on how the system interacts with its users to provide value.
- It helps us to ensure that we consider all the different ways the system can be used.

It is important to view the use cases and actors as intimately interrelated: The system exists to provide value to the actors, and the use cases describe how the system provides that value.

Start by Identifying the Actor Goals

For each actor identified, try to list the things that the actor needs to achieve by using the system. Sometimes you will need to combine these "proto use cases" because they are really different aspects of the same thing or slight alternatives or variations on some other use case. See Figure 4-4.

The actor is key to finding the correct use case, especially because the actor helps you avoid use cases that are too large. In the case of the ATM, focusing on several actors—the Bank Customer, the ATM Operator, and the Bank System—allows us to split the behavior of the system into a number of smaller subsets, making the system easier to understand and less complex. Each of these actors has individual demands on the system and therefore requires a separate set of use cases.

A use case should describe a task that has an identifiable value for the actor. This is very important in determining the correct level or granularity for a use case. "Correct level" refers to achieving use cases that are not too small;

Figure 4-4 Identifying what actors need from the system

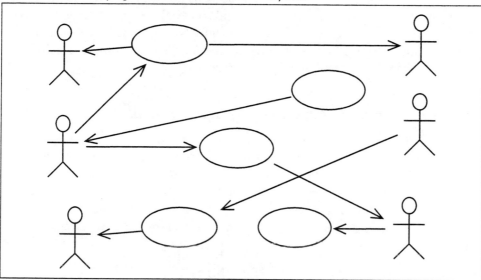

a use case that is too small does not, by itself, produce value for at least one of its actors. As an example, consider again the ATM, and ask yourself whether "Authenticate Bank Customer" (or "Verify PIN") produces value for the Bank Customer; ask yourself whether you would be satisfied if the ATM allowed you to put in your banking card and enter a personal identification number (PIN), only to be told that you had entered the correct PIN. Such a use case clearly has no value on its own—it only adds value as a verification mechanism in some larger context. That larger context is a "real" use case of the system.

Consider the Information Needs of the System and Its Users

As well as looking at the things that the actors wish to achieve, it is also worth considering the information that they and the system will need access to in order to perform their tasks.

Think about the information the actor will need to obtain from the system. This can help to identify additional use cases focused on the provision and capture of this information. You will also need to consider whether there are any occurrences within the system that the actors will need to be informed about and how the system will know who is to be informed. This can lead to the identification of registration- and notification-style use cases.

From the system's point of view, think about where the information it will need to carry out the use cases will come from. Is this information to be stored within the system or will an actor supply it? Regardless of where or how the information is stored, there will have to be use cases responsible for its entry into and retrieval from the system. You will also need to consider if there are any external events or changes that the system will need to be informed about. Again, there will have to be use cases to allow the actors to notify the system of external events.

Don't Worry About Commonality (at least at first)

Some use cases will appear to have common parts; this is to be expected. At this point, it is premature to worry about the structure of the model, because you haven't yet discovered the entire content of the use cases. Wait until after the flow of events has been outlined before you bring up any discussions about use-case relationships. The techniques available for managing commonality between use cases are covered in Chapter 10, Here There Be Dragons.

Don't Confuse Use Cases with "Functions"

The unfortunate visual similarity between use-case diagrams and dataflow diagrams sometimes leads people to define use cases that are really just functions or menu items. Whatever the reason, it's probably the single largest mistake that people new to use-case modeling make. See Figure 4-5.

Figure 4-5 Incorrect use of use cases as menu options or functions

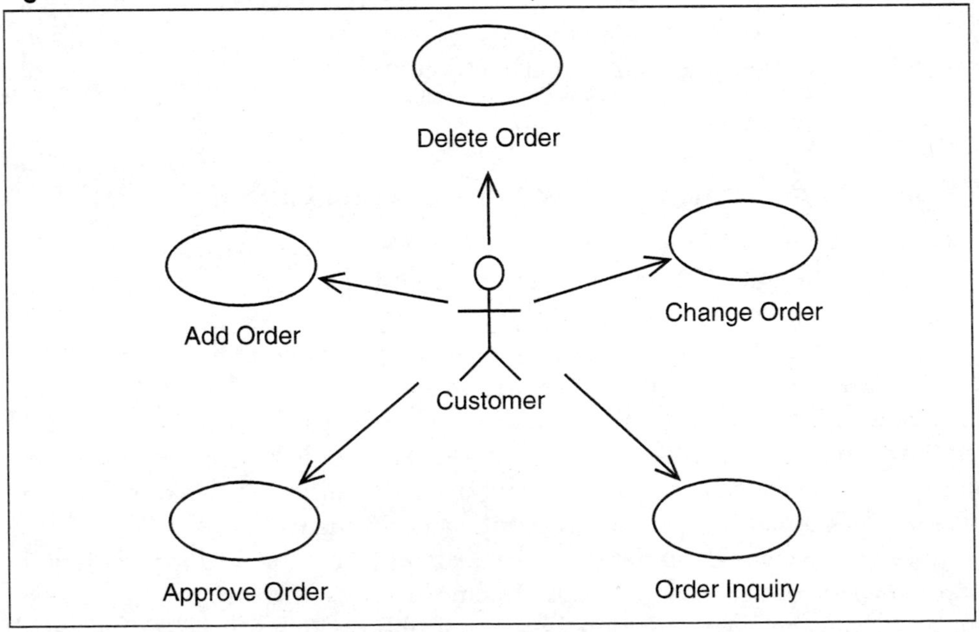

What's wrong with Figure 4-5? Think back to our definition of a use-case description ("a story about some way of using the system to do something useful"). Are all of these "use cases" independently useful?

The answer, of course, is no. The figure depicts things that the system must do, but they are all related to one single thing that the customer wants to do on the system: placing an order. All of the remaining things are alternate flows in that one use case—they are things that might be done in the course of placing an order. Where there is only one useful thing being done, there is only one use case. The "solution" shown in Figure 4-5 is an example of functional decomposition, or (as one colleague puts it) an example of the "circled wagons" formation—one actor at the center of a circle of use cases. This problem is a common one. Why are people drawn to these sorts of solutions? We have an intrinsic need for order, and where none exists we impose it. In the case of functional decomposition, we have a natural tendency to try to break the problem down into smaller and smaller chunks, in a naïve belief that by so doing we can simplify the problem. This perception is wrong; when we decompose the use cases, we have actually compounded the problem.

Here's why.

The purpose of a use case is to describe how someone or some thing will use the system to do something that is useful to it. It describes what the system does at a conceptual level so that we can understand enough about the system to decide if the system does the right thing or not. It helps us form a conceptual model of the system. Now ask yourself: Would I want to use this system *only* to inquire into the status of an order if I had never placed an order? It's not very likely. Or would I need to change an order if I had never placed an order? No, probably not. All of these things are only useful to me if I have placed an order; all of them are necessary to the system's ability to allow me to place an order.

Decomposing the system into smaller use cases actually *obscures* the real purpose of the system; at the extreme, we end up with lots of isolated, disconnected bits of behavior. We can't tell *what* the system does. It's just like looking at a car that's been taken apart—maybe you can tell that it's a car, and you know that the parts must be useful somehow, but you really can't tell how. When working with use cases, remember that use cases are a way to think of the overall system and organize it into manageable chunks of functionality— chunks that do something useful. To get the right set of use cases, ask yourself the question, "What are the actors really trying to do with this system?"

In case you're wondering what the improved version of the Figure 4-5 would look like, see Figure 4-6. These two use cases would encompass all the "functions" that the earlier diagram split out as use cases. You may ask why this is better. The answer is simple—it focuses on the value that the customer

Figure 4-6 Use cases that combine functions to reflect the real value to the actor

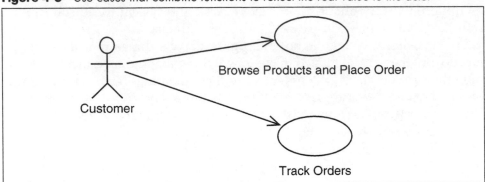

wants from the system, not on how we subdivide and structure the functionality within the system.

Focus on Value

The creation of lots of small use cases is a common problem, especially for teams with a strong background in (or covert sympathies for) functional decomposition. The names of their use cases read like a list of functions that the system will perform: Enter Order, Review Order, Cancel Order, Fulfill Order. This may not sound so bad at first, but there are likely to be many more. Even a small order-entry system generates a list of hundreds of use cases—ones for entering products, reviewing products, adjusting inventory, and on and on. If we stay on this path, we are soon drowning in use cases; if we have a "really big" system we end up with many hundreds of use cases, maybe thousands.

So what's so wrong with this?

The problem is that the value of these use cases is lost. A use case is supposed to result in something of value to the actor, and at one level being able to enter an order is something that has value. But if the order is never fulfilled, would it still have value? Probably not.

Consider entering an order and modifying or perhaps even canceling it—all of those things are related to the real thing a customer wants to do, which is to receive the goods being ordered. They are also all necessary to what the company wants, which is to receive payment for the goods shipped. If the system appears to the users as a large set of disconnected functions to be performed without any apparent relationship, the system is going to be hard to use. Too many systems are just jumbles of features. Use cases help us to focus on what is really important—the things that have real value—and to define the system around those things. Use cases do not present a functionally decomposed picture of the system.

Example

Consider an e-commerce system you have used on the Web. When you go to the site, your goal may be to find information about products, select products to buy, and arrange payment and shipping terms for those products. In the course of doing those things, you may change your mind, enter incorrect information and have to change it, change your mailing or shipping address, and a number of other things. If the site does not allow you to find products and order them in an appealing way or to correct information you provide, you probably won't even complete your order, let alone return to the site again.

So be aware of the value the users of the system expect to obtain from the system, and define the system use cases to reflect these values.

Derive the Use Cases from the System's Vision

When identifying use cases, look to the product vision statement for inspiration. Ask yourself for whom the system is being built and what problems the system is expected to solve, and then make sure that the system provides use cases that deliver this value. If the stakeholders for the system are not users of the system, ask yourself who will use the system on their behalf. Sometimes important stakeholders of the system are not users of the system. They expect to get value from the system even though they do not directly use it. They will need to be as involved in the creation and validation of the use-case model as the users themselves. Often, these various stakeholder perspectives will shape the structure and content of the use-case model as much as the users.

As you identify use cases, make sure that the use cases are compatible and complementary to the product vision statement and provide the behavior required to satisfy the stakeholder needs. Make sure that the use cases are capable of delivering all of the features defined for the system and conform to any constraints placed on the system. Great care must be taken to ensure that the vision and the use-case model are complementary and compatible. It is very easy to get carried away when use-case modeling and identify lots of use cases that, although they sound like good ideas at the time, do not actually contribute to fulfilling the project's vision or conform to the project constraints.

If there is a business model of the system (a description of the business's processes, potentially expressed in the form of business use cases[4]), this can

---

[4] For a discussion of how use cases can be used to model business processes, see Jacobson et al., *The Object Advantage.*

serve the same purpose as the vision. You can derive use cases and actors from the workers used to describe the business processes. The responsibilities of the workers may need to be supported by the system, in which case there will be use cases that describe how the system supports the worker in performing the business process.

Don't Forget the Supporting and Operational Use Cases

Once an initial set of use cases have been identified to support the primary actor goals, many other use cases will be identified that are required to support the system in the provision of these key use cases. These use cases are required to:

- Place the system into a suitable state that the use cases can be fulfilled
- Allow the tracking of the state of the system and the key use cases
- Exploit the information gathered by the system while carrying out the key use cases

It is very difficult to find these use cases at the outset of the modeling activities before the key use cases have been identified and outlined. Instead, the use-case model will evolve and become more detailed as more and more of the actors and use cases are outlined and explored.

Supporting use cases are often overlooked because they do not represent what typically are the primary goals of the system. Neglecting these use cases may produce a system that cannot be easily used, installed, or upgraded. Although these things do not provide the core value of the system, they are essential to the smooth operation of the system.

Make sure you address the use cases required to run and maintain the system, such as system start-up and stop, adding new users, backing up information, and adding new reports. If the system itself is to be configurable, customizable, or upgradeable, then use cases will need to be defined to offer these facilities to the actors undertaking these tasks.

Example

Consider a rule-based insurance sales system that allows insurance companies to distribute information about new products and insurance brokers to set up their own preferences and sales rules. As well as use cases related to the selling of insurance products, use cases will be required for the receipt and installation of new products from the insurance companies and the configuration of the sales rules by the brokers.

Evolve the Set of Use Cases Alongside the Set of Actors and the Supplementary Specification

Remember that the activities related to the finding of use cases go hand in hand with those involved in the finding of actors. Exploring the requirements embodied by the use cases can lead to the identification of more actors, which can, in turn, lead to the need for more use cases. You should also make sure that every actor participates in at least one use case. Actors that do not may be superfluous, or some use cases may not have been identified. Do not expect to find all of the use cases for a system on the first pass.

While identifying the use cases, you may also identify requirements that do not easily fit into the use-case model. These should be captured as part of the Supplementary Specification, which should be evolved in parallel with the use-case model.

DOCUMENTING USE CASES

Associate the Use Cases to Their Actors

After you have identified a use case associated with one or more actors, create a diagram that shows the actors and the use case. Actors that initiate the use case should be shown with an arrow pointing from the actor to the use case. In cases where the system initiates contact with the actor, draw the arrow from the use case to the actor. An example of this is illustrated in Figure 4-7. The arrows represent associations between the actors and use cases that act, in effect, as *conduits* for information. These conduits are pathways for communication between the actor and the system.

When interpreting use-case diagrams, the arrows should *not* be interpreted as directional flows of data. In almost every system, there is a bidirectional exchange of information between actor and use case. Some diagrams may even be shown without arrowheads on the associations; this is perfectly acceptable in the UML, but we prefer to use arrowheads to indicate the initiator of the communication and recommend that you do the same.

Figure 4-7 The *Withdraw-Cash* use case from the ATM use-case model

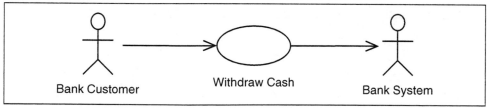

Bank Customer   Withdraw Cash   Bank System

Name the Use Cases

The name you give to a use case is important, and it should be chosen carefully. Names shape how we think about things, and the name you choose can make understanding the use case easier or more difficult. While you are brainstorming, allow the use cases to have long names. A newly identified use case may have a name as long as a sentence; this is a good start on the brief description of the use case, and it can be shortened later on. At this stage, it is more important to capture information, not to be succinct or pithy. An active use case name (one that implies action, such as *Enter an Order*) is a better choice than a passive name (such as *Order Entry*). Active names imply that something gets done, reinforcing the idea that use cases do something useful. Passive names end up sounding like functions or functional areas within an organization.

It's usually possible to use active naming, but sometimes it requires a little creativity. Some examples are

Passive name	Active name
Risk Assessment	Assess Risk
Flight Scheduling	Schedule Flight
Resource Management	Manage Resources

You might wonder, "What's so bad with passive names?" When passive names sound like a functional area within an organization, the use case becomes confused with the activity of the functional area. Functional areas within an organization do many things, and it would be unusual for a single use case to capture all the things that people within the functional area need from the system. Passive names usually send ambiguous messages about the value they provide. For example, what is the value delivered by "Customer Service"? Using passive phrases also makes it more difficult to notice when use cases are missing. For example, what about the situation where a customer wishes to register a complaint or return faulty goods? The passive could be obfuscating the problem. For example:

Passive name	Active names
Customer Service	Register Complaint Return Faulty Goods Request Store Credit Card

We know immediately the purpose of "Return Faulty Goods," but we can't tell much of anything about the purpose of "Customer Service." Another characteristic of better-quality names is the ability to concatenate the actor and use case names to produce a meaningful sentence. For example: "Customer Customer Service" is pretty meaningless, whereas "Customer returns faulty goods" is completely understandable.

Are passive names completely without merit? The answer is no, they can be used to group together a collection of use cases with similar intent and purpose. This kind of use case packaging is looked at in more detail in Chapter 6, The Life Cycle of a Use Case.

Give Every Use Case a Brief Description

Each use case must include a paragraph that describes the purpose of the use case and the value produced for its actors or stakeholders. The brief description justifies the use case's existence.

The brief description should be drafted at the time the use case is identified. A lot of time can be saved in the long run if a few sentences are captured early on that describe the purpose and value of the use case; much confusion is spared when everyone can easily understand the value that a specific use case provides. For each use case, make sure that the brief description captures

- The stakeholders for whom the use case produces value. This is often captured by the actors, but it is a good idea to explicitly call this out.
- The specific value provided for those stakeholders.
- A short synopsis of what the system does to produce this value. Don't repeat the actual use-case description; if you do, you create a maintenance and synchronization problem for yourself. Instead, focus on capturing the essence of the use case.

Keep the description succinct, but ensure that it is clear and unambiguous. Doing so when you identify the use case pays dividends later on by improving clarity and communication.

Example

| Brief description for the use case *Withdraw Cash* in an ATM system |

This use case describes how a Bank Customer uses an ATM to withdraw money from his or her bank account.

Outline the Use Cases

It is very difficult to assess the complexity or fully understand the scope of a use case just by looking at its brief description. The goal of the use case may be very simple and clear, but the narrative it contains may be very complex and convoluted. There is little relationship between the complexity of the brief description and that of the use case it describes.

Remember it is not uncommon for the length of the use-case descriptions in a single system to vary from as short as half a page to as long as 30 pages. Each use-case description has to be long enough to clearly tell its story. It has to explain the basic and alternative flows in a form that satisfies all of the stakeholders. For a very simple, data-capture use case with few or no alternatives, it can be a few sentences long, and in other cases—say, for a complex interaction involving many actors with many alternatives—it will require a lot of text.

To get a better idea of the complexity and scale of a use case, you should produce an outline of the use case to complement the brief description. The focus of the outline is to capture the scale, structure, and complexity of the use case rather than the requirements that it will contain. This outline will provide the starting point for the use-case description. See Figure 4-8. Start by listing the steps of the basic flow. Write down the different actions in order. Don't try to figure out how things are done—just work with the basic flow of events and don't worry about alternatives. Enumerate the steps 1, 2, 3, 4, ... Try not to get too mired in the detail of the use case, generally 5 to 10 steps is sufficient to outline the basic flow.

Once you've agreed on the steps in the basic flow of events, walk through it and identify alternative steps. Enumerate the alternative flows A1, A2, A3, A4, ... At this stage the outline is just serving as a sketch of the use case. The intention is that this sketch will be fleshed out and elaborated when the real use-case authoring starts. This step in the evolution of the use case is a very informal and broad-brush stroke. It is just brainstorming to obtain an idea of the shape of the use case and the effort that will be needed to complete its authoring.

Figure 4-8 Outlining a use case

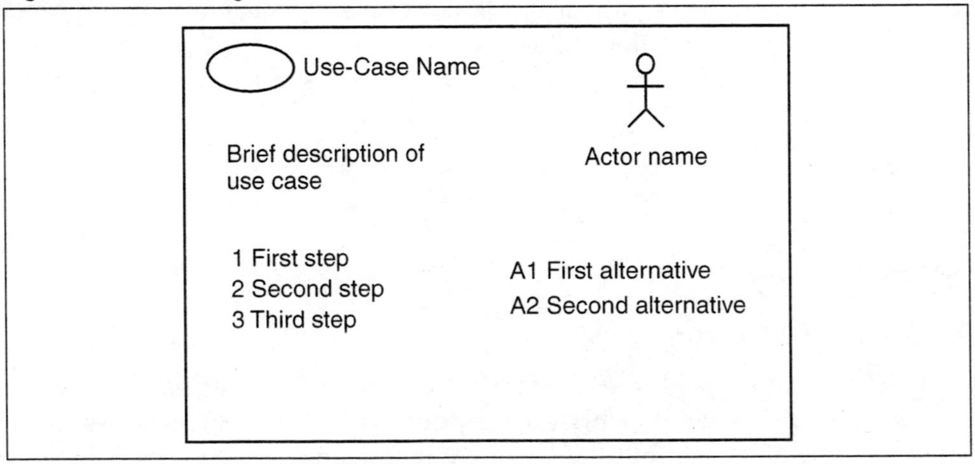

The outlining of the use cases in this way will enable the stakeholders and use-case authors to focus on the true requirement-related issues and provoke a lot of discussion about the appropriateness of the set of use cases selected. This discussion is essential to the healthy construction of an effective use-case model. The outlines will make the use-cases more real to the stakeholders and allow them to more effectively join in discussions about the model. There is no point in sitting alone and trying to outline the use cases without first obtaining input from the stakeholders.

Example

The initial outline for the use case *Withdraw Cash* in an ATM system could be

Basic Flow

1. Insert Card
2. Validate Card
3. Validate Bank Customer
4. Select Withdraw
5. Select Amount from List of Standard Amounts
6. Confirm Transaction with Banking System
7. Dispense Money
8. Eject Card

List of Alternative Flows

A1   Card cannot be identified

A2   Customer cannot be identified

A3   Withdraw not required

A4   Nonstandard amount required

A5   No money in the account

A6   Attempt to withdraw more than daily amount

A7   No connection to the banking system

A8   Link goes down

A9   Card stolen—the card is on the hot-card list

A10 The ATM is out of money

A11 The card cannot be dispensed

A12 A receipt is required

A13 The withdrawal is not from the card's primary account

And so on......

As can been seen from the example, decisions are already being made about what is the core functionality of the use case and what is extra, complementary functionality. For example, if it was required that receipts are always dispensed, then A12 would not be an alternative flow but would be included as a step in the basic flow.

The outline will also allow us to start to do some scope management on the use cases, as we can descope some of the nonessential alternative flows. Perhaps there is no requirement for Bank Customers to be able to make withdrawals from any accounts other than the primary account associated with the card. If this is the case, then A13 is not required and can be descoped.

Trace the Use Cases to Stakeholders and Stakeholder Roles

Generally, there are more stakeholders and stakeholder representatives interested in a use case than those that can be deduced directly from the actors involved in the use case. It is important to record the relationship between the use cases and the stakeholders and stakeholder roles that have an explicit interest in the use case. This will help ensure that you are involving the correct people in the development and review of the use cases. In many cases, the stakeholders will have secondary goals for the use cases above and beyond those of the actors directly involved in them. Explicitly recording these relationships will help ensure that these different viewpoints are not overlooked and ignored. Introducing this traceability will allow you to ensure that the interests of each stakeholder are represented in at least one use case.

Trace the Use Cases to the Features and Constraints

The use cases collectively provide all of the behavior required of the system. It is essential that they are in accord with the vision, and the objectives and high-level requirements that it contains. Tracing the use cases to the features and constraints defined for the system provides validation of both the use-case model and the vision itself.

There are always a number of high-level requirements that cannot be connected to any use case:

- They can be general requirements that do not affect any specific use cases—trace these into the Supplementary Specification.
- They can be requirements that have been forgotten and that will require additional use cases to be added to the model.

There may also be use cases with no requirements. This could be because the use case is not required or because the functionality was overlooked when the vision was constructed. This situation will need to be resolved with the help of the stakeholder representatives, as there may be issues related to the customer's awareness of what it needs and its willingness to pay for functionality it didn't request.

Note: The relationship between the high-level requirements (needs, features, and constraints, etc.) and the use cases is many-to-many. A single feature may give rise to multiple use cases, and a single use case may contribute to the delivery of many features. We will look at the nature of the traceability inherent in use-case modeling in more detail in Chapter 7, The Structure and Contents of a Use Case.

Knowing which needs, features, and constraints are traced to which use case also provides essential context for the people asked to complete the authoring of the use cases. This information will complement, and provide justification for, the brief descriptions and outlines produced when the use cases were first identified.

SUMMARY

The key to a successful start with use cases is to identify the purpose and the boundary of the system. Like a good business enterprise, a good system has a clear and well-defined mission.

When we understand what we want the system to do, we have to ask ourselves, "To whom does the system provide value?" The people with whom the system interacts, or other systems with which the system interacts, are the actors of the system (or maybe we should say the interactors with the system). The system exists to provide value for its actors, so it is appropriate that we focus on their needs.

To identify actors, work from the specific to the general. Start by identifying specific people and user types that will use the system, and then try to define more general roles that these people play. While doing this, avoid falling into the trap of simply using job titles to define the actors. Job titles may change, but frequently the roles that people play with respect to the system do not.

When defining actors, be careful not to forget the external systems that interact with the system being defined—these systems are actors, too. At the same time, don't try to define every kind of device as an actor; if you do, you lose focus on the real users of the system.

The following questions sum up what to look for when identifying actors and provide a useful starting point when trying to identify a system's actors:

- Who will use this system?
- Who, or what, will supply, use, or remove information?
- Who is interested in a certain requirement or area of functionality?
- Who is involved in the undertaking of the system's use cases?

- What other systems are required to interact with this one?
- What external resources does the system require?
- Who or what starts the system?
- Who will support and maintain the system?

After you have identified some of your key actors, look at the things these actors need from the system to start identifying the use cases. A use case should provide unique and independent value to one of its actors. If you find that you need to "execute" several use cases in sequence to have something useful, then you've gone wrong somewhere. Focusing on value is the key to finding meaningful use cases.

The following questions sum up what to look for when identifying use cases and provide a useful starting point when trying to identify a system's use cases:

- For each actor you have identified, what are the goals that the system will fulfill?
- Will the actor need to inform the system about sudden, external changes?
- Can all features be performed by the use cases you have identified?
- What use cases will start, stop, configure, support, and maintain the system?
- What information must be modified or created in the system?
- What events will the system need to be informed about?
- What occurrences must the system track and inform the actors about?
- Does the use-case model represent the interests of all the stakeholders?

Use the vision and the high-level requirements that it contains to drive and validate the use-case model. Trace the stakeholder types and stakeholder roles to both the actors and the use cases. Trace the user types to the actors and the features and constraints to the use cases. Make sure that the use-case model and the vision are complementary and in accord with each other.

Evolve the set of actors and use cases alongside each other. The identification of actors leads to the identification of additional use cases and vice versa. The two concepts complement each other and should be identified in an iterative and incremental fashion, starting with the identification of the primary actors and the key use cases.

After you have identified and briefly described actors and use cases, you've made a good start, but it's only a start. The real value of a use case is in the use-case description. We'll discuss this in detail in Chapter 7, The Structure and Contents of a Use Case. The real work is in the construction of the detailed use-case descriptions. We'll discuss this in more detail in Chapters 8, Writing Use-Case Descriptions: An Overview, and 9, Writing Use-Case Descriptions: Revisited.

Chapter 5

Getting Started with a Use-Case Modeling Workshop

Workshops are an excellent way to bring people together and accomplish a great deal in a short period of time. When properly planned and executed, workshops can produce dramatic results. In this chapter we describe how to get started with use cases using a workshop approach, which is in our experience the best and fastest way to get results. It also provides the best way to establish a common understanding of the problems to be solved and to build a team to jointly find solution to these problems. The concrete outcome of the workshop is a basic use-case model consisting of actors and use cases, brief descriptions for both, and definitions of the relationships between the actors and the use cases in which they participate.

Other workshops that can be useful in the context of the use-case modeling process include workshops to establish the vision and workshops to address specific issues identified with a particular use case. We focus on getting started with finding use cases and actors using a workshop because we know of no better way to do this. While there are many ways to define the vision and to resolve use-case description issues, finding actors and use cases is something that is so critical to the use-case modeling effort that it must be done as a group effort, and it must be done well.

REASONS FOR HAVING A WORKSHOP

As well as being the best way to find the actors and use cases, there are many other reasons why it is beneficial to start the use-case modeling activities with a use-case modeling workshop.

To Transfer Expertise

If the team is unfamiliar with the use-case modeling approach, there is no better way for them to learn how to put the concepts into practice than to have an experienced mentor lead the team through a workshop to identify actors and use cases. In the course of the discussions, team members will gain practical experience in applying the techniques, and they will gain confidence in how to move forward. A successful workshop helps to transfer expertise to the team, making sure that everyone understands the concepts surrounding the use-case model in the same way. A later section discusses how to find the right mentor and how to engage the mentor in the modeling effort.

To Build a Team

The workshop will often be the first opportunity for the new team members to work together toward their shared goal of delivering the system. The mood will be a mixture of excitement and apprehension. There is also typically some degree of skepticism about what, to the team, may be a number of new techniques. A competent facilitator will help to minimize the fears and channel the enthusiasm. In addition, it is essential that management support the effort and communicate confidence in the team, in the results to be achieved, and in the techniques being used. At the same time, it is important that management's expectations are appropriately set; use cases are not magic—just because you use them does not guarantee results.

A facilitated workshop can be an effective team-building activity. Developing the use cases can help to build team rapport and trust, as well as provide a basis for communication and shared understanding throughout the project. The sense of shared achievement that can occur can impart a momentum to the project that will help carry it through the rough spots later on down the road.

To Create Shared Understanding

Not the least challenging in use-case modeling is ensuring that everyone has the same understanding of the use-case concepts. Beginning with a workshop led by a recognized expert in use-case modeling concepts will ensure that everyone starts off with the same understanding of use cases. We have witnessed many project teams that stumbled because they could not come to agreement on what a proper use case is and how it is described. Having an expert there to establish and reinforce the concepts helps to prevent these differences in understanding from getting in the way of progress.

To Tap into the Creative Power of a Group

No one of us knows everything, nor does any one of us have an ability to see things from every perspective. It's not a matter of right or wrong—each one of us has preconceptions and blind spots that prevent us from seeing the full picture of a particular problem. But what one of us cannot do alone, a group of us can do with ease, provided we know how to work together.

If one of us, working alone, were to try to think of all the actors and use cases for a system, we would invariably miss something important. Different types of people have different preconceptions—user advocates tend to focus on how people will use the system, operations people tend to see how the system will be maintained in its environment, and software developers tend to forget about the people entirely and immerse themselves in the technology. By ensuring that we have a diversity of perspectives, we will derive a better and more complete result.

PREPARING FOR THE WORKSHOP

One of the keys to running a successful workshop is to ensure that the workshop is properly planned and that all of the attendees are properly prepared. This is especially true for the initial use-case modeling workshops where the techniques and general approach will be new to a large number of the attendees and the team itself may well be working together for the first time on the project.

Train the Participants

Although people do not need to be use-case modeling experts in order to participate in the workshop, it is useful if they have a basic understanding of use-case modeling and its purpose. This could be gained by reading the first chapter of this book or by attending an introductory presentation given by one of the project's more experienced use-case modelers.

Only facilitators need to be expert in the techniques. They need in-depth knowledge in order to successfully lead and direct the modeling efforts. The only other attendees who need to have more than a basic level of knowledge are those who are expected to take the use cases forward by writing the use-case descriptions.

In an ideal world, all the participants would be trained in the basic techniques of use cases, requirements gathering, and brainstorming before the workshop. Sometimes, there is a desire to combine an abbreviated training session with the workshop itself, and this can work, but there is a hidden peril: Learning the basic concepts of use cases and requirements gathering can confuse the issues, diminishing the value of both the training and workshop aspects of the combined session. A better approach is to follow a training session *immediately* with a workshop session, so that new skills can be exercised immediately. This advice is still valid even when the training has used the attendees' domain as a running example.

Understand the Vision

Prior to holding a workshop to find actors and use cases, there must be a coherent and consistent vision for the system that is to be built. The stakeholders who participate in the shaping of the vision are not typically the same people who participate in finding actors and use cases. As a result, if the vision is not well understood prior to the use-case modeling workshop, the effort will largely be wasted; the team will spend most of its time trying to decide what the system is supposed to do. If you don't have a shared vision for the project, it is not yet time to hold the use-case modeling workshop. Refer back to Chapter 3, Establishing the Vision, for a discussion of how to establish the vision and which stakeholders need to be involved.

In order for the vision to be useful, it needs to be understood by the use-case modeling team. While documents are wonderful ways of recording information, they are not always the best way to convey information. The best way to share the vision is usually through a presentation—having one or more of the principal stakeholders present the vision to the team. This enables the team to ask clarifying questions and to get information directly from the source. Often, the best person to give the presentation is the executive sponsor of the project.

In addition to the vision, it is usually beneficial for project team members to understand the business case and objectives for the project. By understanding how the system will drive customer and business benefits, the project team will have a better basis for finding actors and use cases. If the project has formal vision and business-case documents, these should be circulated to the attendees before the workshop. These will act as reference material during the workshop and back up the messages communicated by the project vision presentation.

Keep the Group Small and Involved

Free, unfettered communication is key to success in any workshop; if there are too many people, communication will be complicated by the logistics of managing a larger group; if there are too few people, there will not be enough diversity to have all perspectives present. The ideal group size is somewhere between five and eight people, not counting the facilitator. A group of sixteen people will never get anywhere, and even in a group of eight there will be several people who do not participate much. The key thing is to make certain that enough diversity of opinion is represented and that there are enough participants to do the work of writing use cases when the appropriate time comes.

Under no circumstances should people be allowed to "sit-in" on the workshop as an inexpensive form of training. Despite all protestations to the contrary, these "invisible" participants are a distraction to everyone, and once the discussions start they inevitably attempt to join in. If you are scheduling a workshop, don't be persuaded that it's a good idea to allow "observers"; there should be no observers in a workshop, only participants.

Vary the Composition of the Group

The key to a successful workshop is achieving a balance in skills and personalities, a common theme of this book. You need to form a small group consisting of people with diverse backgrounds, interests, and personalities. In addition, there needs to be a spirit of mutual respect and cooperation, with a sense that everyone has something to contribute. A trained facilitator is also usually required to make sure that the discussion stays focused on the issues, but more on this in a moment.

A use-case workshop is an organized brainstorming session. In order to achieve good results, a wide range of knowledge needs to be represented among the participants:

- An understanding of customer and user requirements and expectations
- An understanding of the technological issues present in the anticipated implementation
- An understanding of how system capabilities will be verified
- An appreciation of the user education, documentation, and human factors issues surrounding the system

All skills and knowledge must be represented:

- If there are too many user advocates, the resulting use cases will be written only in terms of the user's experience, with the description of what the system does more or less absent.
- If there are too many developers, the use cases will likely be unrecognizable to the user due to overemphasis on structure and technical details.

- If there are no testers, it may later prove difficult to verify whether the system does what it is supposed to do.
- If there are no architects, it may prove difficult to identify all of the other systems with which the system is to interact.
- If usability issues are ignored, the resulting system may be technically satisfactory (it satisfies all requirements), but may be difficult or impossible to use.

In forming the list of workshop participants, refer back to the discussion of stakeholder types and representatives presented in Chapter 3. The use-case modeling workshop should include representatives for each of the major stakeholder roles identified. If the group is getting too large, consider selecting people who can fulfill more than one stakeholder role and represent more than one stakeholder type. This may require them to research issues so that they are adequately prepared. If so, make sure to allow for enough preparation time.

Select a Facilitator

Into the middle of this mix is thrown the facilitator. The facilitator is part moderator, part diplomat, and part goodwill ambassador. Above all, facilitators are expert in managing group elicitation/brainstorming sessions and use-case modeling in general. Typically, you will need to hire someone to do this the first few times—having an outside "expert," perceived as neutral by all parties, is often key to obtaining the trust needed to successfully facilitate a use-case workshop.

The facilitator should spend time interviewing the participants *before* the workshop. Getting to know them, understanding their concerns, areas of expertise, and perhaps even agendas (hidden or otherwise) enables the facilitator to anticipate conflicts and to understand perspectives before entering the arena of the workshop. The trust gained here by listening and taking time to allay concerns is well worth the effort.

In the workshop itself, the facilitator will need to act as a catalyst, initiating discussion, engaging participants, and sometimes controlling participants who tend to monopolize the discussion or fail to respect the opinions of other group members. The facilitator will need to know when and how to summarize discussions and how to drive issues to closure. The facilitator must above all avoid dictating a particular solution—the entire group must feel the result is something for which they feel responsible; the group must be able to carry on even after the facilitator leaves. We discuss more about this later in the chapter, under the heading of Finding a Mentor.

Set Objectives for the Workshop

In order to achieve good results, appropriate expectations must be set. The participants of the workshop should have, from the outset, a clear understanding of what needs to be achieved by the end of the workshop. The main results of the workshop should be

- An initial use-case model, with *actors* and *use cases* identified, given names, and provided with brief descriptions. It is inevitable that while discussing the use cases you will start to sketch out the flow of events of the use cases, at least at a high level; if this happens, write down the discussions and you will have a good start on the flow of events. (This underlines the importance of having an appointed *recorder* for the meetings so that the discussions can be captured without interruptions.)
- The start of a *glossary of terms* or a *domain model* to capture the key concepts that the project team will have to deal with in creating a solution. The purpose of capturing these concepts is to establish a baseline for everyone's understanding of the key concepts or abstractions with which the system must deal. These are useful starting points for the analysis work performed later on.
- Some initial sketches of the user interface and some storyboards for how those interfaces will be used by the use cases to meet the needs of the stakeholders. The purpose of producing these is not to start designing the user interface; they are much too crude to serve that purpose. These sketches tend to be produced as a natural by-product of discussing how the system will work. To the extent that they are produced, they should be saved so that they can be refined later when the actual business of defining the user interface is undertaken.
- A list of risks and issues that need to be resolved. The existence of such a list allows risks and issues to be raised and captured without having the issues derail the discussions.
- A work plan for allocating the work of writing the use-case descriptions, including following up with additional workshops to detail and investigate specific areas of the model or to write and review specific use-case descriptions.[1]
- A plan for following up on the results of the use-case modeling effort, to make sure that the results are ratified by the other stakeholders and that the effort remains focused and on track.

---

[1] If the team has never written or reviewed use cases before, a workshop to help them to do the first one is often helpful to get them started down the right path. Subsequent chapters deal with the topics of writing and reviewing use-case descriptions.

Armed with these items, the team will be ready to move ahead to the real work of use-case modeling—writing use case descriptions.

It is reasonable to expect that the use-case modeling workshop can be conducted in a day, provided that there is agreement on the vision and the business case going into the workshop. Sometimes getting this agreement can be complex and time-consuming, but it is important that it occur before the use-case modeling workshop; failure to do so usually results in confusion and unsatisfactory results.

If the stakeholder community is particularly large and complex, it may take time to ratify and validate the results of the initial workshop with all of the stakeholders and stakeholder representatives involved in the project. It is worth using the initial use-case modeling results to ensure that everybody is in agreement about the extent of the solution and the direction in which the project is heading. There is no point spending a lot of time writing detailed use-case descriptions if there is still no agreement on the boundaries, purpose, and shape of the system to be built.

Schedule the Workshop and Organize the Facilities

Scheduling the workshop includes finding a satisfactory date and time for all participants and ensuring that facilities are adequate and that proper supplies are on hand. The meeting room itself should be large enough to accommodate the participants. It should be equipped with:

- Two large white boards (one is sufficient but two is better)
- Flip charts
- Tape
- Two colors of self-stick notes
- White-board pens (multiple colors)
- Pencils or markers
- Walls on which to attach paper—preferably in a "war room" that you can use and leave undisturbed for two or three weeks

It is also useful to have a computer and a projector to allow reference to information that is in electronic form, such as the vision, the business case, or other background information.

Although it may seem trivial to talk about this preparatory work, conference rooms at many companies are in short supply and high demand, making it important to ensure that the right room with the right resources is available.

FINDING A MENTOR

When exploring a new area, it always helps to have someone who has been there before. A good mentor can help you get started faster while avoiding the common pitfalls and can help you to be more productive. Ideally, the facilitator of the use-case workshop will be an experienced mentor, an expert in facilitation and the application of requirements gathering and use-case modeling.

All this is fairly obvious. What is less obvious is how to find a mentor with the right characteristics, and subsequently, how to put them to good use. Many teams fail because they misapply the mentor's skills, using the mentor as a crutch. The mentor is mainly a teacher and coach, but more on that in a moment.

Find an Effective Communicator

First and foremost, a good mentor needs to be an effective communicator. As most experts on communication will tell you, this means listening first, understanding the issues, and communicating an effective approach based on that understanding. There is not a magic one-size-fits-all approach to applying use cases and requirements-elicitation techniques to a project; the mentor must listen, understand, and adapt. A good mentor will seek to understand the situation first and will ask a lot of questions before proposing solutions.

Once the problem is understood, however, the mentor needs to speak with authority and conviction. Nothing undermines the confidence of a team more than a mentor who equivocates or weakly presents a position. Although there are usually few absolutes in a mentoring engagement, when mentors answer a question with the typical preamble of "well, it depends . . .," they need to clearly articulate the issues and trade-offs, typically based on their own experience. If the mentor provides vague guidance, the team will quickly realize the mentor doesn't really know either and that they are both lost. A large part of being a good mentor (and a leader) is projecting a sense of confidence and enthusiasm.

Find a Skilled Motivator and Manager

A related skill is the ability to manage situations. Running workshops and mentoring teams frequently involves being able to "shut down" overly dominant team members in an appropriate way, allowing the more passive team members to contribute. The dominant team members are not usually aware that their strongly stated opinions can often be intimidating to other group members, who then feel that they cannot contribute (or perhaps cannot even get a word in edgewise). At the same time, dominant team members are often excellent contributors with tremendous energy and enthusiasm. Properly channeled, this enthusiasm is a great asset to the team. It's a sensitive balancing act, and the mentor must understand how to motivate and manage the team without ever having direct authority. It's a subtle skill.

It's common to encounter a team with one or a few dominant, self-appointed experts in "use cases" or other related techniques. Often, these people have read a few books and articles and are keen to demonstrate their superior knowledge. Paradoxically, they require the most management and redirection. They tend to have dominant personalities and also tend to be somewhat insensitive to the needs of other group members. Their interruptions also tend to be disruptive to the mentoring sessions—they tend to dominate discussions and often lead the group into discussions for which they are not ready, such as additional (and abstract, rarely used) concepts like use-case inclusion, extension, or generalization.[2] The mentor must find an effective way to gain control of the situation, channeling the enthusiasm of these individuals while making sure that the needs of the group as a whole are met. At some point, there will be the inevitable collision of wills, and the mentor must handle it sensitively, in a face-saving way, while maintaining control over the situation.

The mentor must also manage the managers in the organization, to gain their support and trust and to ensure that they trust and support the team. Learning a new technique takes some time, and the team is likely to falter and stumble a bit at first. Having a mentor makes this stumbling period shorter, but it does not eliminate it. Many times, managers expect instant results and typically fail to take the learning curve into account when they schedule activities. A good mentor will work with managers to establish realistic expectations and to ensure that critical learning efforts are not undermined by shortsighted and impatient desires to see quick results. Managers need to understand that progress is not linear and that time spent establishing fundamental skills early on leads to faster progress later in the project. Failure to establish fundamental skills will impede progress and endanger the project.

Find a Mentor with Full Life-Cycle Experience

In the words of the great New York Yankees catcher Yogi Berra, "If you don't know where you are going, you might end up somewhere else." It's very hard to employ use cases effectively unless you know where they are leading. Experience with analysis, design, and implementation, as well as testing and

---

[2] Don't worry about these concepts; they are discussed later in the book. They are deliberately left until later so that we can gain a solid understanding of use-case fundamentals.

documentation, all contribute to a better understanding of how well written use cases can contribute to those activities. Knowing how much detail to include often requires understanding the different constituents of the use cases—developers, testers, and technical writers all have a stake in the information presented in the use cases, and their needs need to be considered.

It's rare today to find people who have full life-cycle experience, but it's essential to have at least broad exposure to all of the disciplines of software engineering in order to be an effective mentor. Expertise in user-centered design or requirements is important, but use cases represent a common thread that runs throughout the project. The effective mentor needs to understand the various disciplines at work on a real project.

Don't Use the Mentor as a Crutch

Finally, the mentor should be used as a teacher or a coach, not as one who will do the work of writing use cases. It's often tempting to "hire" expertise and immediately put that expertise to work, but it undermines the development of the team's skills. If the mentor is always there to do the work, to answer the hard questions, or to make decisions, the team will never learn to trust its own judgment and its skills will never develop. The mentor must actively work to wean the team from dependence on the mentor; sometimes this means the mentor must let people make their own small mistakes so that they can learn from them. The mentor's presence should gradually taper off after an initial daily involvement. As the team learns to work on its own, the mentor can just be available for reviews and discussions but should not be a daily presence on the project.

STRUCTURING THE WORKSHOP

For the workshop to be effective and reach its stated objectives, it must be planned and structured. This subsection presents a typical outline for an initial use-case modeling workshop.

Define the Ground Rules for the Workshop

A few procedural comments are usually in order to make the workshop run smoothly. Some of the basic rules for running workshops that we have found useful are the following:

- **Give everyone a chance to express an opinion fully.** This means that when someone is talking, the rest of the group lets them finish the idea without interruption.

- **No one monopolizes the discussion.** This means that sometimes the facilitator must limit the excessive participation of some group members to allow everyone to be able to participate.
- **Reach conclusions by consensus.** All decisions should be made by consensus and reflect the opinions of the entire group; decisions that cannot be made due to lack of consensus probably indicate a lack of information. It is preferable to table issues and pursue them after the workshop rather than waste precious workshop time discussing issues that cannot be resolved immediately.
- **Identify issues and move on.** Issues should be identified but not necessarily resolved. If an issue cannot be resolved quickly, it should be captured and assigned to an owner for investigation and resolution outside the workshop.
- **No "cheap shots" or personal attacks.** When discussions become heated they can sometimes become personal. The facilitator must be vigilant and regain control of the discussion, focusing it on the problem to be solved rather than outside issues.
- **Stick to the schedule.** The workshop needs to stick to its schedule. Breaks are necessary, but the meeting must resume on schedule. If you wait for tardy people to come back to resume the workshop, it is unfair to the people who return from breaks on time. Make sure everyone understands the time limits for breaks and respects their fellow participants.
- **Stick to the point.** Always bear in mind the objectives of the meeting and try not to get sidetracked into other areas, such as debating the project's vision, discussing the finer points of use-case relationships, or drilling down into a single use case at the expense of identifying the other actors and use cases of the system.
- **No outside distractions.** Participants should participate; if they want to catch up on their e-mail, they should not be in the meeting. Reading e-mail during a meeting is disrespectful to the other participants of the meeting. The same is true for cell phones—they should be turned off during the meeting.

Make sure everyone understands and agrees to the ground rules for the meeting, and then make sure that they adhere to these ground rules during the meeting. The team will appreciate it and the results from the meeting will be better. At this stage, it is also worth recapping the objectives of the workshop to ensure that everybody has the correct focus going into the session.

Understand the Problem

The main theme of Chapter 3 was establishing the vision for the system, or, put another way, ensuring that you understand the problem being solved. The use-case modeling workshop should leverage that effort.

Prior to the workshop, ensure that workshop participants are familiar with the vision and the business case. This typically will involve scheduling a presentation by one of the key stakeholder representatives to walk through a presentation of the vision and the business case. At the beginning of the workshop, present a few slides or lead a discussion that recaps the key elements of the vision: the stakeholders, what the stakeholders need from the system, and the business-value proposition that drives the solution. A presentation is preferable if the workshop participants are not well versed in the vision, and a discussion is preferable to get the team participating and discussing issues. Limit this discussion to no more than a half hour, and use it to assess the readiness of the team to participate in the modeling workshop. If there is not agreement on the goals for the system, the team is probably not ready for the use-case modeling workshop.

Define the Boundary of the System

Chapter 4 discussed how to determine the boundary of the system and the effect the boundary of the system has on the actors and use cases of the system. Having a firm grasp on the boundary of the system is essential to the success of the project—at some point, you will have more to do than you have time and resources to accomplish and you will have to adjust the scope of the system. This issue aside, you also need to have a firm idea of those things for which you are responsible, and those things for which you are not.

If the team has difficulty defining the boundary of the system, sometimes drawing a context diagram will help. Context diagrams have been around for some time and are used by a number of methodologies.[3] The basic idea of a context diagram is that it shows interaction between a system and things outside the system. A use-case diagram can be thought of as a kind of context diagram.

A context diagram is an abstraction of the system. For example, it can be a server with a database and a number of clients, or a number of circuit boards with their special tasks marked out. This view is usually easy to illustrate and such a diagram comes about naturally: Team members almost instinctively take a white-board pen and start drawing diagrams that look something like Figure 5-1.

---

[3] The Software Engineering Institute provides a good overview of the general use of context diagrams at http://www.sei.cmu.edu/domain-engineering/context_diag.html

Figure 5-1 A simple context diagram for a fire detection system

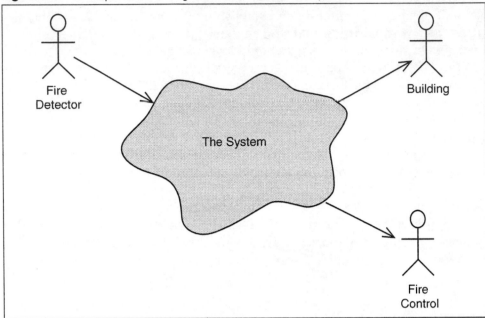

The context diagram need not be very formal—we use it simply to make sure that everyone is looking at the same problem in the same way; the notation can be as simple as needed. The goal is to get agreement on what is inside the system and what is outside. By showing this, and using it as a basis for discussing what the system will and will not do, we provide a way for the different team members to talk about what they see the system doing. As this discussion proceeds, be sure to write down what people say; this will help drive the identification of actors and use cases.

Context diagrams have different applicability to different kinds of systems. If you are working with a technical system, the context diagram is often expressed as some set of nodes or devices that communicate with one another. Even before it is expressed, the content of the context diagram is in everyone's head. Rather than fighting this, draw the diagram of how the team members envision the system, and then let this discussion turn around to one in which the system boundary is set. If you are working with an administrative system, the context diagram may not be as obvious to everyone. In this case, a chart describing the manual routines may be more useful. The graph may describe how one business entity is moved from one person to another and what each is supposed to do with it. To visualize the process of order and delivery, the graph may show a schematic view of the customer office, our office, the storage, and the customer storage.

The context diagrams need not be maintained through the life of the system—their usefulness is in generating ideas and discussion. Once this discussion is underway, the diagrams have done their duty and will effectively transform into more permanent artifacts, such as the use-case model itself.

Identify Actors

Once the boundary of the system is defined, focus on identifying the actors for the system. Chapter 4 dealt in detail with what this means and how to do it, so we won't repeat the details here, but there are some other techniques that can be useful if the team is having trouble getting started.

First, try to identify who or what will use the system. Start initially with actual people who will use the system; most people have an easier time focusing on the concrete versus the abstract. As users are identified, try to identify the role the user plays while interacting with the system—this is usually a good name for an actor.

Second, consult the vision document and the user types defined therein. As you go through and identify actors, make sure that all the user types are covered. If you identify a new type of user, make a note to go back and revise the vision accordingly.

Third, when defining actors, do not forget about the other systems that interact with the system being designed. The icon for an actor is misleading here—it seems to imply "person," but the concept of actor encompasses systems as well. Focus first on finding the "human" actors, though; most groups will do better when they focus on the familiar first, then consider the more esoteric.

Finally, when identifying actors, be sure to write a short description for each actor. Usually, a few bullet points capturing the role the actor plays with respect to the system and the responsibilities of the actor will help when the time comes later on to determine what the actor needs from the system.

Don't worry about the structure of the use-case model, or about relationships between actors; simply capture the people or things that will use the system. Focus on identification, and be prepared to find a lot of actors. Don't worry too much about filtering the list now; the identification of use cases (see the following subsection) will do that. Identifying actors will tend to occur throughout the day, but the initial identification of actors should be limited to no more than an hour. The goal of this part of the work is to be thorough without getting bogged down in discussions that don't contribute directly to development of the use-case model.

Identify Use Cases

When identifying actors and use cases, nearly everyone is able to express a few sentences about what the actor or the use case does; all you need to do is to capture these, refining them later. As with identifying actors, identifying use cases is best done in a group. As soon as someone identifies an actor, that person should be able to describe what the actor does in relation to the system; as soon as a use case is identified, its value for the actors should be evident. In fact, it is nearly impossible to keep people from providing brief descriptions in addition to the name of the actor or use case; all you really need to do is to write it down so that it is not forgotten. As you do this work, you will find out that there are some things that everybody thought were clear that are not actually clear at all; new use cases will appear, some will disappear. Use a flip chart to capture the brief description, and possibly the outline, of each use case identified. What you end up capturing in the brief description might be things that you think are self-evident, but remember that in many cases what is self-evident during a use-case workshop is not when weeks and months have passed. Also, what is obvious to the people attending the meeting may not be to other stakeholders.

Very often, the best way to express the use-case description is to briefly outline the flow of events. This outline will evolve into the flow-of-events description of the use case, but for now it is sufficient to capture it as part of the brief description. At this point, don't focus on identifying alternative flows—just focus on the main things the system does. If you happen to identify alternative flows as part of outlining the main flow, make a note of the alternative flow but don't spend extra time looking for alternatives. The purpose of this exercise is to convey the essence of the behavior of the system described by this use case. The idea here is to spend a very short amount of time to add a lot of value—do not ponder endlessly on what the perfect definition would be. At this stage, spend no more than 10 minutes for each actor or use case.

Consolidate the Model and Validate the Results

After you have made a first pass through the actors and use cases, take some time to consolidate the results and validate them against the vision. As noted in Chapter 3, the Vision document is a key driver for the project. Among other things, the vision describes features that the system must provide in order to meet the needs of the stakeholders. Walk through the feature list and make a note of which use cases provide the behavior that supports each feature. Sticky notes can be used to capture the information—just write the feature ID on a note and stick it to the white-board area or flip-chart page that describes the use case. There are always a number of features or requirements that can't be connected to any use case:

- They can be general requirements that can't be connected to any use case (those that describe general qualities of the system). Put these on the list for the Supplementary Specifications.
- They can be requirements that have been forgotten and require either new use cases or changes to the existing model.

Also take some time to assess the suitability of the emerging model. Get everyone to consider whether there is anything missing or if there is anything unnecessary in the model. It is always worth taking a little time to take a break from identifying more actors and use cases to consider the shape of the model and whether it is already complete. As part of the consolidation note which areas of the model people are happiest with, which areas they are uncertain about, and which areas are missing. Use the rest of the available workshop time to fill out the missing areas and to drill down into the areas of uncertainty. Some areas of uncertainty may be caused by there being insufficient expertise within the group; these areas should be identified and left for a follow-up workshop to tackle. Other areas of uncertainty can be addressed by either reworking the set of actors and use cases or fleshing out the outlines of the use cases to clarify their extent and purpose.

Wrap Up the Workshop and Plan the Next Steps

Allow for at least an hour at the end of the workshop to evaluate your results and to establish a plan for the next steps. As well as doing a final consolidation and validation of the model, make sure to ask the following questions:

- Are there use cases with no requirements? Has the team been a little too creative and added things the stakeholders don't really want, or has something important been forgotten?
- Have all features been traced to at least one use case?
- Have all user types been traced to at least one actor?
- Have all nonfunctional requirements been handled?
- Have all the actors and use cases been given brief descriptions?

The goal of the initial use-case modeling workshop is to capture the outline of the use-case model and provide a firm foundation for the commencement of the more detailed use-case modeling activities. It will also identify areas of uncertainty that require other workshops and areas of stability where detailed use-case modeling activities can be commenced.

When wrapping up the workshop it is important to clearly identify the areas of the model that are stable and where consensus has been reached.

These areas can be driven forward and the use cases they contain assigned to teams of use-case authors for more outlining or detailed specification. For key, significant use cases, it is worth organizing a workshop involving all the interested stakeholder representatives to outline the use cases and brainstorm the alternative flows. For less-significant use cases, it may be appropriate to have the use-case authors write them alone. Rather than tackling the use cases individually, a more effective technique is to take a set of related use cases and set up a workshop to outline them all simultaneously. Where areas of the model are uncertain or unstable, additional workshops may be required to drive these forward. These may involve different sets of stakeholder representatives than attended the initial workshop.

Make sure all issues have owners and establish milestones for further discussion and resolution of the issues. Again, these may require additional workshops with different sets of stakeholder representatives. In addition, schedule a walkthrough of the use-case model with key stakeholders to ensure that the results of the workshop are satisfactory. This may take some time—in at least one case, we found that it took several weeks to get confirmation from the stakeholders that the workshop produced a model of what they wanted (they eventually did agree).

SUPPORTING ACTIVITIES

There are some activities that need to be carried out throughout the workshop that do not fit nicely into the structure presented here. These activities support the identification of the actors and use cases, ensuring that all of the information generated by the workshop is captured in the correct form and can be taken forward alongside the use-case authoring activities.

Capture Terminology in a Glossary

Most teams spend a significant amount of time arguing about terminology, and if they don't, perhaps they should. We recall one team who spent over a day defining what a *customer* was. It may sound trivial until you try it yourself.

Good results rest on shared understanding, and without agreement on key definitions, you'll find yourself arguing over things that you really agree on or thinking you have agreement when both sides mean something different. The key is to know how to start and when to stop—the goal is not to create a glossary for its own sake, but simply to augment other work as it proceeds.

As the workshop proceeds, keep a list of terms that need to be defined. They are usually obvious—they are the ones that generate discussion. Typical candidates are things that eventually turn into entities in the analysis process, for example:

- Customers
- Orders and items on orders
- Products
- Special domain-specific terminology
- Technical terms

The idea is to capture the key concepts that are needed to understand the use cases. Don't go out of your way to look for the terms, but if some discussion arises, record the results in the evolving glossary. It's especially important to define terms that are used in many places in the use cases, in requirements, or in other project documentation—failure to get agreement on these terms can lead to later unpleasantness. The glossary of this book can be used as an example of how to represent common terms that may be used in several places or whose definitions need to be captured in one place. The glossary should contain only definitions; it should not turn into explanations of how to use the concept being defined. The glossary should be updated continually throughout the project and should represent the interests of all project members—users, developers, testers, managers, and documenters. The glossary may eventually evolve into product documentation, but the main purpose with respect to use cases is to promote clarity and shared understanding.

When you use terms defined in the glossary in use cases or other documentation, don't repeat the definition; let the glossary do its work. Define the terms in one place, and use references where you feel you need to point the reader to the definition. Sometimes this means nothing more than using a different font to indicate a term is defined elsewhere. When capturing information on flip charts, during a workshop, underlining is an effective and easy way of denoting which terms are glossary terms.

Example

Here are a couple of examples that one might find in the car maintenance trade. Note the important business rules that they may contain.

Quote A quote defines an offer price to a customer for an item of work, including parts and labor, but not tax. The price is not contractually binding and is subject to change during the work.

Part A part is a replacement component for a vehicle. The original vehicle manufacturer may approve the part, in which case it is guaranteed for 12 months. If it not an approved part, it is guaranteed for 3 months.

Take a close look at these definitions. You will notice that they may raise other questions. For example, what is a "component," a "vehicle," or a "tax"? These and other words or phrases may also need to be defined if they are interpretable and crucial for true understanding. Please note however, we usually do not need mathematical preciseness, we're not trying to prove a theorem here. Remember the purpose of the glossary is to support our understanding of the domain in which we are working and help define the requirements for the system.

Capture Nonfunctional Requirements

Throughout the workshop, there will be requirements on the system that you may not be able to readily capture in a use case. Typically, these requirements are not related to the behavior of the system (that is, they are *nonfunctional*), but rather have to do with usability, reliability, performance, and supportability of the system, among other things. When one of these requirements applies to a particular use case, make a note of it. If you are using white boards or flip charts, an easy way to do this is to write the requirement on a "sticky note" and attach it to the use-case description. Later, you will probably enter these requirements in a requirements management tool, establishing traceability between the nonfunctional requirement and the use case. Doing this will make it easy to understand the dependencies between requirements and the use cases. Nonfunctional requirements traced to specific use cases are presented in Supplementary Specification reports in the Rational Unified Process.

Capture Issues, Risks, and Assumptions

Often, risks and issues will come up that cannot be resolved with a brief discussion. This is usually because insufficient information exists at the time to resolve the issue; continued discussion of the issue will not result in progress. When this situation occurs, clearly articulate the issue and record it. Before the end of the meeting, assign the issue to someone to research and schedule a time for the group to meet to discuss the issue and bring it to resolution. Don't waste time arguing about things when the cause of the problem is lack of information. In other cases, the group will have to make assumptions in order to progress. Again, these should be recorded and resolved outside the workshop.

HANDLING COMMON PROBLEMS

In the course of the workshop, there are a number of common problems that may occur. Some of these problems are related to working in groups toward a common purpose, but some are unique to use-case modeling. These are discussed in greater detail here along with strategies for overcoming the problems.

Avoid Functional Decomposition and Dataflow Modeling

If you employ context diagrams as a brainstorming technique, be aware that the typical "context" for these diagrams is in association with dataflow diagrams. In dataflow diagrams, it is possible to decompose the diagrams into multiple levels, showing successively greater detail. Use-case diagrams do not work this way at all—there are no "high-level" use cases that decompose into lower-level use cases. In this respect, it is unfortunate that use-case diagrams look so much like dataflow diagrams.

It is wrong to confuse the notions and notations of dataflow modeling and functional decomposition with those of use-case modeling; the two approaches have absolutely nothing to do with one another. More to the point, the "arrows" between actors and use cases *do not* represent the flow of information. The "arrows" or associations represent communication, which is frequently bidirectional; the direction of the arrows (if they are shown at all, the arrowheads are optional) represents the direction of the initial communication between actor and system.

Even more emphatically, use cases do not "call" other use cases or communicate with other use cases. Attempts to show this are just plain wrong; if you find yourself needing to do this, you are going down the path of turning use cases into functions. Remember, a single use case must provide a complete experience that results in real value for at least one of its actors; if you need to link use cases together in order to provide value, your use cases have degraded into functions.

The main value of the context diagram is to get the team focused on the *actors* of the system, which gets them to focus on defining the boundary of the system. Keep the focus on the boundary and don't let the discussion drift into discussing the system itself. Very often, the discussion of the boundary can lead quite naturally to a detailed description of some behavior of the system itself. That behavior is important, but in due time. The purpose at this point is to set limits for the system before moving on.

Maintain Focus

Success in many things related to software development requires focusing on one or a few specific issues, driving them to at least a preliminary conclusion and then moving on. Teams that try to consider too many aspects of the system at once find that nothing ever gets decided, and weeks and months pass by without real progress. It's often better to make a decision based on the best available information and move on. Once more information becomes available, the decision can be adjusted. Too often, discussions continue on the basis of speculation while no decisions are made. If there's not enough information, the decision should be to get more information, but further discussion based on conjecture and supposition is not productive. The best teams realize this and focus on moving ahead. When issues arise that cannot be resolved with a brief discussion, clearly articulate the issue, record it, and move on. Don't waste time arguing about things when the cause of the problem is lack of information or the wrong attendees at the workshop.

Sometimes the team will conclude that a requirement is unclear, or that there is something wrong with the vision, or that there is something wrong with some part of a use case. Treat these as issues—identify the problem and briefly discuss it, but if the issue cannot be quickly resolved, table the issue for further investigation and move on. Handling issues in this way will keep the team from being distracted by things that cannot be resolved.

Synthesize, Don't Analyze

The difference between analysis and synthesis is not often considered but it is significant. *Analysis* means to break something down into its constituent parts, whereas *synthesis* means to create something from a less-ordered set of constituent parts; analysis and synthesis are actually opposite approaches. Our methods of teaching logic typically involve teaching analysis, and we have a long history of breaking down large problems into smaller problems in order to solve them. The use-case approach takes advantage of this by breaking the functionality of the system into sequences of things that add material value for some stakeholder (and calling these things *use cases*). But that is where the analysis stops—we do not continue to break the use case down into smaller use cases.

Instead of breaking down the system's requirements into smaller and smaller parts, the use cases work to group requirements together into units of work that together do something useful for a stakeholder of the system. These units of work we call *use cases*, and their value is very much related to the fact that they provide some comprehensive value for a stakeholder. By doing this, it allows everyone to focus on ensuring the system provides value. If we were to break the use cases down into smaller use cases that do not provide direct value, we would lose this benefit and the real value of use cases would be lost completely.

Don't Describe What Happens Outside the System

Actors do not interact with each other, only with the system. The purpose of the use-case model is to capture the interactions of the actors and the system, to describe what the system does in response to events initiated by the actors (that is, external events). Interaction between actors may be important to the business (the loan officer may have to talk to the department head in order to approve the loan), but if the system does not enable or facilitate this interaction, the designers of the system should not care about it. If you don't do this right, you risk spending too much time on the actor interaction, which is defocusing. Your task is to define system requirements, not how the business is run.

However, if it turns out you need to clarify the business processes in order to understand system requirements, you should consider building a set of business models. Set aside project time to do this, and use the appropriate techniques for it. This is a more effective use of your time.

Don't Just Draw Pictures

Use-case diagrams have an aura of significance about them. After many years of encountering software design techniques, we are drawn to approaches with rich visual interpretations, so much so that we often see things that aren't there.

A use-case diagram, such as the one shown in Figure 5-2, conveys some useful information: It tells us that there is a kind of user of the system called the "customer," and that the customer uses the system to do several things—transfer money, withdraw money, and check balances. But that's about it; just from the diagram we cannot tell how the use cases start, or even what they do. They provide a way to get started, and a way to present an overview of the system, nothing more. Yet many teams spend hours on their use-case diagrams, polishing and refining them as if they convey great quantities of information. They don't.

The diagram provides a quick summary of the relationships between the actors and the use cases, but it's only a summary picture. The real value in the use cases is deeper, in the descriptions. With the diagrams, say what needs to be said quickly and clearly, and then move on to the heart of the matter—the descriptions.

Based on the information in Figure 5-2 alone, can we build a system? No, not unless we already know a lot about the system. Can we even tell what the system does? No; but because many of us *think* we know what an automated banking machine does (having used one), we may be fooled into thinking that we know what these use cases do. In truth, the diagram does not tell us very much at all; certainly not enough to design the right system (the one that the

Figure 5-2 A simple use-case diagram for an automated banking machine

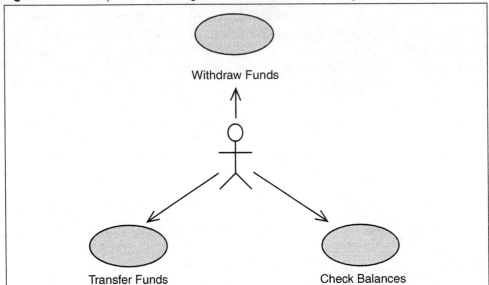

customer wants to use, and that does what the bank needs it to do). Use-case diagrams, which only present "stick figures and ovals" with only short names, have very little value. It's not possible to tell much of anything about what the system is supposed to do from a set of short "sound bites." Just because you know the system has to "Transfer Funds" doesn't tell you anything about what it should do when transferring the money. If this is all the use-case modeling you are going to do, then save your time and spend it elsewhere. Don't go through the motions just because someone has told you "you must do use cases"; if you're going to do it, do it right.

A brief description, up to a paragraph long, that describes the role played by the actor or the responsibilities of the use case starts to clarify what the actor or use case does in the context of the system. The brief description describes the role the actor or use case plays in the system. For an actor, it describes what the actor expects to obtain from the system; for the use case, it describes the value the system provides to the actors.

Don't Mix Business Use Cases and System Use Cases

The system and the business that uses the system are two separate things. The system should serve the business, but mixing business and system actors and use cases is just plain confusing. The use-case model of a system does not capture the business process, although it certainly must support the business process. If you mix the two together, the system boundaries, and therefore the requirements for the system, will be confused and it will be harder to get a good view of the system.

Use cases can be used to define business processes, but these are then "business use cases."[4] The actors in a business use-case model are *outside* the business, they are *customers, shareholders, suppliers,* and other parties that participate in some business relationship.

Determine what you're describing—a business or a system—and be consistent. You may want to do both, if there is a need to understand the context in which the system is to be used. The following are situations where a business use-case model might be useful:

- To clarify the context of the system and gain agreement on the requirements.
- If you are going to build several related systems to support one organization. A business use-case model helps clarify what each system needs to be responsible for and what the relations need to be between the systems.
- If you are building an application that will be used by several organizations. You may need to gain an understanding of the differences in how they work so that the system you build can be made flexible.
- If you are building a system to support a completely new line of business. This usually will be preceded by a business definition effort.
- If the software development effort is part of a larger business reengineering effort.

To make a business use-case model really useful, you also need a business "design," which shows how the business use cases are realized by people and assets of the organization. Based on this more detailed model, you are well equipped to make decisions about what to automate and then define system use cases based on those decisions.

SUMMARY

Getting started is often the hardest part of any project, and the introduction of new techniques can make things more complex if not managed well. Use cases can help to simplify the definition of the system, but they are not magic—anything done well takes hard work. If you follow a few simple rules, things will go much better:

---

[4] A good introduction to the topic of using use cases to describe business processes appears in Jacobson et al., *The Object Advantage.*

- Build a team to do the identification work. The start of the project is a good time to bring people from different disciplines together and forge them into a working unit.
- Don't forget about the actors that are other systems—they are easy to overlook.
- Don't just draw pictures—make sure to capture names and brief descriptions of the actors and use cases.
- Use a glossary to capture concepts, and supplement it with a domain model if the concepts are interrelated.
- Do not, under *any* circumstance, introduce relationships *between* use cases. At the *getting-started* stage of the project, this is asking for trouble.

Once you have at least a few actors and use cases identified and briefly described, you are ready for the next step—writing descriptions of the behavior of the use case.

It is important to remember that the techniques we have discussed so far are just part of the process of building a system. If done well, this stage gives us a strong foundation for a successful project. We should at least have a great understanding of the fundamental value and purpose of the system, the actors with which it will interact, and what they expect from it. The next step will be to build on that foundation and describe the use cases in detail.

Part II

WRITING AND REVIEWING
USE-CASE DESCRIPTIONS

Part I, Getting Started with Use-Case Modeling, introduced the basic concepts of use-case modeling, including defining the basic concepts and understanding how to use these concepts to define the vision, find actors and use cases, and to define the basic concepts the system will use. If we go no further, we have an overview of what the system will do, an understanding of the stakeholders of the system, and an understanding of the ways the system provides value to those stakeholders. What we do not have, if we stop at this point, is an understanding of exactly what the system does. In short, we lack the details needed to actually develop and test the system.

Some people, having only come this far, wonder what use-case modeling is all about and question its value. If one only comes this far with use-case modeling, we are forced to agree; the real value of use-case modeling comes from the descriptions of the interactions of the actors and the system, and from the descriptions of what the system does in response to the actions of the actors. Surprisingly, and disappointingly, many teams stop after developing little more than simple outlines for their use cases and consider themselves done. These same teams encounter problems because their use cases are vague and lack detail, so they blame the use-case approach for having let them down. The failing in these cases is not with the approach, but with its application.

The following chapters describe how to write use-case descriptions, how to manage detail, and how to structure the model to make it easier to understand. We also discuss how to review use cases, including how to organize and staff the reviews. The intent of these chapters is to reveal how the use-case descriptions unfold from the basic modeling effort and how the structure of the use-case model emerges from the contents of the use-case descriptions.

The goal of Part II is to equip you with the knowledge needed to write good use-case descriptions, managing detail appropriately and avoiding the pitfalls of too much or too little structure. Part II also represents a transition from a "group" style of working to a more solitary style. While it is best to identify actors and use cases as a group, it is impractical to write use-case descriptions as a group; writing is almost always principally an activity performed by one person, with reviews of the material conducted as a group. Finally, we conclude Part II with a discussion of how and when to review use cases.

So let's continue on our journey into the world of use cases.

Chapter 6

The Life Cycle of a Use Case

So far, we have seen the basic concepts behind the use-case modeling approach to eliciting and capturing software requirements and looked at how to get started in applying them. Before we look at the mechanics of authoring full use-case descriptions, we need to have a better understanding of the life cycle of a use case and how well-formed, good quality use cases can drive and facilitate the other, downstream software development activities. We also need to put what we have learned into a broader perspective with regard to software development and team working.

Use cases have a complex life cycle—they undergo a series of transformations as they mature through a number of development stages, from discovery to implementation and eventually to user acceptance. One way that this life cycle manifests itself is in the style and form adopted for the use-case descriptions. To speak of a single way of representing a use case is to miss the point—there are different presentation approaches and styles that are useful at different points in the use case's evolution. There is no one single form that is "better" in the absolute sense; they all play a role. This is why you will often see use cases expressed in different formats by different authors in different use-case texts.

Use cases also play a broader role, outside of the requirements space, in driving the analysis, design, implementation, and testing of the system. This is why you will also read about use cases being realized in design and tested by testers. Sometimes the use cases are so embedded in the design process of the system that the impression is given that the use cases are a development artifact rather than a requirements one. This misconception often leads to developers trying to manipulate the use-case model in a misguided attempt to design the system using use cases.

To fully understand the role and purpose of use cases, and consequently the most appropriate form to use, we need to look at the life cycle of a use case from a number of different but complementary perspectives:

- **Software development:** how the use case is reflected throughout the full software development life cycle
- **Use-case authoring:** how the use case and its description evolves through the authoring process
- **Team working:** the activities involved in creating a use case model and how these impact on team and individual working practices

THE SOFTWARE DEVELOPMENT LIFE CYCLE

As well as facilitating the elicitation, organization, and documentation of requirements, use cases can play a more central and significant role in the software development life cycle. This is especially true for many of the object-oriented and iterative development processes for which use cases are recommended.

From a traditional object-oriented system model, it's often difficult to tell how a system does what it's supposed to do. This difficulty stems from the lack of a "red thread" through the system when it performs certain tasks.[1] Use cases can provide that thread because they define the behavior performed by a system. Use cases are not part of traditional object orientation, but over time their importance to object-oriented methods has become ever more apparent. This is further emphasized by the fact that use cases are part of the Unified Modeling Language.

In fact, many software development processes, including the Rational Unified Process, describe themselves as "use-case driven."[2] When a process employs a "use-case driven approach" it means that the use cases defined for a system are the basis for the entire development process. In these cases the life cycle of the use case continues beyond its authoring to cover activities such as analysis, design, implementation, and testing. This life cycle is shown,

---

[1] Ivar Jacobson introduced the notion that use cases can tie together the activities in the software development life cycle; see *Object-Oriented Software Engineering, A Use-Case Driven Approach*, 1992, ACM Press.

[2] See, for example, Philippe Kruchten's *The Rational Unified Process: An Introduction* or Jacobson et al., *The Unified Software Development Process*.

Figure 6-1   The software development life cycle*

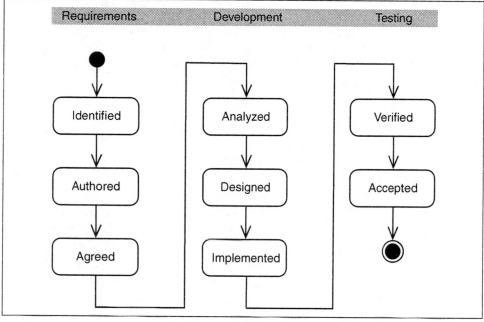

* This life cycle diagram is not intended to imply that analysis cannot be started until all the use cases have been agreed on or even until any use cases have been agreed on. The diagram is just saying that you cannot consider the analysis of a use case to be completed before the use case authoring has been completed and the use case itself agreed on.

in simplified form, in Figure 6-1. Figure 6-1 is arranged to emphasize the three main applications for the use cases:

- **Requirements:** the identification, authoring and agreement of the use cases and their descriptions for use as a requirement specification. This is the focus of this book.
- **Development:** the analysis, design, and implementation of a system based on the use cases. This topic is outside the scope of this book.[3]
- **Testing:** the use-case-based verification and acceptance of the system produced. Again, the details of how to undertake use-case-based testing is outside the scope of this book.

---

[3] For more information on using use cases to drive the analysis and design of software systems, we would recommend Doug Rosenberg and Kendall Scott's *Use Case Driven Object Modeling with UML: Practical Approach* and Craig Larman's *Applying UML and Patterns: An Introduction to Object-Oriented Analysis and Design and the Unified Process*.

It is this ability of use cases to unify the development activities that makes them such a powerful tool for the planning and tracking of software development projects.[4]

To fully understand the power of use cases, it is worth considering this life cycle in a little more detail. Use cases can play a part in the majority of the disciplines directly associated with software development.

- **Requirements:** The use-case model is the result of the requirements discipline. Requirements work matures the use cases through the first three states, from Identified to Agreed. It also evolves the glossary, or domain model, that defines the terminology used by the use cases and the Supplementary Specification that contains the systemwide requirements not captured by the use-case model.

- **Analysis and Design:** Use cases are realized in analysis and design models. Use-case realizations are created that describe how the use cases are performed in terms of interacting objects in the model. This model describes, in terms of subsystems and objects, the different parts of the implemented system and how the parts need to interact to perform the use cases. Analysis and design of the use cases matures them through the states of Analyzed and Designed. These states do not change the description of the use cases, but indicate that the use cases have been realized in the analysis and design of the system.

- **Implementation** (also known as code and unit test or code and build): During implementation, the design model is the implementation specification. Because use cases are the basis for the design model, they are implemented in terms of design classes. Once the code has been written to enable a use case to be executed, it can be considered to be in the Implemented state.

- **Testing:** During testing, the use cases constitute the basis for identifying test cases and test procedures; that is, the system is verified by performing each use case. When the tests related to a use case have been successfully passed by the system, the use case can be considered to be in the Verified state. The Accepted state is reached when a version of the system that implements the use case passes independent user-acceptance testing. Note: If the system is being developed in an incremental fashion, the use cases need to be verified for each release that implements them.

---

[4] If a project manager's perspective on use cases is desired, we recommend Walker Royce's *Software Project Management: A Unified Framework.*

These relationships are directly reflected in the life cycle of the use case just described and are illustrated in Figure 6-2.

Use cases can also help with the supporting disciplines, although these do not impact upon the life cycle of the use cases themselves:

- **Project Management:** In the project management discipline, use cases are used as a basis for planning and tracking the progress of the development project. This is particularly true for iterative development where use cases are often the primary planning mechanism.
- **Deployment:** In the deployment discipline, use cases are the foundation for what is described in user's manuals. Use cases can also be used to define how to order units of the product. For example, a customer could order a system configured with a particular mix of use cases.

Although primarily a requirement-capture technique, use cases have a significant role to play in the ongoing planning, control, development, and testing of the system. It is this unification of the software development process that makes use cases such a powerful technique. To get the full benefit of

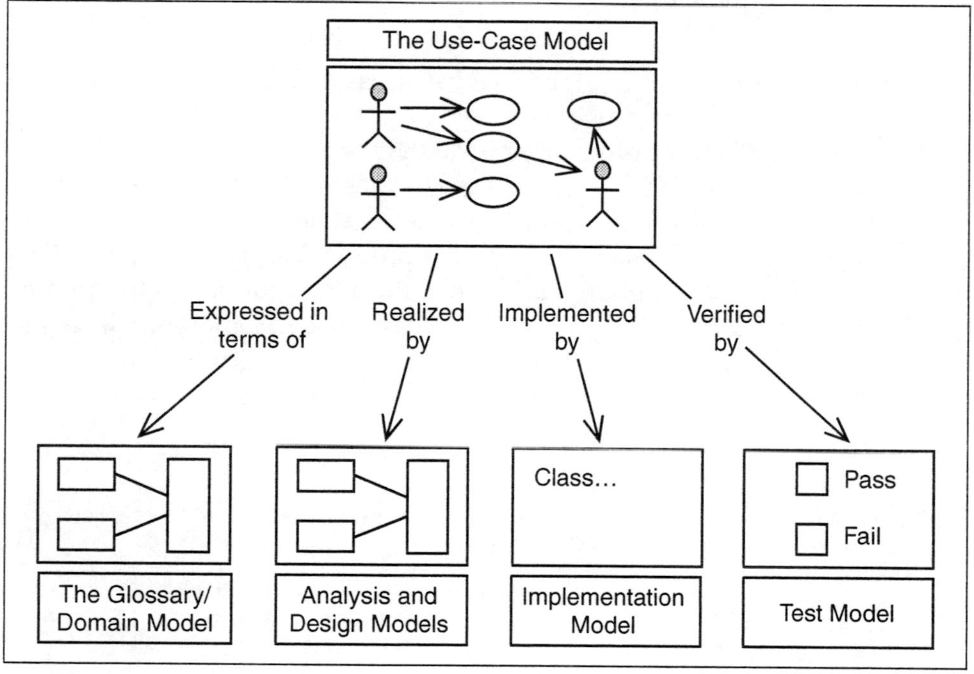

Figure 6-2 The use-case model and its relationship to the other software development models

using use cases, they should be placed at the heart of all the software development and project planning activities.[5]

THE AUTHORING LIFE CYCLE

Of more direct relevance to the people involved in the writing of use cases is having a clear understanding how the use case and its description evolves through the authoring process. We have seen the following use-case formats in use in various different projects and texts:

- Use cases that look like just brief descriptions—a short paragraph that describes something that the system does
- Use cases that look like outlines—a numbered or bulleted list of events and responses
- Use cases presented in the form of a table of actor actions and system responses
- Use cases that present a purely "black box" view of the system, focusing on the actions taken by the actor and the system's response
- Use cases presented as structured English, using sequential paragraphs of text and a more expansive, narrative form, like many of the examples presented in this book

There are also many different popular styles of use case, such as *essential use cases*[6] and *conversational style*[7] use cases.

What are all these use cases, and how do they relate to one another?

It is our contention that these are all just states in the evolution of a use case. Figure 6-3 provides a visual summary of the states of a use case during its evolution from its initial discovery to the production of its fully detailed and cross-referenced description. Each of these different forms is appropriate at different points in the evolution of a use-case model. Different use cases will evolve at different rates. It is not uncommon for an early version of the

---

[5] For more information on how use cases can shape and drive the entire software development process, we would recommend the following texts:
- Philippe Kruchten, *The Rational Unified Process: An Introduction*
- Jacobson, Booch, and Rumbaugh, *The Unified Software Development Process*
- Jacobson, Christerson, Jonsson, and Overgaard, *Object Oriented Software Engineering: A Use Case Driven Approach*, the original books that popularized use cases.

[6] Larry Constantine is most often associated with this formulation of use cases; see L. Constantine, "The Case for Essential Use Cases," *Object Magazine*, May 1997. SIGS Publications.

[7] Rebecca Wirfs-Brock has notably promoted this technique; see R. Wirfs-Brock, "Designing Scenarios: Making the Case for a Use Case Framework," *Smalltalk Report*, Nov-Dec 1993.

Figure 6-3 The authoring life cycle[*]

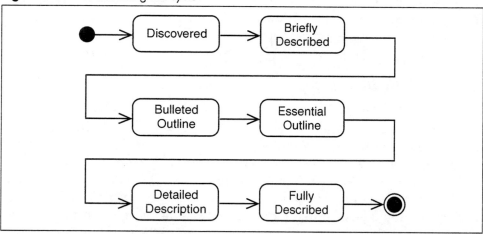

[*] The states shown in the authoring life cycle can be considered to be substates of Identified and Authored states in the software development life cycle shown in Figure 6-1. Discovered and Briefly Described are substates of Identified; the others are substates of Authored.

use-case model to contain a number of key use cases that are fully described and other, less important use cases that are still in the briefly described state or even awaiting discovery. It is worth taking a detailed look at each of these states, how they are manifested in the use-case description, and the role that they play in the evolution of the use case.

State 1: Discovered

A use case will begin as just a name (for example, *Browse Products and Place Orders*), perhaps on a diagram with an associate actor (for example, Customer), as in Figure 6-4. This name is a placeholder for what is to come, but if

Figure 6-4 A newly discovered use case.

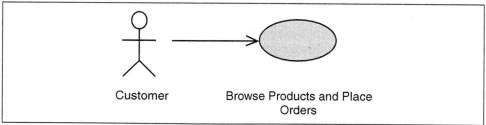

Customer   Browse Products and Place Orders

this is as far as the description goes, it is not very useful. The use-case diagrams produced at this stage really act as no more than a visual index, providing a context for the use-case descriptions that are to come.

State 2: Briefly Described

Almost immediately, usually while the name is being discussed, people will start briefly describing the use case; typically, they can't help it. Even as a name is being proposed, people will start to elaborate on the name (for example: *This use case enables the customer to see the products we have to offer and, we hope, to buy them. While browsing, they may use a number of techniques to find products, including direct navigation and using a search facility.*) These discussions should be captured more formally as the brief description of the use case.

Example

Brief description for the use case *Browse Products and Place Orders* in an on-line ordering system

This use case describes how a Customer uses the system to view and purchase the products on sale. Products can be found by various methods, including browsing by product type, browsing by manufacturer, or keyword searches.

This brief description is important, and it may be as far as the use case evolves, especially if the required behavior is simple, easily understood, and can be expressed in the form of a prototype more easily than in words. But if the behavior is more complex, particularly if there is some defined sequence of steps that must be followed, more work is needed.

State 3: Bulleted Outline

The next stage in the evolution of the use case is to prepare an outline of its steps. The outline captures the simple steps of the use case in short sentences, organized sequentially. Initially, the focus is on the basic flow of the use case—generally this can be summarized in 5–10 simple statements. Then the most significant alternatives and exceptions are identified to indicate the scale and complexity of the use case. This process was discussed in detail in Chapter 4, Finding Actors and Use Cases, as it is an integral part of establishing the initial shape and scope of the use-case model.

Example

Outline for the use case *Browse Products and Place Orders*
Basic Flow

1. Browse Products

2. Select Products

3. Identify Payment Method

4. Identify Shipping Method

5. Confirm Purchase

Alternative Flows

A1   Keyword Search

A2   No Product Selected

A3   Product Out of Stock

A4   Payment Method Rejected

A5   Shipping Method Rejected

A6   Product Explicitly Identified

A7   Order Deferred

A8   Ship to Alternative Address

A9   Purchase Not Confirmed

A10 Confirmation Fails

etc....

Bulleted outlines of this form are good for getting an understanding of the size and complexity of the use case, assessing the use case's architectural significance, verifying the scope of the use case, and validating that the use-case model is well formed. They also provide a good basis for exploratory prototyping aimed at revealing requirement and technology-related risks.

If the use cases are to act as the specification of the system and provide a basis for more formal analysis, design, and testing, then more detail is required.

State 4: Essential Outline

So-called *essential* use cases are at another point in the use case's evolutionary timeline. Essential use cases focus on only the most important behavior of the system and leave much of the detail out (even omitting the mention of a PIN when describing the ATM's Withdraw Cash use case, for instance) in order to focus on getting right what the system must do. This is important early in the use-case identification process, when it is easy to get mired in details that will become important later but are not essential to defining the system as a whole.

The defining characteristic of this format is that it presents a pure, external, "black-box" view of the system, intentionally focusing on its usability. The strength of this approach is that it places usability "front and center" and in so doing ensures that the needs of the user are placed first. This format helps describe user intent and actions, along with the observable response of the system, but it does not elicit details about what is happening inside the system. It also ignores the specifics of the user-interface (because this information is better and more easily presented in prototypes and user interface mock-ups). The description is often presented in a two-column format:

Example

The essential form of the use case *Browse Products and Place Orders*	
User Action	*System Response*
1. Browse product offerings	Display product offerings
2. Select items for purchase	Record selected items and quantities
3. Provide payment instructions	Record payment instructions
4. Provide shipping instructions	Record shipping instructions
5. Complete transaction	Record transaction and provide receipt

The mistake made with essential use cases is forgetting that they will continue to evolve, adding detail and increasing in both scope and number, as the project progresses. Not every use case will pass through the Essential Outline state. Many use cases will progress straight from the bulleted outline to the more detailed formats, if they evolve beyond the bulleted outline form at all. Typically, the essential use-case form is used to provide an early embryonic description of the most important use cases in the system. The descriptions will then continue to evolve. You do not develop a set of essential use cases, then move on to a separate set of conversational use cases, and then move on to a another, different set of more detailed use cases. They are the same things at different points in their evolution.

Essential use cases are very effective for facilitating user-interface and user-experience analysis and design, especially where a system's visual metaphor needs to be established, typically early in the project's life cycle. Too much detail in the use cases often limits and constrains the creativity of the user-interface designers. The stripped-down essential outlines capture the essence of the required dialog without forcing the designers into any particular technology or mode of interaction. This allows them to start to explore the presentation options for the system, which, once defined, may impact in turn on the style and level of detail adopted in the final-form, fully detailed use-case descriptions.

Some people recommend that use-case authoring stop at the essential outline state, but if the use cases are to be used to drive the other aspects of systems design, act as the basis for formal integration and system testing, or be used as the basis for contractual relationships, more detail is required.

State 5: Detailed Description

The next step in the authoring life cycle is to start adding to the outline the detail required to complete the specification of the system. In this state, the use case is evolving, as more and more detail is added to flesh out the outline. If the use case expresses a strong sense of a dialog between an actor and the system, then the description may be in the *conversational form*; otherwise, it will be in the *narrative form* and simply list the steps in order.

The Conversational Form

The conversational form of use-case description is most useful when the system and actor engage in a well-defined dialog in which the actor does something and the system does something in response.

Example

The conversational form of the use case *Browse Products and Place Orders*	
User Action	System Response
1. Browse product offerings	Display product offerings, showing categories selected by the user
2. Select items for purchase	For each selected item in stock, record selected items and quantities, reserving them in inventory.
3. Provide payment instructions	Record payment instructions, capturing payment terms and credit card type, number, and expiration date using a secure protocol.
4. Provide shipping instructions	Record shipping instructions, capturing billing address, shipping address, shipper preferences, and delivery options.
5. Complete transaction	Record transaction and provide receipt containing a list of the products ordered, their quantity and prices, as well as the billing and shipping addresses and the payment terms. The credit card information should be partially omitted, displaying only the last 4 digits of the credit card number.

This *conversational* format is excellent for a number of situations: where there is only one actor and where the system and actor engage in an interactive dialog. It can be expanded to include a considerable amount of detail but will often become a liability. It is difficult to use when there is more than one actor (as often happens in real business systems) or when there is a simple actor action (like pressing on the brake pedal) with a complex response (such as controlling the antilock braking system).

The Narrative Form

The most common format for a detailed use-case description is the *narrative form*. In this form, the outline is again expanded by adding detail but the tabular format is replaced by a more narrative description.

Example

The narrative form of the use case *Browse Products and Place Orders*

1. The use case starts when the Customer selects to browse the catalogue of product offerings. The system displays the product offerings showing the categories selected by the Customer.

2. The Customer selects the items to be purchased. For each selected item that is in stock the system records the items and quantity required, reserving them in inventory.

3. The system prompts the Customer to enter payment instructions. Once entered, the system records payment instructions, capturing payment terms and credit card type, number, and expiration date using a secure protocol.

4. The system prompts the Customer to enter shipping instructions. Once entered, the system records the shipping instructions, capturing billing address, shipping address, shipper preferences, and delivery options.

5. The system prompts the Customer to confirm the transaction. Once confirmed, the system records the transaction details and provides a receipt containing a list of the products ordered, their quantity and prices, as well as the billing address, shipping address, and payment terms. Credit card information is partially omitted, displaying only the last 4 digits of the credit card number.

This format is more flexible, allowing the system to initiate actions and supporting the interaction with multiple actors if required. This is the format that we prefer, as it more readily supports the ongoing evolution of the use case into its final form and the use of subflows to further structure the text.

Using the Detailed Description

Regardless of the form chosen for the detailed description, it is a state that the majority of use cases will pass through as they evolve toward the fully detailed description. In fact, this is the state that most allegedly "completed" use cases are left in as the use-case modeling efforts run out of steam. Unfortunately, it is dangerous to evolve the use cases to this state only and not to complete their evolution. The detailed description loses the benefits of brevity and succinctness offered by the bulleted and essential outline formats and lacks the detail required of a fully featured requirements specification. We do not recommend stopping work on the use cases when they have reached this state. If it is not necessary to evolve a use case to its full description, then stop at the outline format and don't waste time adding incomplete and ambiguous detail just for the sake of it.

State 6: Fully Described

The final state in the evolution of a use case is Fully Described. This is the state in which the use case has a complete flow of events, has all of its terminology fully defined in the supporting glossary, and unambiguously defines all of the inputs and outputs involved in the flow of events.

Fully described use cases are

- **Testable:** There is sufficient information in the use case to enable the system to be tested.
- **Understandable:** The use case can be understood by all of the stakeholders.
- **Unambiguous:** The use case and the requirements that it contains have only one interpretation.
- **Correct:** All of the information contained within the use case is actually requirements information.
- **Complete:** There is nothing missing from the use cases. All the terminology used is defined. The flow of events and all of the other use-case properties are defined.
- **Attainable:** The system described by the use case can actually be created.

Fully described use cases support many of the other software development activities, including analysis, design, and testing. One of the best checks of whether the use-case description is finished is to ask yourself if you could use the use case to derive system tests. The best way to tell if the use cases fit the purpose is to pass them along to the analysis and design team for analysis and the test team for test design. If these teams are satisfied that they can use the use cases to support their activities, then they contain sufficient levels of detail.

Example

An extract from the fully described use case *Browse Products and Place Orders*
Basic Flow

1. The use case starts when the actor Customer selects to browse the **catalogue of product offerings**.

{Display Product Catalogue}

2. The system displays the **product offerings** highlighting the **product categories** associated with the Customer's **profile**.

{Select Products}

3. The Customer selects a **product** to be purchased entering the number of items required.

4. For each selected item that is in stock the system records the **product identifier** and the number of items required, reserving them in inventory and adding them to the Customer's **shopping cart**.

{Out of Stock}

5. Steps 3 and 4 are repeated until the Customer selects to order the **products**.

{Process the Order}

6. The system prompts the Customer to enter **payment instructions**.

7. The Customer enters the **payment instructions**.

8. The system captures the **payment instructions** using a **secure protocol**.

9. Perform *Subflow Validate Payment Instructions*

. . .

Note that this fully described use case uses the narrative format. If the use case has only one actor and the system and actor engage in an interactive dialog, then the conversational style could also be used.

As you can see, there is much more to be said about the formatting and authoring of fully described use-case descriptions. This is the subject of Chapter 7, The Structure and Contents of a Use Case; Chapter 8, Writing Use-Case Descriptions: An Overview; and Chapter 9, Writing Use-Case Descriptions: Revisited.

TEAM WORKING

Another interesting perspective on the life cycle of a use case is that related to team working and the activities that are undertaken to produce the use-case model. We have seen that use cases have an important role to play in the software development life cycle and also have an authoring life cycle of their own. In Chapters 3, 4, and 5, we also looked at how the use-case model starts to emerge from the vision of the system via a series of workshops and other group-focused activities. In this section, we will look at the use-case modeling process and how this impacts on individual and team working.

You may wonder why we have saved this more formal look at the use-case modeling process for the second part of the book rather than presenting it earlier. Well, basically, we wanted you to have a good understanding of the concepts before we started to talk about all of the activities involved in creating a use-case model. So treat this section as part recap of what you have already learned and part teaser for what you will learn in Part II.

The Use-Case Modeling Process

Figure 6-5 illustrates the activities involved in the development of a use-case model. This is a simplified subset of a full requirements process[8] and emphasizes the major activities involved in the evolution of the use-case model, which is being used as the primary requirements artifact. It is interesting to look at this workflow from the perspective of group and individual activities. In Figure 6-5, the group activities are shown in gray and are focused on preparing the groundwork for the evolution of the use-case model and its supporting Supplementary Specification by establishing the vision, scoping the system, addressing areas of uncertainty and instability in the requirements definition, and consolidating and reviewing the use-case model as a whole. The diagram can give the wrong impression that the majority of the effort in use-case modeling is related to group activities and that the model can be accomplished by simply holding a series of workshops and brainstorming sessions with the user and stakeholder representatives.

In fact, more time is typically spent on the individual use case and Supplementary Specification authoring activities than is spent on all of the group activities put together. Figure 6-6 shows the relative amounts of effort expended on group and individual activities across the life of a project, which would typically iterate through the process many times. Note that the figure shows the relative amounts of effort and is not intended to be indicative of the total amount of effort required at any point in the project. The graph illustrates where healthy projects spend their time and should not be taken as a definitive statement. The amount of time the group activities will take is dependent on the ability of the group to focus and reach decisions. If all the

---

[8] For a fully documented Requirements Life Cycle that is seamlessly integrated with all of the other software development disciplines, see the Rational Unified Process.

Figure 6-5 The use-case modeling process[*]

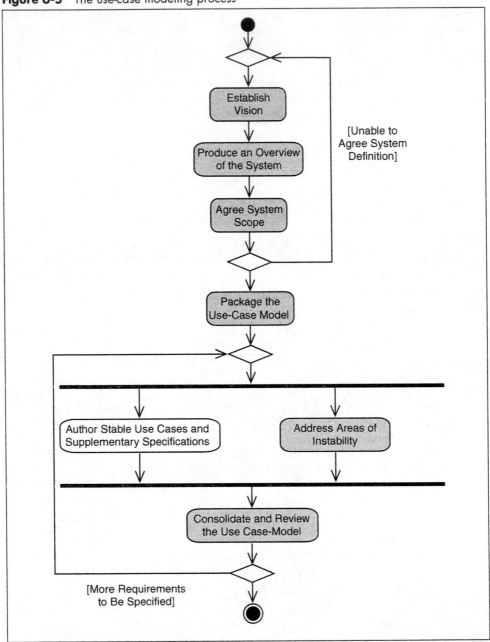

[*] Note: The use-case modeling process is not as waterfall / linear as this figure may imply. If applying the process iteratively, then you only need agreement that a single use case is in scope and its purpose is stable before you start to author it; there is no need to have a full scope definition in place. This process can in fact be applied in every iteration, with just enough envisioning and scoping of the system to select the use cases to be worked on in the iteration.

Figure 6-6 Ratio of group and individual activities for a typical project

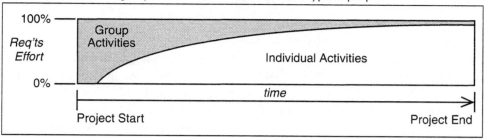

stakeholder representatives disagree with each other and spend all of their time fighting and arguing, the project may never achieve enough stability for it to be worth undertaking the authoring of the use cases. These issues were addressed in Part I: Getting Started with Use-Case Modeling. The amount of time that the individual authoring activities will take is dependent on the complexity of the solution and the capabilities of the individuals involved. These issues are addressed in more detail in Chapter 8, Writing Use-Case Descriptions: An Overview.

It is worth taking a detailed look at each of the activities shown in Figure 6-5 and the roles that use cases and the use-case model play in undertaking them.

Establish the Vision

Establishing the vision is a group activity aimed at getting all of the stakeholders to agree about the purpose and objectives for both the project and the system to be built. The best way to achieve this is to use traditional requirements-management techniques to produce a high-level system definition and to ensure that there is agreement on the problem to be solved. Typically, this is done via a series of workshops involving the project's major stakeholder representatives. This topic was covered in detail in Chapter 3, Establishing the Vision.

The use-case model can help in establishing the vision by defining the system boundary and providing a brief overview of the system's behavior, but it is really no substitute for a vision document. If this stage is skipped, then no real attempt is made to analyze the problem before starting on the definition of the solution. This is really only applicable for small-scale, informal, low-accountability projects with a very small set of stakeholders and where the developers and the users work very closely together. Without undertaking any problem analysis, it can be difficult to know when the use-case model itself describes a suitable solution.

Produce an Overview of the System

The initial use-case model, containing the key actors and use cases with brief descriptions and outlines, provides a very good overview of the functionality of a system. This should be complemented with an initial draft of the key Supplementary Specifications and an outline glossary or domain model. At this stage, there is no need to fully detail any of the use cases, although it is a good idea to have identified the majority of the significant alternative flows for each of them. We are just looking for enough information to allow the scoping of the system with regard to the current project. This activity is best done as a group activity in a series of use-case modeling workshops, as described in Chapter 5, Getting Started with a Use-Case Modeling Workshop, and using the techniques described in Chapter 4, Finding Actors and Use Cases.

Reach Agreement on System Scope

The next activity is to reach agreement on the scope of the system. To do this, the proposed use-case model needs to be examined in light of the vision and any other high-level requirements documentation produced as part of the project.

Use cases are a very powerful aid when attempting to manage the scope or the system. Use cases lend themselves to prioritization. This prioritization should be undertaken from three perspectives:

1. **Customer Priority:** What is the value placed on each of the use cases from a stakeholder perspective? This will identify any use cases that are not required by the stakeholders and allow the others to be ranked in order of customer priority.
2. **Architectural Significance:** Which of the use cases are going to stress and drive the definition of the architecture? The architect should examine the use cases and identify those use cases that are of architectural significance.
3. **Initial Operational Capability:** What set of use cases would provide enough functionality to enable the system to be used? Are all of the use cases needed to provide a useful system?

By considering these three perspectives it should be possible to arrive at a definition of system scope, and order of work, that satisfies all parties involved in the project.

If these three perspectives do not align (that is, the use cases the customer most wants are not those of architectural significance and do not form a significant part of a minimally functional system), then the project is probably out of balance and likely to hit political and budgetary problems. A lot of expectation management would be required to bring these three perspectives into alignment and place the project on a healthy footing where the customer and the architectural goals are complementary rather than contradictory.

Beyond the use cases themselves, we can also use the flow-of-events structure for scope management. In most cases, the basic functionality of the majority of the use cases will be needed to provide a working system. The same cannot be said of all of the alternative flows. In the ATM system, is it really necessary to support the withdrawal of nonstandard amounts or the use of the secondary accounts associated with the card? In many use cases, the majority of the alternative flows will be "bells and whistles" that are neither desired by the customer nor necessary to produce a useable system. This will be discussed in more detail in Chapter 7, The Structure and Contents of a Use Case, when we discuss the additive nature of use-case flows.

Once the scope for the project has been agreed on, the use cases that have been selected for initial implementation can be driven through the rest of their life cycle to completion and implementation. If iterative and incremental development is being undertaken, then the use cases can be assigned to particular phases and iterations.

Package the Use-Case Model

As the scope of the system and the structure of the use-case model start to become apparent, it is often a good idea to package up the use cases and actors into a logical, more manageable structure to support team working and scope management. Using the UML, packages can be used to structure the use-case model.

The UML defines the package as

A general-purpose mechanism for organizing elements into groups.

Graphically, the package is represented using a folder icon, as shown in Figure 6-7. In a use-case model a package will contain a number of actors, use cases, their relationships, use-case diagrams, and other packages; thus, you can have multiple levels of use-case packages (packages within packages), allowing the use of hierarchical structures where appropriate. Often, the use-case model itself will be represented as a package that contains all of the elements that make up the model.

There are many reasons for using use-case packages to partition the use-case model:

- **To manage complexity.** It is not unusual for a system to have many actors and use cases. This can become very confusing and inaccessible to the stakeholder representatives and developers working with the

Figure 6-7 The graphical representation of a package

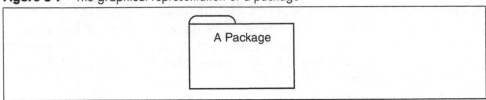

model. A model structured into smaller units is easier to understand than a flat model structure (without packages) if the use-case model is relatively large. It is also easier to show relationships among the model's main parts if you can express them in terms of packages.

- **To reflect functional areas.** Often, there are families of use cases all related to the same concepts and areas of functionality (for example, customer service, operations, security, or reporting). Use-case packages can be used to explicitly group these use cases into named groups. This can make the model more accessible and easier to manage and discuss. It also helps to reduce the need for enormous "super" use cases that include massive sets of only loosely-related requirements.
- **To reflect user types.** Many change requests originate from users. Packaging the use-case model in this way can ensure that changes from a particular user type will affect only the parts of the system that correspond to that user type.
- **To support team working.** Allocation of resources and the competence of different development teams may require that the project be divided among different groups at different sites. Use-case packages offer a good opportunity to distribute work and responsibilities among several teams or developers according to their area of competence. This is particularly important when you are building a large system. Each package must have distinct responsibilities if development is to be performed in parallel. Use-case packages should be units having high cohesion so that changing the contents of one package will not affect the others.
- **To illustrate scope.** Use-case packages can be used to reflect configuration or delivery units in the finished system.
- **To ensure confidentiality.** In some applications, certain information should be accessible to only a few people. Use-case packages let you preserve secrecy in areas where it is needed.

The introduction of use-case packages does have a downside. Maintaining the use-case packages means more work for the use-case modeling team, and the use of packaging means that there is yet another notational concept for the developers to learn. As the need for packaging is directly related to the size and complexity of the use-case model, this is an optional activity and may be skipped for smaller models.

If you use this technique, you have to decide how many levels of packages to use. A rule of thumb is that each use-case package should contain approximately 3 to 10 smaller units (use cases, actors, or other packages). The following list gives some suggestions as to how many packages you should use given the number of use cases and actors. The quantities overlap because it is impossible to give exact guidelines.

- 0–15: No use-case packages needed.
- 10–50: Use one level of use-case packages.
- > 25: Use two levels of use-case packages.

Packages are named in the passive, as opposed to the active names used for the use cases themselves, typically representing some area of the system's functionality or some organizational element of the business that is going to use or support the system. For example, the ATM functionality could be split into two packages, Customer Services and Operations, both of which are supported by the back-end banking systems, as shown in Figure 6-8. The dashed arrows are UML dependency relationships, which, in this case, indicate that model elements in the Customer Services and Operations packages access model elements in the Back End Systems package. This allows us to see how independent the packages are from one another, which is essential if the packaging is to support team working and model management. Packages are a

Figure 6-8 A possible package structure for the ATM use-case model

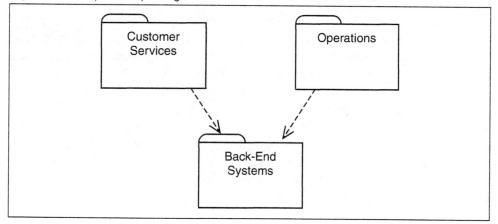

standard UML model element and are not any different for use-case models than they are for any other UML model.[9]

Once the packaging has been put in place, it is usually difficult to change without causing great disruption to the people working with the model. For this reason, it is not advisable to attempt the packaging too early in the evolution of the use-case model. Packaging the model is again primarily a group activity that is undertaken, with the help of the stakeholder representatives, as part of the final use-case modeling workshop or review.

Address Areas of Instability and Author Stable Use Cases and Supplementary Specifications

Once the scope of the system has been established and the use-case model structured to facilitate the further development of the use cases, we are faced with two parallel activities:

1. The detailed authoring of the requirements for those areas of the model where there is stability. This is an individual activity and is the subject of Chapter 8, Writing Use-Case Descriptions: An Overview, and Chapter 9, Writing Use-Case Descriptions: Revisited. It is in the authoring of the detail that most of the effort related to use cases is expended.
2. Continuing to run additional workshops to address those areas where there is still instability in the use-case model. This entails running use-case modeling workshops (as described in Chapter 5, Getting Started with a Use-Case Modeling Workshop) with more detailed objectives and a more specialized selection of stakeholder representatives.

Typically, when the use-case model is being constructed initially, there will be some areas of the model with which everybody agrees and others where consensus is harder to reach during the early project brainstorming and use-case modeling workshops. There is no need to wait for agreement on every area of the use-case model before proceeding to the authoring of detailed use-case descriptions. Once agreement has been reached that a use case is required, it can be driven through the authoring process to produce the fully detailed description and through the software development process to facilitate the design and implementation of the software. It is counterproductive to start doing detail work for use cases whose scope, purpose, and intention are still under debate. To evolve these beyond the essential outline stage

---

[9] For more information on packages and package relationships, we would recommend the *Unified Modeling Language User Guide* by Booch, Rumbaugh, and Jacobson.

is likely to cause large amounts of scrap and rework. The level of detail provided by the outlines should be sufficient to allow scoping and other decisions to be made.

The first use cases to stabilize and then proceed through the authoring process should be those of architectural significance, those that explicitly help to attack project risk, and those essential to the initial release. Once the authoring of any of these use cases is complete, they should be passed over to the designers so that they can progress through the rest of the software development life cycle. In the same way that there is no need for all the use cases to have been identified and outlined before detailed authoring starts, there is no need for all the use cases to have been authored before analysis, design, and the other downstream activities start. It is our recommendation that use cases be passed on to the other project teams as soon as they become available. This allows the downstream activities to start as soon as possible and will provide the use-case authors with the immediate feedback on their work that they can use to improve the quality of the use-case model as a whole.

Consolidate and Review the Use-Case Model

As the use cases, the Supplementary Specifications, and the use-case model evolve, it is worth taking some time to consolidate and review the team's work as a whole. This should be a group activity and should focus on achieving consistency and completeness across the whole of the requirements space. This is also the time when you may want to do some more detailed structuring of the use cases themselves. These topics are covered in more detail in Chapter 10, Here There Be Dragons, and Chapter 11, Reviewing Use Cases. It is also worthwhile to check the detailed requirements work against the vision for the system to make sure that they have not diverged as the use-case model has evolved.

These suggestions are not intended to imply that all of the use cases are to be reviewed in one go at the end of the process. Walkthroughs and reviews are an essential part of the authoring process, as we shall see in Chapter 11, Reviewing Use Cases. Here we are talking about looking at the model as a whole rather than at the individual use cases.

SUMMARY

There is a common misconception that use cases have one form or can be stated in only one way. Practitioners are therefore confused when they see use cases stated in different ways. Many of the differences between use cases stem from the fact that a use case has a life cycle, and it will take different forms at different points in that life cycle.

The life cycle of a use case can be considered from many perspectives. It is important that people working with use cases understand the life cycle from the broader team working and software development perspectives as well as the use-case authoring perspective.

For the purposes of this book, the most important life cycle is use-case authoring. Initially, use cases begin as drawings that show the use cases and the actors who interact with the system during the use case. The use cases are little more than "ovals" and very terse names. This is sufficient for identification, but not much more. Very quickly, however, they evolve into brief descriptions, short paragraphs that summarize the things that the use case accomplishes. This brief description is sufficient for clarification, but more is still needed. The brief descriptions quickly give rise to outlines of the flows of events. Initially, these are just bulleted lists illustrating the basic flow and identifying the significant alternative flows. These bulleted outlines give an indication of the size and complexity of the use cases and are very useful for initial prototyping aimed at revealing requirements and technology-related risks.

For user-interface-intensive systems, the flows are often elaborated to cover the important things the user sees and does when interacting with the system. These "essential" use-case outlines are the primary drivers of the user interface's design. This level of description, while more than sufficient for users and interface designers, is greatly lacking for software developers and testers.

Additional evolution adds more information about the internal interactions, about testable conditions, and about what the system does, providing a more complete picture of the behavior of the system. These complete descriptions drive the development and testing of the system.

It's important to keep in mind that these are not "different" use cases, but the same use case from different perspectives and at different points in time. This "unified" view makes understanding and employing use cases easier.

The key to deciding how detailed to make your use cases is to consider two factors:

1. How unknown the area of functionality covered by the use case is. The more unknown, misunderstood, and risky the functionality described by the use case, the more detail is required.
2. What use is to be made of the description. It is very difficult to know when the use-case descriptions are complete if the downstream activities that the use cases are going to support are not also understood.

The following table summarizes the purpose, risks addressed, and down-stream activities for each of the use-case authoring states:

Authoring State	Primary Purpose	Risks Addressed	Downstream Activities
Discovered	Identify the use case	• Not knowing the boundary of the system	• Scope management
Briefly Described	Summarize the purpose of the use case	• Ambiguity in the model definition	• Scope management
Bulleted Outline	Summarize the shape and extent of the use case	• Not knowing the extent, scale or complexity of the system • Not knowing which use cases are required	• Scope management • Low-fidelity estimation. • Prototyping aimed at addressing requirements and technological risks.
Essential Outline	Summarize the essence of the use case	• Ease of use	• User interface design • Prototyping aimed at addressing requirements and technological risks
Detailed Description	To allow the detail to be added incrementally	• None—it is not recommended that use cases in this state be used outside of the authoring team	• None—this is purely an intermediate step.
Fully Described	Provide a full requirements specification for the behavior encapsulated by the use case	• Not knowing exactly what the system is supposed to do • Not having a shared requirements specification	• Analysis and design • Implementation • Integration testing • System testing • User documentation • High-fidelity estimation

Chapter 7

The Structure and Contents of a Use Case

In Chapter 2 we presented formal definitions of the fundamental elements of a use-case model, described the additional artifacts that are required to enable a use-case model to form a complete software requirements specification, and had a brief look at the contents of the use-case descriptions. Before we delve into the mechanics of writing detailed use-case descriptions and completing the use cases documentation we need to take a closer look at the structure and contents of a use case.[1]

Table 7-1 provides a summary of all of the properties of a use case. We have already discussed the importance and role of the name, brief description, and special requirements properties when we looked at the basic building blocks of the use-case model in Chapter 2, Fundamentals of Use-Case Modeling. We also provided a brief introduction to the flw of events, relationships, preconditions, and postconditions, but there is still a lot more to learn about these particular use-case properties. In this chapter, we will take a closer look at these as well as examine two new properties, extension points and diagrams, introduced for the first time in Table 7-1.

First, we will take a more formal look at the relationship between a systems use cases and the systems state. This will complete our understanding of how use cases interact and how preconditions and postconditions are used in practice. Next, we look more closely at the structure of the flw of events, the significance of this structure, and its implications for other software development activities that depend on the use cases. We will also introduce the

---

[1] This chapter builds on the work of Ivar Jacobson, who originally identified the concepts presented in this chapter.

Table 7-1 The Properties of a Use Case

Property Name	Brief Description
Name	The name of the use case. Each use case should have a name that indicates what is achieved by its interaction with the actor(s). The name may have to be several words long to be understood. No two use cases should have the same name.
Brief description	A brief description of the role and purpose of the use case.
Flow of events	A textual description of what the system does in regard to the use case (not how specific problems are solved by the system). The description is understandable by the stakeholders. The flw of events is structured into a basic flw, alternative flws, and subflws.
Special requirements	A textual description that collects all requirements, such as nonfunctional requirements, on the use case that are not considered in the flw of events, but that need to be taken care of during design or implementation.
Preconditions	A textual description that defines a constraint on the system when the use case may start.
Postconditions	A textual description that defines a constraint on the system when the use cases have terminated.
Extension points	A list of locations within the flw of events of the use case at which additional behavior can be inserted.
Relationships	The relationships, such as communication relationships, in which the use case participates.
Diagrams	Diagrams that illustrate aspects of the use case, such as the structure of the flw of events or the relationships involving the use case.

final set of use-case properties: extension points and diagrams. This will complete our understanding of the nature of the flw of events. Finally, we will take a brief look at scenarios and use-case realizations. These concepts are related to, and often confused with, use cases. Understanding them, and their role in software development, will help us remain focused when use-case modeling. You will have to wait until Chapter 10, Here There Be Dragons, to learn more about use-case relationships.

USE CASES AND SYSTEM STATE

To discover and define effective use cases, you must understand the relationship between the use cases and the state of the system and how these are related to events happening outside the system. The reason for this is that the use cases describe the behavior of the system, behavior that results in changes in the state of the system. In order to understand how use cases start and how use cases end, you must consider the state of the system.

The System and External Events

Thus far, we have spent a lot of time talking about the use-case model of the system and the requirements of the system without specifically defining what we mean by a system. The Collins *Modern English Dictionary* defines a system as

> A group of things or parts working together or connected in some way as to form a whole [a solar *system, system* of motorways].

The UML contains the following definition of system:

> (1) A collection of connected units that are organized to accomplish a specific purpose. A system can be described by one or more models, possibly from different viewpoints. Synonym: physical system.
> (2) A top-level subsystem.

So far as this book is concerned, the system is the thing that is being developed. The system itself may be composed of a number of smaller units[2] and may, if necessary, collaborate with any number of peer systems. The key thing about a system is that it clearly forms a whole. We can clearly see what is part of the system and what is outside the system. *The system has a distinct boundary.* The system boundary defines the border between the system (our proposed solution) and the environment that surrounds, and interacts with, the system.

Because of the existence of the system boundary, most systems can be treated as black boxes that respond to stimuli from their surrounding environment. The system takes inputs from the surrounding environment and processes them to produce outputs (see Figure 7-1). One way of defining the system is to document all of the possible inputs and their corresponding outputs. A small subset of systems performs pure transformations on the input data, producing the same output for the same input at all times. The vast

---

[2] A system at one level of abstraction may be a subsystem of a system at a higher level of abstraction (the earth can be considered a system but is itself part of a larger system: the solar system).

Figure 7-1 Input-output representation of an information system

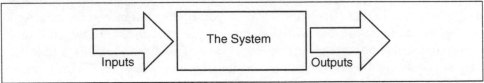

majority of systems are more complex and vary the output depending on the state of the system and the state of the environment surrounding the system.

Systems can also be treated as stimulus-response machines.[3] In this case, rather than considering only the input/output relationship, we consider the events in the environment that the system will respond to, the state that the system is in, and the events that the system will generate to effect change in the surrounding environment, as shown in Figure 7-2. Use-case models are a variation on the stimulus-response model of systems. The actors represent people, or other systems, that interact with the system. The actors are outside the system but are essential to the definition of the behavior of the system, as they are the source of the events detected by the system and the target for any events generated by the system (see Figure 7-3).

In a use-case model, the detected and generated events are categorized as

1. **Major Events:** Those that start a use case
2. **Minor Events:** Those that are generated as part of an ongoing interaction between the system and an actor

Figure 7-2 A stimulus-response model

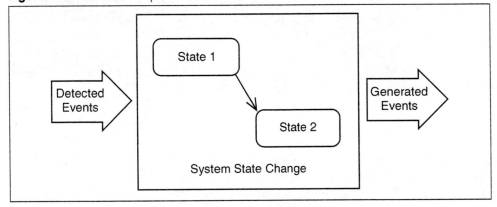

---

[3] See Cooke and Daniels *Designing Object Systems* for a discussion of systems as stimulus-response machines.

Figure 7-3   Actors and a stimulus-response system

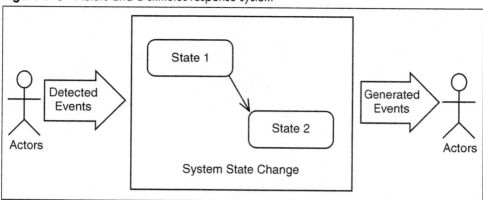

It is this classification of events that enables use cases to focus on the value provided by the system, to put requirements into context, and prevent the unnecessary multiplication of use cases, which would happen if a use case was produced for every event detected by the system.

The use-case description must clearly describe the event that will start the use case. The *communicates* relationships clearly denote the source of the initial event (the actor that starts the use case) and whether the use case starts interactions with any additional, supporting actors. To see the details of the events, and the corresponding dialog between the use case and its actors, we will have to look to the detail of the use-case description. As we shall see, this description includes the definition of all of the inputs and outputs that make up the dialog as well as details of how the behavior of the system is affected by the underlying state of the system.

If we revisit our simple telephone system example, last seen in Chapter 2, we can superimpose a box representing the system boundary onto the diagram. This is shown in Figure 7-4. This presentation illustrates the stimulus-response nature of the use-case model and is preferred by many use-case modelers, as it clearly shows the boundary of the system.

The System State: More about Preconditions and Postconditions

Sometimes, the system must be in a particular state in order for the use case to be executed: An automated teller must possess funds to dispense, an engine must have fuel, and a user must be authorized to use the system. Sometimes these conditions can be verified by a simple test, and sometimes there will be a use case to verify or establish the condition. Whatever the case, it is inconvenient, distracting, and even wrong to force every use case that depends on these conditions to repeat the description of how the system is put into the

Figure 7-4 The simple telephone system showing the system boundary

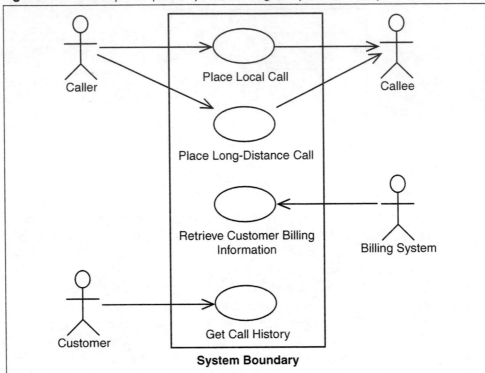

desired state. Instead, we simply want to declare the required condition, or state, in which the system must be; we call this declaration the *precondition*.

Examples of Preconditions

- *The user must be authorized to use the system (or, alternately, the user is logged-in).*
- *The system must have sufficient cash available to process a typical transaction.*[*]
- *The communication channel to the host system is open and available for use.*

> [*] As we get further into the details of writing use cases, we will see that all of the descriptive text that we write is dependent on the existence of a well-understood and documented set of underlying definitions. The reference to a "typical transaction" is OK as long as there is a definition of a typical transaction somewhere.

The precondition is a statement about the condition or conditions that are required in order for the use case to be performed. Often, these preconditions are established by the execution of other use cases, so why do we use preconditions stated in terms of the desired result, instead of saying, "*The use case 'Authenticate User' has been executed*"?

There are three reasons. First, we want to make the use-case descriptions as much as possible into independent stories of what the system does to provide value for one or more actors. If one use case becomes dependent on other use cases, it makes the use case harder to understand. Second, just because the use case *Authenticate User* has been executed, that doesnt mean the user executing the current use case has been authenticated. Perhaps the result of the execution of *Authenticate User* was to allow the user to access the system but with reduced privileges, or perhaps a different user executed it several months ago. Finally, there may be more than one way for the system to reach the desired state. We may have more than one way to authenticate the user (we could use a user identifier and password scheme, or we may use a special card combined with a personal identification number (PIN), or we could even use a retinal scan if we want to be really exotic). Each one of these could be a different use case with a different flw of events, all resulting in the same state—the user is authorized to execute transactions in the system.

The preconditions themselves are "necessary but not sufficient"for the use case to be performed. The precondition must hold if the use case is to be started but is not going to result in the use case being started automatically just because it becomes true. Starting a use case requires an actor to do something. The precondition merely states the conditions under which the use case can be started. The states that the precondition refers to should also be "externally visible"—in other words, be a condition that the actors would understand. Preconditions must not refer to the design of the system; they should be applicable regardless of how the system is implemented.

Postconditions are statements about the state (or condition) in which the system is at the conclusion of the use case. Postconditions are not triggers for other use cases; they are just summarizations of fact. They help ensure that the reader understands what the result of executing the use case has been. In the example of the use cases that authenticate the user, the postcondition is that *the user is authorized to execute transactions in the system* or *the user has been barred from using the system*.

Sometimes we try to make things more complicated than they really are. Preconditions and postconditions are simply statements of the condition (or state) in which the system is when the use case starts and ends. In addition, preconditions and postconditions are optional features of a use case—they may be omitted if the system state is not important to how the use case starts or ends. They are seldom required for every use case in a system, but when they are needed, its typically obvious. If no precondition is defined, then there is no restriction on when the use case can be started. If no postcondition is defined, then there are no explicit constraints on the state of the system when the use case ends.

How Use Cases Interact

Use cases do not directly communicate with one another (they are, after all, just *descriptions*). The only way for use cases to interact is via the state of the underlying system. Use cases can check the state of the system at any time, or wait for the state of the system to change, or can be dependent on the state of the system via the use of preconditions. There is no way of directly relating use cases. In fact, there is nothing in the definition of a use case that allows the sequencing of use cases in a direct way. This is by design. Each use case is intended to be independent of other use cases; use cases are independent *sequences of behavior that results in something of value to a user of the system.*

Sometimes, a group of headstrong developers will subvert the use case into a design tool, decomposing the system behavior into use cases. They produce use cases that may sound something like *Login, Select Products, Enter Order Information, Enter Shipping Information, Enter Payment Information, and Confirm Order* if the system provides on-line order capabilities. These "things" certainly describe behaviors that the system must support, but ask yourself this: Is each of these things independently valuable? Would you ever do just one without the others? The answer is, of course, no; there is no need to enter shipping information if there is no order.

The team has most likely taken a wrong turn. This is usually confirmed by their expressed need to somehow *sequence* the use cases. Lacking an association that might allow one use case to "call" another use case, clever modelers sometimes turn to the use of preconditions and postconditions. This troublesome cleverness is founded upon the idea that the *precondition* for one use case could be said to be the successful completion of another use case. Or the postcondition for a use case could be the execution of another use case. So, like a row of dominoes, the use cases fall one-by-one in a sequence.

The first problem with this is that the need to strictly sequence use cases is a symptom of a poor set of use cases—steps or functions masquerading as use cases. To solve this problem, the use cases should be grouped together so that they become a single use case that provides some value to the use of the system. So the preceding "use cases" merge into a single use case, *Browse Products and Place Orders.*[4]

The second problem with using preconditions and postconditions to sequence use cases is that the solution is hard to maintain because the dependencies are hard to see. Even if the use cases are at the right level of granularity, it is better to state precondition dependencies in terms of some *state* or

---

[4] You may have already noticed that this set of mini use cases are just the major steps of the *Browse Products and Place Orders* use case we examined in Chapter 6, The Life Cycle of a Use Case.

condition that must exist before the use case can begin. That state may occur, of course, as the result of some other use case completing, or there may be several different use cases that all result in the system being in the same state. Stating precondition dependencies in terms of some condition that must be satisfied is more robust and is unlikely to be affected by changes to the use-case model, such as splitting or combining use cases.

The Side Effects of Using Preconditions

The use of preconditions can have a direct effect on the shape of the use-case model as a whole as well as the shape of the individual use cases.

Using Preconditions Can Reduce the Amount of Validation in a Use Case

The precondition defines a state in which the system must be before the use case can be performed; as a result, the flw of events of the use case does not test the precondition. An alternative to stating a precondition is to include the test specifically in the flw of events of the use case. Only use preconditions where they help to clarify the required behavior.

Example

> If one of the automatic teller machine's use cases has the precondition *"The communication channel to the host system is open and available for use,"* then the use case cannot be started unless the connection is available. An alternative to using the precondition is to test the state of the connection inside the use case.
>
> *The use case starts when the actor* **Customer** *inserts the* **bank card**.
>
> *If there is no connection to the* **financial institution**, *then the system informs the Customer that the service is not available and the use case ends.*

The dangers of using preconditions to reduce the amount of checking to be done within a use case include

- The checking specification can often be forgotten. In most cases, it is very easy to deduce what the check should be. What is more difficult to deduce is what action should be undertaken when the condition does occur. If the test is undertaken by the use case, then corrective actions can be defined.
- Use cases can be created that can never be started. Remember the pre-condition **must** be true for the use case to be executed. If preconditions are overused, it is not unusual for use cases to be given preconditions that are impossible for the system to achieve.

Using Preconditions Can Lead to the Identification of More Use Cases

If we were to revisit our simple phone system example, we could look at the precondition for the *Place Local Call* use case:

Example

In order for local calls to be made:

• The handset must be registered to an active account.

This simple application of a precondition raises issues about the completeness of our use-case model:

1. How does a handset get registered to an account?
2. How is an account activated or deactivated?

In this case we would need to add at least one use case to our simple telephone system model:

Example

To allow accounts to be managed and handsets to be registered to accounts, a new use case needs to be added to the model. This is shown in Figure 7-5.

The use of preconditions can help with the assessment of the completeness of the use-case model by explicitly calling out important system states and making them more visible to the use-case developers and reviewers.

THE NATURE OF THE FLOW OF EVENTS

People find several things about the flw of events confusing:

• The structure of the flw
• The relationship between the complexity of the use-case model and the complexity of the system being described
• The relationship between flws, scenarios, and use-case realizations

Figure 7-5 Additional use case to allow the management of customer accounts and associated devices in the simple telephone system model

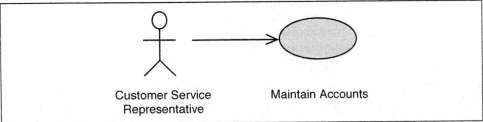

Customer Service
Representative

Maintain Accounts

In this section, we address these issues. (Note: This section uses lots of short extracts from the *Browse Products and Place Orders* use case last seen in Chapter 6, The Life Cycle of a Use Case. A more complete version of this use case can be found in Appendix A.) Additional examples can be found at www.usecasemodeling.com.

The Structure of the Flow of Events

Unfortunately, the UML treats the entire flw of events as a single property of a use case and has little to say about how it should be structured. As we have seen throughout this book, a good structure of the flw of events makes the use-case description easier to understand and therefore more useful. By this point, you should be comfortable with the concepts of the basic flw, sub-flws, and alternative flws. In this section, we will look at their structure and definition in more detail.

Defining a Flow of Events

As seen in Chapter 6, The Life Cycle of a Use Case, there are many styles for writing up the flws of events. We recommend adopting the narrative style, numbering each step and titling each self-contained section in newspaper style. This will enable the reader to see an overview of the flw without having to read all the details and to unambiguously refer to a step when it is being reviewed.

When you detail each step in the outline, be sure to describe the flw of events, not only what the system is doing. A suggestion for how to enforce this is, where possible, to start every step with The [actor] . . . 'or The [system] . . . .'Each time the interaction between the actor and the system changes focus (between the actor and the system), the next segment of behavior should start with a new paragraph. This ensures adherence to the spirit of the purpose of a use case and makes analysis of the use case far easier.

Example

The *Browse Products and Place Orders* use case includes the following behavior:

1. The system displays the **product offerings**, highlighting the **product categories** associated with the Customer's **profile**.

2. The Customer selects a **product** to be purchased, entering the number of items required.

3. For each selected item that is in stock, the system records the **product identifier** and the number of items required, reserving them in **inventory** and adding them to the Customer's **shopping cart**.

4. Steps 3 and 4 are repeated until the Customer selects to order the **products**.

The majority of actions in the flw of events are system controlled. That is, after the user's initial request to begin the use case, the system controls the interaction: The system asks for information and the user supplies information; the system asks for a decision and the user takes it; and so on.

General guidelines for the contents of a flw are

- •Describe how the flw starts and ends.
- •Describe what data is exchanged between the actor and the use case.
- •When first referring to an actor, precede the name of the actor with the identifier 'Actor.' For example, use 'Actor Customer' rather than just 'Customer' to clearly distinguish the actor from a reference to any similarly named entity.
- •Do not describe the details of the user interface, unless they are necessary to understand the behavior of the system.
- •Describe the flw of events, not only the functionality. To enforce this, start every action with 'The actor . . . 'or 'The system . . . .''
- •Describe the events that belong only to the use case and not what happens in other use cases or outside of the system.[5]
- •Describe what the system does, but be careful—remember the flw of events should present what the system does to perform the required behavior, not how the system is designed.
- •Detail the flw of events—all 'whats' should be answered. Remember that test designers are to use this text to identify test cases.
- •Describe things clearly enough that an outsider could easily understand them.
- •Use straightforward vocabulary. Dont use a complex term when a simple one will do.
- •Write short, concise sentences.
- •Avoid adverbs, such as *very, more, rather,* and the like.
- •Avoid vague terminology, such as *information, etc., appropriate, required, relevant,* and *sufficient.*
- •Use correct punctuation.
- •Avoid compound sentences.
- •Make sure that the sequence of events is clear. If the order of the events is not important, make sure that this is clearly stated. If the order of the events described for the use case does not have to be fixed, do not describe it as though it does have to be fixed.

---

[5] If you need to describe events that dont belong to the use case, to make the use case more accessible to the stakeholders, make sure that they are clearly distinguished from the rest of the flow of events and marked as being a comment. We would suggest using quotation marks and italics to distinguish any comments inserted into the use-case description.

- Use terminology consistently throughout the use-case model. To manage common terms, put them in a glossary.
- When using glossary terms in the flw of events, clearly distinguish them from the other text by making them bold.

These guidelines apply to all the different kinds of flw: the basic flw, subflws, and alternative flws.

Defining the Basic Flow

The basic flw of events should cover what "normally" happens when the use case is performed. The basic flw should be named "Basic Flow" and be the first flw to be described in the use case's flw-of-events section. The basic flw should start by clearly defining the actor and event that the actor initiates to start the use case. It should then describe the normal way that the actor (or actors) and the system interact to derive value from the system. Finally, it should describe how the use case ends.

Example

> The *Browse Products and Place Orders* basic flow case starts with the paragraph:
>
> > The use case starts when the actor Customer selects to browse the **catalogue of product offerings**.
>
> It ends with:
>
> > The system asks the **Customer** if there are any more **products** to be ordered.
> >
> > If the **Customer** wants to order some more products, the use case resumes from {**Display Product Catalogue**}.
> >
> > If the **Customer** does not want to order any more products, the use case ends.

Defining Subflows

Complex flws of events should be further divided into subflws. The main goal in doing this should be improving the readability of the text.

A subflw should be a segment of behavior within the use case that has a clear purpose and is "atomic," in the sense that either all or none of the actions described are performed. You may need to have several levels of subflws, but if you can, you should avoid this as it makes the text more complex and harder to understand. Remember that the use case can perform subflws in optional sequences or in loops or even several at the same time.

For clarity, subflws should be named and numbered. Number the subflws S1 . . . SN and give them active names that sum up their purpose.

Example

The *Browse Products and Place Orders* use case contains the following subflows:

- S1 *Validate Payment Instructions*
- S2 *Validate Shipping Instructions*
- S3 *Execute the Financial Transaction*

To reference a subflw from another flw of events, use the syntax:

> Perform subflw   *<subflow name>*

Example

The following extract from the *Browse Products and Place Orders* use case illustrates the use of the three subflows named in the previous example:

7. The Customer enters the **payment instructions**.

8. The system captures the **payment instructions** using a **secure protocol**.

9. Perform ***Subflow Validate Payment Instructions***.

{Invalid Payment Instructions}

10. The system prompts the Customer to enter **shipping instructions**.

11. The Customer enters the shipping instructions, supplying at least the **billing address**, **shipping address**, **shipper** preference, and **delivery options**.

12. The system captures the **shipping instructions** using a **secure protocol**.

13. Perform ***Subflow Validate Shipping Instructions***.

{Invalid Shipping Instructions}

14. Perform ***Subflow Execute the Financial Transaction***.

The guidance for writing flws outlined in the preceding Defining a Flow of Events section also applies to subflws.

Using Extension Points

Extension points are named places in the flw of events where additional behavior can be inserted or attached. Extension points may be private (used only within the use case in which they appear) or public (used by other extending use cases). Chapter 10 will describe the use of public extension points. Extension points presented in Chapters 7–9 are private extension points. Within the flw of events, extension points are shown in bold and enclosed in curly brackets:[6]

---

[6] There are other ways of showing extension points, but this is the one we prefer and is therefore the one that we have used throughout this book.

Example

The use case *Browse Products and Place Orders* includes the following extension points:
- {Display Product Catalogue}
- {Out of Stock}
- {Process the Order}
- {Order Processed}

There is no specific naming convention for extension points. They are least intrusive if they sum up some aspect of where the position is in the use case or what the use case has achieved.

Extension points can occur anywhere in the flw of events, although we prefer them to be on their own line and not embedded in a chunk of text.[7] One good way to use extension points is as headings in the text to delimit self-contained sections of flws.

Example

**The Basic Flow of the *Browse Products and Place Orders*
Use Case Including Extension Points**

The {Display Product Catalogue}, {Select Products}, and {Process the Order} extension points are used as headings, whereas the {Out of Stock} and {Order Processed} extension points reflect the state of the use case.

With extension points, the basic flow now becomes

1. The use case starts when the actor Customer selects to browse the **catalogue of product offerings**.

{Display Product Catalogue}

2. The system displays the **product offerings** highlighting the **product categories** associated with the Customer's **profile**.

{Select Products}

3. The Customer selects a **product** to be purchased, entering the number of items required.

4. For each selected item that is in stock, the system records the **product identifier** and the number of items required, reserving them in **inventory** and adding them to the Customer's **shopping cart**.

{Out of Stock}

5. Steps 3 and 4 are repeated until the Customer selects to order the **products**.

{Process the Order}

6. The system prompts the Customer to enter **payment instructions**.

. . .

---

[7] Note: There is another way of defining extension points separately from the flow of events, but the technique is harder to use, harder to maintain, and, most important, actually renders the flow of events harder to read. A sophisticated editing tool could enable the extension points to be suppressed or displayed at the user's convenience, providing the best of both worlds.

There are three kinds of extension points.[8] They can be used to define

- **A single location, the most straightforward of usages.** In this case, the extension point defines a single point in the flow of events; this is indicated by placing the extension point at a unique position in the flow of events.

Example

In the preceding example basic flow of the *Browse Products and Place Orders* use case including extension points, the {**Display Product Catalogue**}, {**Select Products**}, and {**Process the Order**} extension points all represent single locations in the flow of events.

- **A set of discrete locations.** In some cases you wish to place the extension point in multiple places within the flow of events. The extension point will therefore represent a state that several of the flows of events can reach rather than a position in the flow of events. This is indicated by the extension point appearing in multiple places in the flow of events.

Example

In the *Browse Products and Place Orders* use case, the {**Out of Stock**} extension point could appear in multiple places in the flow of events if there were multiple places where the use case is dependent on the system not being out of stock.

- **A region.** In some cases you may want to mark up a region of a use case, in effect marking the set of all of the locations between two defined points in the flow of events. Without sophisticated tool support, this actually requires the introduction of two extension points. The region could be between any two extension points, but typically there is a clearly matched pair of extensions points whose names are intuitively related.

Example

In a use case for a system that controls a pump to dispense fuel, you could delimit the section of the flow of events where fuel is being dispensed with the extension points {**Pump Activated**} and {**Pump Deactivated**}

In the *Browse Products and Place Orders* use case basic flow, the flow of events between the two extension points {**Select Products**} and {**Process the Order**} could be treated as a region.

---

[8] As detailed in Rumbaugh, Jacobson, and Booch, *The Unified Modeling Language Reference Manual*.

The beauty of extension points is that their location can be changed without affecting their identity or requiring any changes in the flws of events that reference them. As we shall see in the next section, the primary use for extension points is for defining alternative flws.

Defining Alternative Flows

The alternative flws of events cover behavior that is of optional, exceptional, or truly alternate character in relation to another flw of events. Alternative flws are always dependent on some condition occurring at an explicit point in another flw of events. If the alternative flw is not conditional, then it is not an alternative.

There are three kinds of alternative flw:

- **Specific Alternative Flows:** These are alternative flws that start at a specific named point in another flw of events.
- **General Alternative Flows:** These are alternative flws that can start at any point within the use case.
- **Bounded Alternative Flows:** These are like general alternative flws but can only occur between two named points.

We will look at examples of these after we have examined the syntax for declaring the different kinds of alternative flw.

Alternative flws are named and numbered. Number the alternative flws A1 . . . A n and give them active names that sum up their purpose. The first line of the alternative flws flw of events identifies the point at which the alternative will be activated and the conditions under which it will occur. This clause is always of the form:

At {*extension point*} when <*some event occurs*> . . .

or

At {*extension point*} if <*some condition is true*> . . .

Note: If required, both the {*extension point*} and the <*condition*> can be compound clauses, although great care should be taken to ensure that it is actually possible for them to be true simultaneously. The last line of the alternative flw, and any other exit points within it, must state explicitly where the actor resumes the flw of events. This will be either the original extension point where the alternative flw was triggered or another extension point elsewhere in the flw of events, unless the use case ends. For optional behavior, this is usually the original extension point; for truly alternative behavior, this is usually another extension point; for exceptional behavior, this is usually the end of the use case. (Note: The flw of events can only be resumed at an extension point that identifies a single location or the extension point from which it was started.) If the use case ends in the alternative flow, explicitly state The use case ends 'in the alternative flows flow of events.

Examples of Alternative Flows

In the use case *Browse Products and Place Orders*, there are many alternative flows, including A3 *Handle Product Out Of Stock* and A1 *Undertake a Keyword Search*.

Example 1

> **A specific alternative flow**
>
> A3 *Handle Product Out Of Stock*
>
> At {**Out of Stock**} if there are insufficient amounts of the **product** in the **inventory** to fulfill the Customer request.
>
> The system informs the user that the order cannot be fulfilled.
>
> . . . the flow continues to describe the offering of alternative amounts and products to the Customer . . .
>
> The flow of events is resumed from the point at which it was interrupted.

Example 2

> **A bounded alternative flow**
>
> A1 *Undertake a Keyword Search*
>
> At any point between {**Display Product Catalogue**} and {**Process Order**} when the Customer selects to undertake a keyword search.
>
> The system prompts the Customer to enter the **product search criteria**.
>
> The Customer enters the **product search criteria**.
>
> . . . the flow continues to describe what the Customer and the System do to complete the search. . .
>
> The flow of events is resumed at {**Select Product**}.

Unfortunately, there are no general alternative flows in the *Browse Product and Place Orders* use case, but if there were, they would have the pseudo extension point 'At any time in the flow of events . . . ,' and they would have to either resume from the point where the original flow was interrupted or end the use case.

Managing Scope Using Alternative Flows

You may well be wondering why we have focused so on the structure of the flow of events, especially on exception points and alternative flows. Why dont we just do everything using subflows and *if* statements as one long and continuous narrative? The reason is related to the way that use cases are used to manage the scope of the system. You want to be able to define meaningful subsets of functionality that will actually deliver value to the customer. You also want to be able to take subsets of functionality away without breaking the system and/or failing to provide any value at all.

If we consider things only at the level of entire use cases, we will not be able to do very much scope management because the use cases will tend to be large and relatively indivisible. By adding structure within the use-case description using alternative flws, we introduce a way to remove scope from the system by removing alternative flws. The very purpose of alternative flws is to permit behavior to be removed without affecting the basic flw or other alternative flws, because alternative flws are often optional and address behaviors that are outside of the normally expected behavior.

Consider the *Cash Withdrawal* use case as it was outlined in Chapter 4:

Example

Basic Flow
1. Insert Card
2. Validate Card
3. Validate Bank Customer
4. Select Withdraw
5. Select Amount from List of Standard Amounts
6. Confirm Transaction with Banking System
7. Dispense Money
8. Eject Card

List of Alternative Flows

A1   Card cannot be identified

A2   Customer cannot be identified

A3   Withdraw not required

A4   Nonstandard amount required

A5   No money in the account

A6   Attempt to withdraw more than daily amount

A7   No connection to the banking system

A8   Link goes down

A9   Card stolen—the card is on the hot card list

A10 The ATM is out of money

A11 The card cannot be dispensed

A12 A receipt is required

A13 The withdrawal is not from the card's primary account

and so on . . .

What is the impact of not delivering "A3 Withdraw not required" and "A4 Nonstandard amount required" and "A12 A receipt is required" and "A13 The withdrawal is not from the card's primary account"? Would you still have a usable system that delivers the value of the use case (the ability to withdraw cash)? Yes, you would. Not all of the alternative flows represent core functionality. In fact, you may well discover that some of them are not required at all; they may cost too much or may not provide enough value to warrant further development.

In comparison, what would be the impact of not delivering part of the basic flow? Would you be able to deliver a usable system if you failed to deliver the capability to validate the card or confirm the transaction with the banking system or dispense the cash? No, you would not. Without the entire basic flow the use case cannot deliver any value at all.

The alternative flows allow you to incrementally add functionality on top of the basic flow as the use case evolves or to remove functionality as the time and money run out. You can also clearly see the impact of not including a use case or an alternative flow: If it is not included, you will not get the value that it delivers. This does not hold true if you divide the functionality up in a more stepwise (part 1, part 2, part 3) sort of way. If you leave out the second half of the use case, then you do not deliver any of its value.

It is this structure that makes use cases so integral to iterative and incremental development. It allows the targeting of individual sets of flows onto the iterations and the value provided by the system to increase iteration by iteration.

The Complexity of the Use-Case Model Versus the Complexity of the Design

Some people have the idea that a system with a complex design will have a complex use-case model. It may, but the complexity of the required behavior of the system (as expressed in use cases) is really wholly unrelated to the complexity of the design. Design complexity is a function of how hard something is to implement, whereas use-case complexity is a function of how hard the desired behavior is to describe.

A system such as a building monitoring system may have a quite simple use case model, even though the system itself can be quite complex. The main use case is *Monitor Building*, and this is responsible for monitoring for events (fires, break-ins, and so on) and responding to them. A few other use cases exist to maintain the system information, but otherwise, that's about it. The system itself can become quite complex, having to correctly detect events (and screen out false alarms) as well as control and coordinate many different devices. The complexity of the system comes from the problem domain and certain nonfunctional requirements that dictate the required responsiveness of the system, the types of devices that must be used, the need to correctly report fires and detect false alarms, and so on. But the use-case model itself is fairly simple.

Example

Five analysts (business experts) eventually decided that a medium-scale system development effort for a transportation system had only eight use cases—the main two being *Import Goods* and *Export Goods*. Initially, they had assumed that the system was complex and identified over a hundred use cases. These turned out to be functions or features that the use cases provided; once they realized this, the model became much easier to understand.

If you have too many use cases—if your use cases are really functions in disguise—you will struggle to write meaningful use cases. You will find yourself needing to invent ways to string use cases together to provide something the user finds meaningful or valuable. In the need to fill the use cases with content, you will tend to fill them with design and implementation details that obscure the real value of the system to its users. And you will probably end up wondering why use cases are so great—you will have the same problems you do with every other technique: Technical documentation that is incomprehensible to the stakeholders of the system and also very detailed requirements that do little to help you build the right system.

The internal complexity of the system is completely unrelated to the number or length of the use cases. What the use cases reflect is really the complexity of *using* the system, and that should be as simple as possible.

Visualizing the Flow of Events

Although the additive nature of the use cases is crucial to their effective use in requirements management, planning, risk reduction, testing, and other downstream activities, it can make it very hard to get an overview of the entirety of the use case. Sometimes, although the basic flow is clearly defined, the stakeholders need to have an overview of the key alternative flows to fully understand the scope of the use case. This can be difficult when you have to wade through a long list of alternative flows and track back to their extension points to see when and where they will apply. If the stakeholders require some kind of holistic overview of the entire functionality provided by the use case, then the use-case authors need to supply it. One way to do this is to provide some form of visualization of the flow of events to act as a map of the underlying textual definitions.

The most typical way to do this is to use a UML activity diagram or a traditional flwchart. Figure 7-6 shows an activity diagram illustrating the *Browse Products and Place Orders* use case. Figure 7-6 uses the following elements:

UML Element	Meaning
●	Start State—represents the event that starts the flw of events.
(rounded rectangle)	Activity State—represents the performance of an activity or step within the flw of events. Activities allow you to show the subflws and sections of the basic and alternative flws.
⟶	State Transition—shows the ordering of the activities. The transition is triggered by the completion of the activity the activity state represents.
◇	Decision Points—represent extension points where decisions may be taken. The condition to be evaluated at the decision point is shown by a guard condition. Decisions and guard conditions allow you to show **alternative flows** in the flw of events of a use case.
[condition]	Guard Conditions—control which transition (of a set of alternative transitions) follows once the activity has been completed.
◉	End State—shows where the use case ends

Other elements are available for use on activity diagrams:

- **Synchronization bars** that you can use to show parallel subflws. Synchronization bars allow you to show **concurrent threads** in the flw of events of a use case.
- **Swim lanes** that let you show whether the responsibility lies with the actors or the system.

As you can see from the example, the diagram does not capture all of the nuances of the textual flw of events. It is very difficult to show bounded or general alternative flws when using this kind of notation. It also does not show all of the detail of the flw of events, as this would render the diagram overly complex and make it harder to understand than the original flw of events it is supposed to illuminate. It does allow the highlighting of the most significant alternative flws and their relationship to the basic flw. The thing to remember is that this is just an illustration, not the definition of the flw of

Figure 7-6 An activity diagram presenting an overview of the *Browse Products and Place Orders* use case. The basic flow is shown shaded to distinguish it from the alternative flows.

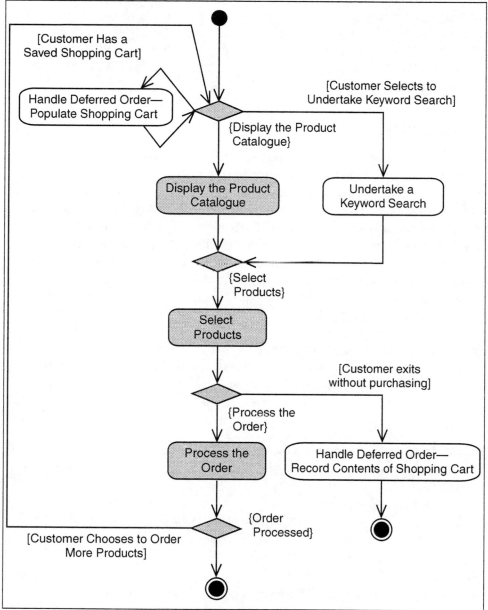

events. Only use these forms of diagram if they make the use case more accessible to the readers and add value to the use case modeling process.

A dangerous side effect of attempting this kind of diagrammatic representation of the flw of events is a tendency to overly decompose the use case to force the text to match the structure of the diagram. These sorts of diagrams should only be added to the use case to provide an informal overview of the general shape and purpose of the use case. Using this kind of pictorial representation does not reduce the amount of text that needs to be written—you still have to write all of the flws of events, and, in our opinion, you should do this first. If this kind of diagrammatic representation is used, it is recommended that you take great care and limit it to providing high-level overviews of the structure of the flw of events.

What Is a Scenario?

Scenarios are *instances,* or specific occurrences, of use cases. Scenarios are useful because they help us think in concrete terms about what a system will do when a particular use case is performed. They help us walk through exactly what will happen to make sure that we have handled everything properly, and they can be useful later on in defining the test cases that are required to test the system to make sure that it performs the way the use cases say it should.

A typical use case will have a main flw of events and several alternative flws of events. A single scenario will walk through one particular path of the use case, exploring a particular way that the use case can be performed from beginning to end. To explore the relationship between a use case and its scenarios, let's consider an example. Assume that we have a simple use case that maintains the temperature in a room (in other words, a use case for a thermostat). Just to make things interesting, let's assume that the room has temperature sensors and that the system makes sure that the average temperature of the room is within the acceptable range.

Example

Monitor and Maintain Temperature use case

1. The use case begins when the Facility Manager engages the temperature control system.

{Determine Temperature}

2. The system determines the **average temperature** of the room by polling the temperature sensors placed throughout the room, summing the **readings**, and dividing by the **number of sensors** deployed.

{Turn On/Off Heat}

3. If the **average temperature** of the room is below the **desired room temperature** minus 5 percent, the system activates the flow of gas, ignites the gas, and turns on the forced-air fan if it is not already on.

4. If the **average temperature** of the room exceeds the **desired room temperature** plus 5 percent, the system deactivates the flow of gas. It also turns off the forced-air fan if the **fan setting** is set to "automatic"; otherwise, the forced-air fan continues to run.

5. The use case continues until the system is deactivated by the Facility Manager.

The variables presented in this use case are highlighted in **bold** in the example: the average room temperature, the sensor readings, the number of sensors, the desired room temperature, and the fan setting. So many variables for such a simple use case!

When you consider scenarios, look at "boundary" conditions, the points at which a small change in the value of some variable causes some very different behavior in the system as a whole. The boundary conditions help you find interesting values for the variables and spot flaws in the use case. For example, what happens if there are no sensors? The system will try to divide by zero and will halt. What happens if the average temperature is exactly equal to the desired temperature minus 5 percent? The system will not turn on the heat, because the average temperature has to be more than 5 percent below the desired temperature. Is this acceptable? What happens if the fan is set to "off" when the temperature falls below the desired temperature threshold? Should the system still turn on the fan? What should it do when the desired temperature threshold is exceeded? Should it turn the fan off? If you focus on the boundary conditions when forming your scenarios, you will find the number of scenarios much more manageable and the scenarios themselves much more useful. From looking at our scenarios, we are forced to really think about the use case and what it says, and by so doing we are better able to spot and fix the flaws in the use case basic flow and the alternative flows.

One final point about use-case scenarios: The number of scenarios can multiply combinatorially if you're not careful. Consider the situation in which there are four completely independent alternate flows (A1A4) plus the main flow. If you were to create independent scenarios for each possible path through the use case, you would have at minimum 1 (main) + 4 factorial, or 25 different scenarios, and this does not even include different boundary conditions. It is clearly impossible to formally document all of these scenarios.

In fact, you rarely have to document (or even identify) all of the scenarios. If the alternative flows are really independent, then you can consider only five scenarios—the main plus each of the four alternatives combined with the main—because the alternative flows wont affect one another. And sometimes alternative flows can be combined into a single scenario (if they occur in different parts of the main flow of events), so the number can drop further. Look for these opportunities to "prune" the number of scenarios, and youll make your life a lot easier.

What Is a Use-Case Realization?

The purpose of the use-case realization is to separate the concerns of the specifiers of the system (as represented by the use-case model and the requirements of the system) from the concerns of the designers of the system. A use-case realization represents the design perspective of a use case. It provides a construct in the design model that organizes artifacts related to the use case but which belong to the design model. The use-case realization is a collaboration of components that realizes (or performs) some use case. The realization describes how the behavior of a use case is performed by the collaboration of elements within the system

The main purpose of the use-case realization is to provide a bridge between the descriptions of the system used by external stakeholders (principally users and customers), such as use cases and requirements, and the descriptions of the system used by internal stakeholders (principally developers and testers), such as designs, code, and test cases. Use-case realizations overcome a problem area that is key in many other development techniques—the discontinuity between requirements and design. By connecting these two major areas of interest, they prevent the design and tests from significantly diverging from the user and customer perspectives of the system.

The separation of the use-case realization from the use case is essential, as it decouples the use case from its implementation, allowing the design to progress without affecting the baseline requirements captured in the use case. It also allows multiple designs to be produced for the same use case. This is particularly important for larger projects or families of systems where the same use cases may be designed differently in different products within the product family. Consider the case of a family of telephone switches, which have many use cases in common but which are designed and implemented differently according to product positioning, performance, and price.

Typically, for each use case in the use-case model, there is a use-case realization in the design model with a realization relationship to the use case. Figure 7-7 shows how this is visualized using the UML. In addition, there is typically at least one test case for every use-case realization. Use-case realizations can be expressed visually, using UML constructs such as sequence and

Figure 7-7 A use-case realization in the design model can be traced to a use case in the use-case model.

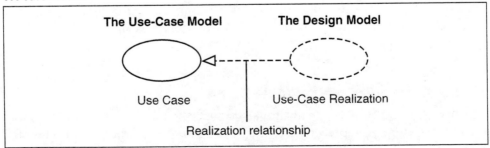

collaboration diagrams, or textually, using structured English. In fact, when people write their use cases with an implementation focus, discussing the components of the system and the way that they work, they are actually creating a textual use-case realization rather than a use-case description.

SUMMARY

In this chapter we have looked in detail at how the contents of a use-case description is structured and defined. We are now ready to look at the mechanics of actually writing some of these detailed use-case descriptions.

Chapter 8, Writing Use-Case Descriptions: An Overview, describes the objectives and challenges related to writing detailed descriptions of use cases and presents strategies for successfully mastering this task. Chapter 9, Writing Use-Case Descriptions: Revisited, discusses the mechanics of writing use-case descriptions, how to handle details, and how to structure the descriptions for readability. The chapter uses an evolving example in which a variety of techniques are progressively and systematically applied to improve the quality of the use-case description.

Chapter 8

Writing Use-Case Descriptions: An Overview

There is an easy trap into which one can fall after identifying use cases and actors, writing some brief descriptions, and drawing some use-case diagrams: *stopping!* At this point, one really knows only that there are people or things that will use the system, and there will be some vague notion of what they want to do with the system, but little more. Although this may be appropriate for simple use cases that have well-understood behavior (that is, there is no risk that *anyone* will misunderstand what the system will do for this use case), most use cases will have at least some additional description, even if it is only an outline of the flow of events.

There is no escaping it—at some point you have to sit down and describe the details of what happens. You can wait until you start designing or even coding to do this, but if you do, you should ask yourself whether mixing up *what* the system does with *how* it does it is really a good idea. Most times it is not a good idea—the *what* and the *how* become so intertwined that it becomes hard to understand whether a particular set of behaviors is really required or whether it is just a side effect of how the system is designed. Once this starts to happen, it is virtually impossible to know whether the system will actually solve any real business problem or whether it is just exploring technology for the sake of it.

This chapter describes the objectives and challenges related to writing detailed use-case descriptions and presents strategies for successfully mastering this task.

WHO WRITES USE-CASE DESCRIPTIONS?

Writing a use-case description is primarily an individual activity, as is most writing. It is possible for people to work in pairs, each reviewing the other's work and each working on different sections of the use case. This has the advantage of providing a broader set of perspectives, which may allow the team to make more progress because it is considering a broader set of alternatives. Another strategy is to have small teams work on related sets of use cases. But ultimately, writing boils down to individuals sitting down with an authoring tool.

Regardless of how the work is divided, a mentoring approach should be taken, with more-experienced team members guiding and assisting the less-experienced ones. This means the mentor should be available to review the work of others, provide constructive criticism and suggestions for improvement, and answer questions when needed. Often, a consultant brought in from outside the company will provide this expertise, but it is probably best over the long run for an organization to develop its own internal mentoring resources. An internal use-case "writers group" is an excellent way to share experiences. When it comes time to doing the actual writing, however, the responsibility for each use case should be assigned to one person. The work on individual sections may be divided, but the overall ownership should be clear.

Reviewing use cases is a group activity, with short but frequent and focused sessions yielding better results than large, comprehensive review sessions. But more on this later, in Chapter 11, Reviewing Use Cases.

Programmers Write Poor Descriptions

What we really mean here is that writing use cases has a different purpose than developing code; a use case is focused on *what* the system must do, whereas code is an expression of how the system will do those things. These are very different. If a person approaches the task of trying to describe what the system does by constantly trying to figure out how it will do those things, attention is divided and the result will suffer. Writing use-case descriptions should not be approached as if it were another way of expressing the design of the system. It should be approached as if one were solving a mystery—the mystery of what the system needs to do in order for it to be useful to the people who will use it.

When working with a small team, there is a tendency to encourage everyone to wear all the hats—team members get to elicit requirements, write use cases, and design and execute tests as well as write the code. This works well for people who regard their challenge as delivering the *right* solution to the problem rather than writing efficient or elegant code. The problem is that someone who cannot move out of the programmer role won't take this sort of holistic view—they just want to crank code. As a result, forcing them to write use cases is often a bad idea on several fronts—they don't like it and as a result they usually aren't very good at it.

Programmers are good at taking a set of requirements, usually stated in precise and unambiguous terms, and making the system satisfy those requirements. They are good at weighing alternative implementation approaches and skillfully making the necessary trade-offs to deliver the desired system. Writing use cases is a more exploratory and visionary skill. The system does not exist yet, and out of the swirling cloud of incomplete and perhaps conflicting requirements, the system that the users want and need must emerge. It is not a deterministic process of pouring requirements or wishes in at one end and—voila!—out pop the use cases.

The *story* analogy used throughout this book is carefully chosen. Deciding what the system does requires vision, creativity, and the ability to describe what does not yet exist—not unlike the process of writing a story. Programmers tend to think too literally and analytically; they immediately start thinking about how the system will work, how its components will be structured, and how the desired behaviors will be implemented. Eventually, this is a good thing, but only if we already have a clear idea of what we need to do. If done too early, or at the expense of establishing a real understanding of what is needed, it can produce systems that are "technically elegant" but unuseable because they do not solve a real business problem. Before you can write code you need to know what the system has to do. It's hard for the programmer to wait.

The Characteristics of a Good Use-Case Author

So, if the programmer is not a good choice, who is? There's no one profile or background, but there are some common characteristics:

- The ability to synthesize (as opposed to analyze)
- The ability to approach a problem systematically
- Some domain knowledge, or at least an understanding of the users of the system
- At least some understanding of software development
- An ability to write well

Each of these is worth spending a few moments discussing.

The Ability to Synthesize

Synthesize means to bring together, whereas *analyze* means to break down. Developers tend to analyze; they want to take everything the system needs to do and gradually break those things down into small units of code that will implement the desired behavior. This is as it should be.

When developing use cases, however, we don't want to break the system down into little increments of functionality; we want to be able to clearly see what the system does and for whom. Declarative requirements don't give us this—they are, in a sense, selective samples from the great "wish list"—they tell us only that the system must satisfy some condition. How it gets to that condition and the intermediate steps that it must go through in order to get there are not explicitly stated. The task of the use-case writer is to comb through these requirements, adding information gleaned from other sources, in order to create a coherent story.

The Ability to Approach a Problem Systematically

Good use-case authors have the ability to understand the system as a whole and create a consistent picture of that system. On this attribute, programmers tend to do quite well, except that their approach is, as noted earlier, typically analytic rather than synthetic. Consistency across use cases, domain entities, business rules, and glossary terms requires that the team members responsible for these elements approach the problem in a systematic way.

Some Domain Knowledge

In order to write effective use cases, you need to know what you're talking about. It's hard to write a detective novel if you don't know anything about the process of solving a crime. It's not necessary to be an expert, but you need to know something about the subject or learn something very quickly. If you are working on a manufacturing system, a few days or weeks in the plant will give you a different perspective on what is really needed. Similarly, if you are writing about a financial trading system, spending a few days observing on the trading floor can explain a lot that simply talking to an expert cannot. There is no substitute for direct experience.

At Least Some Understanding of Software Development

Use cases are about the *what;* software development is about the *how.* The problem, as one of our esteemed colleagues points out, is that one person's *what* is another person's *how.* Ensuring that requirements (including use cases) are precise without inappropriately constraining the developer requires knowledge of both perspectives. The general rule is that if the system *must* behave a certain way, the use case should describe it. If the designer has complete freedom to exercise creativity, the use case should remain silent about the exact details of how the system carries out the use cases. Sometimes it's hard to decide, and this is where judgment comes in. To make these kinds of judgments, use-case developers require at least some understanding of software development, especially the difference between deciding *what* the system must do and deciding *how* the system must do it.

An Ability to Write Well

We're not talking about being the next Ernest Hemingway, but writing clearly and directly is essential to writing good use cases. The ability to organize thoughts and to convey them in simple and direct language goes a long way toward making the use cases useful. Effective use-case writers come from many different backgrounds. Sometimes they are from the user community but have more technical interests. Sometimes they have a technical writing background. And sometimes they come from a programming background, but usually only if they possess broader skills. When assigning the work, make sure to assign the right people to the right task.

HOW LONG DOES IT TAKE TO WRITE A USE CASE?

This is a bit of a "trick question"—there is no standard amount of time for writing a use case; it depends on the complexity of the behavior of the use case. A simple use case that maintains information about employees (names, anniversary dates, benefit plans selected, and so on) will take less time than the use case that controls the environment inside the International Space Station. When we define use cases, we are not trying to divide the behavior of the system into equal-sized units—we are identifying the things of value that the system performs for its actors, and these "chunks" may take small or large amounts of effort to describe.

What *can* be done to gauge the effort required to write a use case is to work bottom up from an outline of the use case, estimating the number of pages of written description that will be required to adequately describe it. This requires judgment and experience, so if you have no prior experience with writing use cases, you will have to experiment a little at first. Once you have an estimate of the number of pages of description, you need to determine how long it will take to write a page. We have found that, on average, one to four pages of written technical documentation can be produced per day, depending on the complexity of the subject matter. If this seems low, consider the time it takes to research issues and discuss content with subject-matter experts, in addition to just writing the text. People working in an unfamiliar problem domain or working on particularly complex behavior will probably take longer to write a use case. Simple use cases can be produced more quickly. These are just guidelines, so take time to calibrate the models to your own problem domain and team.

GETTING STARTED

The actual writing of the use-case description is a solitary rather than a group activity. The group activities have been completed, the use cases have been allocated, and the real work is about to start. This section presents some basic rules of thumb to bear in mind while writing use-case descriptions.

Use a Style Guide

Some of the difficulty of writing use cases can be eased if key decisions on how to work with use cases are made once for the entire project and communicated to team members. The style guide serves as a simple reference on how to handle specific stylistic issues. A template or standard outline provides a good start, but there is more. The major topics that need to be addressed are

- General issues on writing style and presentation
- Decisions on how to represent or describe the user interface
- Decisions on technical aspects of use cases, such as
  - How (or if) to use preconditions and postconditions
  - How (or if) to use associations between actors or between use cases[1]
- Brief examples of appropriate style

The style guide need not be terribly formal, nor need it be terribly complete at first. A key lesson from successful projects is that they are no more formal than necessary, and they *act* on a plan that is good enough rather than forever formulating a perfect plan. Start with a simple style guide and improve it to address specific problems.

Write Simply, Directly, and Deliberately

A use case that can't be understood is, in a word, useless. Writing use cases is, essentially, writing, and writing clearly is hard work. More to the point, most of us are not accustomed to writing clearly and concisely. Here are a few guidelines to writing use cases:

---

[1] We will discuss this topic at length in Chapter 10, Here There Be Dragons.

- **Write in *active voice*.** This means using direct, declarative statements. Say "the system validates the amount entered" instead of the weaker "the amount entered *should be* validated by the system." Not only is the direct approach clearer (it states conclusively what is done rather than what *should* or *might* be done), it is shorter.

- **Write in *present tense*.** This means describing what the system does, rather than what it *will do*. Although this may seem a minor point, saying that the system *will* do something in the future leaves when it will do it ambiguous. This applies to the word *shall* as well, which is often used in requirements documents to indicate something the system must do. Just say what the system does; sprinkling *shall* here and there does not change the fact that the use case describes behavior the system must support.

- **Use *newspaper style*.** Newspapers have over a hundred years of experience in conveying lots of information in a quick, concise way. They do it by using simple, direct sentences and by organizing those sentences in a top-down format that is easy to read. Briefly, they use major headings to communicate the key ideas so that the reader can gain a good understanding of the contents just by reading the headings. Then they fill in the details if the reader wants to go further. Organizing content this way respects readers' time and provides value even if they only have a little time to spend reading. Writing use cases this way encourages feedback, which improves the system.

Beyond these simple rules, there are a number of worthwhile books on writing well. One of the best (and also shortest) is *Elements of Style* by Strunk and White. The simplicity and clarity of the writing is a model for us all, and everyone who writes even a little should read it. Keep in mind that the reader of the use case will rely on the use case to design and build the right system, so every sentence and every word must be carefully chosen to convey meaning very precisely. And remember:

> In anything at all, perfection is finally attained not when there is no longer anything to add, but when there is no longer anything to take away (Antoine de Saint-Exupéry, *Wind, Sand and Stars*, 1968, New York: Harcourt Brace Jovanovich, pp. 41–42).

Treat the Use Case Like a Story

A use-case description is, in a sense, a story of how an actor uses the system to achieve some end result. It has a beginning (the actor does something that starts the sequence of events described in the use case). Once the use case is started, the actor and the system interact, with the system potentially interacting with other actors, until the final result desired by the actor is achieved. If you keep looking for the "story," your use cases will describe something useful and meaningful.

A good beginning makes all the difference. The beginning of the use case is some event initiated by an actor. Use cases do not start spontaneously; the actor must do something. Indicate this by writing, as the first step in your use case, "The use case begins when the actor [Actor] does [something]." It sounds simple enough, almost childish, but these simple words get you to focus on what starts the use case.

All good stories require a plot. The "plot" of a use case is the sequence of steps that the actor and the system take as they interact. More than just a plot, the description of a use case is like the dialog of a play or a movie; it indicates who says or does what and when they do it. It has a typical pattern of: "The actor [Actor] does [xxx]; then the system does [yyy] in response." Of course [xxx] and [yyy] are sometimes very complicated, but it is essential that we describe these things.

Consider the situation of running a small store. Let's say you have hired a student for the summer and you want to teach him to close the store at the end of the day. If you tell the student that he must "close-out the cash register," will he know what you mean? Will it mean to him that he should make sure the cash drawer is closed (not what you mean)? Or that he should just take all the cash out and put it in the safe (also not what you mean)? If you want to make sure that he will do what you want, you must tell him what needs to be done.

This is just what you must do in the use case—you must describe what needs to be done, in detail. A good way to know if you have described something sufficiently is to ask yourself if the users of the system will care how the system does something. If they do, if the way that the system works is somehow both visible and important to them, you must describe it. If it does not matter, the details can be left to "design" and up to the discretion of the developer. If you care how something is done, you should describe it; if you do not, designers can rightly assume that they can choose how it should be done in a way that makes the system easy to design, build, and maintain.

Use cases have a clear ending. A good use case has a purpose—it delivers some result to one or more of its actors, and then it terminates. To make sure that everyone understands when and how the use case ends, make the ending explicit: "The use case [xxx] ends when [yyy] . . . ."

Make a Conscious Decision about the Depth of Detail Required

People often ask, "How much detail should I put in the use-case description?" The answer is that there is no standard answer; it depends on the needs of the development team, the users, and the needs of the teams that will come down the road to maintain the system. To get a sense of the trade-offs, consider the following:

- Testers and the people who will need to maintain the system will need to know what the system was supposed to do so that they can determine whether the system is working as intended. If there is a strong need for quality and maintainability, the use cases will probably need to be quite precise in their descriptions. The longer the system needs to be maintained, the more important become detailed descriptions of what the system does.
- A team that has domain expertise or has a close working relationship with domain experts from the user community can work with less formality. The use-case descriptions may consist of largely outlined flows of events, supplemented by storyboards and/or prototypes.
- Systems with stringent regulatory requirements or that are safety-critical require a greater degree of formality in their specification and verification. Think about it—would you expect any less of a system that may dispense intravenous drugs, measure radiation dosage, or control an aircraft?
- Systems that support a complex decision-making process or automate a complex business process will require a more precise and complete description than those that automate simple processes. An on-line order-entry system is by definition simpler and less risky than a system that controls a gasoline refinery or chemical plant.

The level of detail required varies from project to project, but these fundamental factors are present in most systems. Choosing the right level of detail to balance these forces will help you to focus on what is important. The simplest answer on the level of detail required is that you should continue to expand the description of the use case until all the stakeholders are satisfied that they understand and approve the description of behavior expressed in the use case.

One thing to keep in mind: Not all use cases are equally important. In many systems, a few use cases represent the largest share of complex behavior. If you need to focus your efforts on where they will yield the greatest results, focus on detailing these use cases and leave the simpler (and less risky) use-case descriptions at the "outline" level. The pros and cons of the most popular use-case formats, and the level of detail that they imply, were discussed and summarized in Chapter 6, The Life Cycle of a Use Case.

Describe What Happens When the Actors and the System Interact

The purpose of the use-case model is to capture the interactions of the actors and the system, to describe what the system does in response to events initiated by the actors (that is, external events). As a result, you should focus on what the actor does to the system and what the system does in response to that interaction. The response will have to include what happens *inside* the system. This makes some people uncomfortable; they feel that somehow this is "designing" the system. If done correctly, it is not.

The use case should describe *what* the system does, but not how the user interface or the internal components of the system collaborate to do what it does. In the use case *Browse Products and Place Orders*, we say that the system prompts the user to make decisions and that the user enters information, but we do *not* say the system pops up a *dialog box* to capture the payment details, we do *not* say the system displays a *list box* containing the names of the products, and we do *not* say the user selects the number of items to be ordered from a *drop-down list*. In the ATM example, we say that the system determines that the PIN the customer entered is correct or that the system records the amount of money disbursed, but we do *not* say that the *Card Reader Subsystem* determines whether the PIN entered is correct, and we do *not* say that the *Cash Dispenser Component* records the amount of funds disbursed as *a null terminated string in the transaction database*. We want to capture what the system must do, but we *must* be completely indifferent to how the behavior is implemented.

Don't Rely on Just Text

Text is not always the ideal medium for describing behavior. Just as a flow-chart can sometimes clarify a complex decision-making process and a state chart can clarify the actions and events in a real-time system, certain kinds of behavior are more easily described using visual representations than relying on just text. In addition, diagrams can often clarify the concepts used by the system. Diagrams of classes in the domain model used by the use case can aid in explaining and illuminating the use case by helping to clarify complex concepts.

Another kind of visual aid that can render the use-case description more understandable is a use-case *storyboard*, a sequence of screen shots from a user interface prototype that depicts the flow of events of the use case. The storyboard can be a valuable tool for visualizing the use case. When using storyboards, it is important that the audience understand that the storyboards represent what the system *could* look like; the storyboards are not intended to be exact depictions of what the system *will* look like. They are merely tools intended to bring life to what could otherwise be a very dreary textual description. Finally, there is the activity diagram, mentioned in Chapter 7. As discussed earlier, the activity diagram provides a way to visualize a complex flow of events. Although not a substitute for a detailed description, an activity diagram of the use case's flow of events can provide a useful overview of the basic flow and alternative flows.

In choosing visual aids for the use case, take into account that audiences are different. Some come from the world of the IEEE type of requirements specifications and don't consider requirements to be so unless they're text. Some come from the visual modeling world and consider text hard to penetrate. These people tend to interact while use cases are being built, so you need to find a way to make them both read and comprehend the material. Remember that the reason use cases are created is to focus on a specific purpose of the system and to describe it in such a way that all the stakeholders in the project have some chance of understanding the system that is being proposed.

Prototype the User Interface

As the saying goes, a picture is worth a thousand words. If that's true, a prototype is invaluable. Use prototypes to describe the user interface, leaving the use cases to describe what happens behind the screens.

Use cases, or rather the textual descriptions of use cases, are tedious to write and don't generate much good feedback on whether the user interface is right or not. People need to *see* the interface, or even more importantly, *feel* the user interface before they can really say whether it is right or not. In addition, textual descriptions are particularly clumsy in describing the nuances of navigation. In most user interfaces, the user is relatively free to navigate anywhere, for example, to fill-in fields in any order so long as the information is complete and correct at the time it is submitted to the system. The numerous variations of behavior are nearly impossible to capture in a textual way. What is more, there is little need to; with the excellent prototyping and interface development tools available today, it is faster to prototype the user interface than it is to describe it.

Using a prototype *in conjunction with* a use-case description provides much greater power and flexibility. The prototype can present the look and feel of the interface, and the use case can describe the behavior of the system *behind the screens*. Prototyping is a great approach for visualizing the behavior of the system, especially if the behavior is mostly visual (in other words, mostly things that happen on the screen). If there is a bit more to the behavior, you may need to supplement the prototype with a little supplementary "storyboarding" to explain what happens behind the scenes. Don't try to describe the behavior of navigation within the user interface or the structure of the user interface; use a prototype or mock-ups of the user interface to convey the user experience. Let the use case focus on the flow of events and what the system does in response to user actions. The user interface will often change a great deal, even while the overall flow of events remains unchanged. In addition, text is not a very good vehicle for conveying how someone will work with the product.

Because use cases describe how a user of a system interacts with a system, there is a very natural interrelationship between use cases and user interface (UI) descriptions. Often, quite early in the identification of use cases, it is useful to sketch the UI so that you can visualize how the user and the system interact. As the description of use cases progresses, so too will the definition of UI progress beyond sketches, into more detailed pictures, and finally to one or more prototypes. Thus the UI and the use cases tend to evolve in parallel. It is important to *not* place specific descriptions of the UI into the use case. Often, the UI (the *look and feel*) will change quite substantially long after the flow of events (the *behavior*) of a system has stabilized. Describing the UI in detail in the use cases (for example, click this button, select that menu option) will merely increase the workload on the project team as it tries to keep UI prototypes and the textual use-case descriptions consistent. Leave documentation of the UI to prototypes, where it can be more dynamically defined.

Sometimes, however, visual prototypes are not very useful. If you were developing the software for an embedded system, such as an antilock braking system for a vehicle, there is really hardly any user interface (just the brake pedal), so a visual prototype is almost useless. For this system, you're going to need something more; you're going to need to describe the behavior in a way that everyone who needs to can understand it.

MANAGING DETAIL

There seems to be a strong fear of putting too much detail into use cases. Too much detail *can* be a problem if the details obscure the real flow of the use case. But the details matter; without them, the use case too easily becomes a meaningless document (truly, "a useless case") that tells nothing about the system's behavior. The real challenge is finding ways of managing and presenting detail so that it is captured but does not get in the way.

Assuming that you've made a conscious decision about how much detail to put into the use-case description and you feel that the details are important to capture if the right system is to be built, the following techniques can help you handle the details while keeping the use cases readable.

Good Use-Case Models Have No "Levels"

Use cases tell you what the stakeholders want the system to do, not how the system implements the functionality. People who want to see "levels" of use cases often want to turn the use case into a design tool.

Often, software developers *want* to believe that use cases can be used to divine the architecture of the system directly. Perhaps they are misled by the slight visual similarity between use-case diagrams and other diagrams such as dataflow diagrams or context diagrams that have been historically used for analysis and design of software systems. Perhaps they misinterpret the essentially true statement that "use cases help link requirements to implementation and testing." But however appealing this view may be, it leads down a dangerous path.

The whole point of a use case is to capture a **description** of something that the system must do. It is an expression **of a desired behavior** of the system. The system must behave that way no matter how it is designed and implemented. Its value is in expressing that behavior in a simple and unambiguous way. The more structure we add to that description, the harder it becomes to see the desired behavior.

This is easy to say, but hard to follow.

Software developers often seem to be unable to help themselves: They begin to talk of "levels" of use cases, and soon enough the decomposition starts (think of rotting models and you'll get the general idea of what is really happening). Pretty soon, the model looks a lot like a high-level design of the system and not at all like a description of what the system is supposed to do from an external observer's perspective. In fact, by this point, we're not really sure *what* the system is supposed to do, but we sure know how it does it. In short, we're lost.

So how do we keep from crossing the line from providing good structure to the model to using the model for design purposes?

For starters, **make sure that each use case provides the user of the system with something of value.** Think of an automated banking machine. One thing the user must do with the system is to "log in," or enter a personal identifier that matches the number encoded on the user's automated banking card. Many developers will understand this and say "aha! a use case—'Log in'." But as a user of the system, would you be happy if the system accepted your card, asked you for your identification number, and then returned your card, saying "Congratulations, you've correctly entered your identification number." Of course not! Simply "logging in" has no value on its own; therefore, it's not really a use case with independent value. What a bank customer expects the system to do is, for example, to dispense cash or to deposit cash. These are the use cases. The logging in and the printing of the receipt are only means to accomplish those goals.

There are times when levels of use cases are appropriate. However, before you rush back to your team and introduce multiple levels of use cases, read on.

If your system is actually a "system of systems," where each part of the system can be used independently (or perhaps is already sold independently), then it may be useful to describe the system with a top-level use-case model then create for each smaller system a use-case model. Resist the temptation to go down another level—just keep it at two levels maximum. Two levels of models would describe a *very* large system that consists of many systems in their own right, all collaborating to perform a set of system-level use cases. Each of these systems in turn has its own use-case model. A system that could not be described by two levels of use-case models would be very large indeed. If you are reading this book and learning about use cases for the first time, it is best to avoid describing systems of systems until you have had a good deal of experience in use-case modeling or are being led by an experienced mentor.

Adapt the Description to Your Intended Audience

A valid argument can be made for something that may initially sound similar to "levels" but is really quite different. Different audiences need different information and different approaches to presenting that information. Users may only be interested in seeing how they will interact with the system; when using an automated banking machine, most of us are only interested that the machine dispenses the correct amount of money and prints a receipt. But a subject-matter expert is often interested in far more; the banking network expert *is* interested in what the automated banking machine does to ensure that the transaction is recorded correctly and is communicated to the bank for processing. To the banking expert, these are not just "details" that can be left to the designer to figure out; they are *the* important behavior of the automated banking machine. Designers have *absolutely no freedom* to decide *what* the system does to support security and transaction integrity; they only have the freedom to choose the best way to implement this behavior.

Clearly, the amount of detail presented will vary depending on the audience and its needs, and the designer needs to see *everything* in order to design and build the right system. So the challenge is to present details only when needed, yet in such a way that the details are always there.

Use the Glossary and Domain Model to Capture Definitions

The glossary can be used to describe not only simple definitions but also more complex terms that often require detailed explanations but do not materially add to the flow of events. Anytime you see a lengthy discussion or definition that serves mostly to explain background information, consider putting it into the glossary.

Use-case descriptions need to discuss the specific information that the system manages and uses to make decisions. They need to describe how the system uses that information. The details matter; if the system captures customer information, we need to know what specific information it needs: name, address, order history, and so on. Don't fall into the trap of using vague labels (for example, "customer information") expecting that someone later on will work out the real details of what this means; the specifics are important and represent an important part of the requirements of the system. This creates a problem, though. If we put all these descriptions of data into the use cases, we will figuratively drown in them; we won't be able to "see the forest for the trees." Enlightened use of a glossary will simplify the use-case descriptions by allowing the use case to focus on describing behavior, not terminology.

Use a Domain Model to Manage Detail in the Glossary

Often, glossary terms are related in rather well-defined ways. Consider the following definitions for an on-line order-entry system:

order: A contract between the company and a customer to provide some set of **items** to a particular **customer** location. An order has an order date, a shipped date, and an order number.

item: Specifies a quantity of a particular **product** being ordered. Appears on an **order**. An item consists of the quantity of the product ordered, the quantity of items supplied, and the **product** itself. Customers can specify special instructions for each item on the order.

customer: One who purchases products. A Customer has a name and contact details.

product: Something that can be sold to a **Customer**. A product definition includes a description, a reference number, and a unit price.

Several cross-references appear in the definitions for these terms, and this is our first indication that some well-defined relationships may exist among the concepts. Our second indication of some structure in some of the glossary entries is that each term captures additional information; there is some structure *within* the entries. When glossary terms reveal relationships within and between entries, you should consider using a domain model. This will help to simplify the glossary in the same way the glossary helps to simplify the use-case descriptions.

A **domain model (also called the business object model)** provides a way to capture the relationships among concepts, as well as the structure of information within the concepts.[2] Domain models are typically represented in the form of diagrams like the one in Figure 8-1. The purpose of the domain model is to clarify concepts and to facilitate communication. If half the team starts diving deep into system design, this benefit will be lost. Before a good design can be developed, one must understand the problem. Understanding the key concepts is a big part of this. Most problems are made more complex because team members do not focus on one thing at a time. A domain model does not represent the design of the system; rather, it simply defines in precise terms a set of concepts used in the problem domain. The ability to visualize these concepts often helps the team and various stakeholders agree on the definition of these concepts. The fact that the domain model will eventually give rise to design elements is *not* license to start capturing design information while working on the use cases, with the thought that "it's work you'll need to do eventually, so why not start now?" Focus on doing one thing at a time, and doing it well.

The domain model serves the same purpose as the glossary. By capturing information in the domain model it is possible to remove details from the use case. In fact, the glossary and the domain model are complementary and interchangeable, so much so that if you define a concept in the domain model, you should not also define it in the glossary (to do so would be redundant).

---

[2] Jacobson et al. in *The Object Advantage* use a business object model to capture the dynamics of the entire business process. In this context, the domain model is a subset of this business object model that contains just the parts that identify key business entities and their relationships. The *enterprise data model* is another term used to refer to the parts of the domain model that relate exclusively to the business terms.

Figure 8-1 A simple domain-model diagram illustrating the definitions of order, item, customer, and product in the previous example

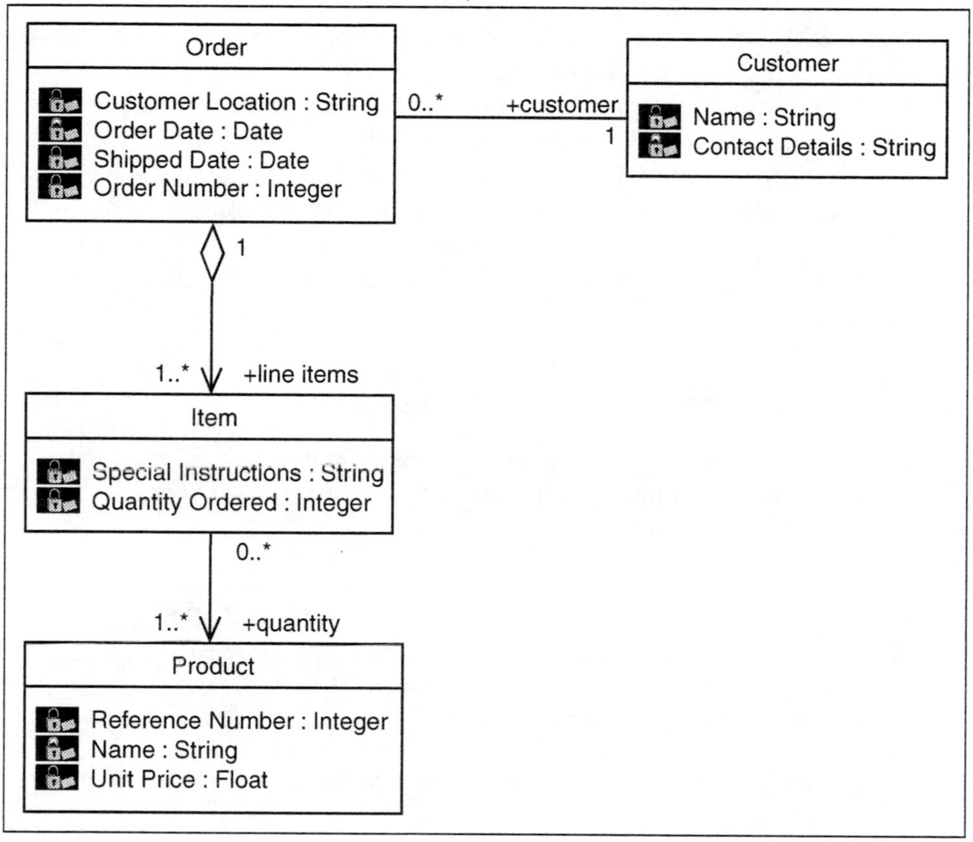

Use the Glossary and the Domain Model Together

Decide where to define a term and then do it in only one place. If a concept is related to other concepts in well-defined ways (for example, orders have items, which refer to products), use the domain model. If the concept is just a defined term, use the glossary. Establish clear guidelines on what to use and when, and then apply them consistently. To make the glossary and domain model accessible, we would recommend leaving a placeholder in the glossary that points to the domain model for all terms defined in the domain model. This allows the glossary to act as a complete index to all definitions.

The main thing about the glossary and the domain model is that they should not become ends unto themselves—they exist only to clarify the requirements and the use cases. It is tempting to say, "Well, since we are doing a domain model, let's define all the things in the problem domain so that we'll have a complete model." This will not get you closer to your goal, which is probably to deliver a specific system. If the glossary and domain models help to clarify the problem domain, thereby making it easier to describe what the system should do, they have done their duty.

As you write your use-case descriptions, remember to keep the glossary and any supporting domain models updated. These supporting artifacts can help you to reduce the complexity of the use-case descriptions by separating important (but sometimes distracting) details from the use-case descriptions. The glossary terms and the domain model elements will appear as terms in the use-case description. If your text editor supports hyperlinks, the links will point to the appropriate glossary or domain model entry. If hyperlinks are not supported, present glossary or domain model elements in a different typeface to highlight them.

Capture Business Rules in a Domain Model

A set of requirements that pose a special problem are *business rules*, which are requirements that constrain how the business itself works, independent of how the solution supports the business.

Examples

- A person must be a member of the cooperative before they can make a purchase.
- A customer may have no more than one outstanding order.
- A product may be sourced from more than one supplier; the product may have different prices depending on the supplier.
- Customers whose bills go unpaid for more than 60 days will be referred to a collection agency.

Many business rules relate to how information is validated.

Examples

- Postal codes in addresses must be valid.
- Product prices must be positive and end in whole-dollar amounts.
- Customers can order only in-stock products.

Other business rules relate to the way that work is performed.

A domain model provides an excellent way to capture many of these rules, especially those that constrain the relationships between things or the validation of information. Simple rules may be captured as requirements and traced to relevant use cases. Minimum and maximum amounts for various information properties and other validation rules can be captured right along with the definition of the information itself. This relieves the use-case authors from the tedium of describing simple validation, and it prevents the reader from getting lost in the detail of reading about simple validation.[3] Use cases excel at describing real flows of events. It would be distracting to have to stop after every other paragraph to describe how data is validated or to discuss the rule for using or updating information in each case. Using the domain model for this purpose simplifies the work and makes the result easier to understand.

Use Subflows *to Simplify Complex Descriptions*

Often, a use-case description will contain sequences of one or more steps that can be given a name. By isolating this behavior into a subflow and simply referring to it by name in other parts of the use-case description, the description can be made easier to understand. Consider the following example:

S1 Login

1. When the user enters the system for the first time, the system prompts them for the password.

2. The user enters this password (the system echoes only '*' characters to the screen as they do so). When the user indicates completion of entering the password, the system compares the password to the one associated with the user's profile.

3. If the password matches, the user is granted access to the system and the use case continues.

   a. If the user does not enter the correct password, the system reports that the password is incorrect.

      i. The user is given two additional opportunities to enter the correct password.

      ii. If the user fails to enter a correct password in three attempts, the system logs the failure attempt date and time along with the user profile information and the user is logged off the system.

   b. If the password matches, the user is granted access to the system and the use case continues; otherwise, the system reports that the password is incorrect.

---

[3] A simple but effective way to capture simple domain-model validation rules is to use operations on the domain-model entities. Each domain class can have an operation *isValid()*, the description of which captures the simple validation rules. The description can be just simple text; there is no need to write the validation rule in any kind of pseudocode since just concepts, not real designs, are presented in the domain model.

By moving this text into a subflow, we simplify the use-case description by allowing this behavior to be referred to by simply saying:

> ... perform subflow **Login** ...

within the use-case description where we need to reference the behavior.[4]

Use Alternative Flows *to Capture Unusual or Complex Behavior*

As discussed in Chapter 7, an *alternative flow* is a separate section of the use-case description that typically presents optional or unusual behavior that is not part of the *normal* behavior of the use case. Alternative flows are used to present the details of alternative behavior and exception handling, but they can also be used to describe complex behavior that is important but which, if presented in the main flow of the use case, might obscure the overall flow of events.

Consider the example of a building security system, specifically the *Monitor Building* use case. The alternative flow, *Report Unauthorized Access*, is certainly a very important alternative flow of the use case, but its complexity might easily obscure the main monitoring behavior of the system. Many teams encountering this kind of problem try to solve it by having two use cases, *Monitor Building* and *Report Unauthorized Access*, but this is unsatisfactory because it leaves monitoring and reporting disconnected: You cannot report what you cannot detect. The better approach is to have a use case whose outline looks like the following:

Basic Flow

1. The use case begins when the actor System Administrator indicates that the system should begin monitoring the surveillance area.

2. The system first ensures that all monitoring devices are reporting properly, running a system diagnostic on the reporting devices. See the subflow *Run System Diagnostic* for the details.

3. The system then waits for events to report on.

4. When the System Administrator turns off monitoring, the use case ends.

---

[4] We will discuss named subflows and alternative flows in greater depth in Chapter 9. In Chapter 10, Here There Be Dragons, we will discuss how to handle the situation in which a subflow is common to more than one use-case description.

A1 *Report Event*

1. When an event occurs, the system first checks to see if the event is one the system is required to report. If it is not, the alternative flow ends and the system returns to monitoring for events.

2. If the event requires only logging, the system records the date and time of the event along with the *event details.*[*]

3. If the event requires notification, the system determines the recipients of the notification and the preferred notification mechanism (pager, e-mail, phone message), prepares the text of the messages, and sends the message to each recipient. The text of the notification message will include the date and time of the event, the event details, and a description of the required response. The system logs the date and time the message was sent, the text of the message, and the identification information for each recipient

4. The system then resumes waiting for subsequent events.

[*] *Event details* would be a perfect item to define in a glossary.

Once these techniques are applied, the use cases often become quite simple and very readable.

Don't Fill Your Use Cases with CRUD

Use cases filled with CRUD (Create, Retrieve, Update, Delete behavior) end up being nothing more than a regurgitation of the CRUD requirements stated in a requirement specification. Often, it is better to write a simple use-case description (typically, an outline is sufficient), then move quickly to developing a prototype to validate the requirements and to make sure that you've got the right user interface, and then move on to design. Use cases for simple CRUD behavior don't add much value to ensuring that the system is doing the right thing. This may sound like heresy, but we don't find that use cases help much here. When the requirements are basically "here's some important concept and here's how to validate it," the requirements are pretty clear and there's no real flow of events (just "enter data, validate it, etc., etc., etc., and then commit the transaction"); there's little chance of getting the requirements wrong.

In the case of CRUD behavior, there is typically little or nothing to the flow of events—some datum is updated, it is validated, and so on. Typically, information can be entered in any order, perhaps with minimal dependencies on other data. When this occurs, you may decide to dispense with the use cases, capture the data in a domain model or business object model along with the validation rules, and move quickly on to some prototypes. The benefit of doing this is that you save time and effort for the really hard use cases that have complex behavior and that have a much greater impact on the architecture of the system. You also use these complex use cases to exercise and validate the domain model to make sure that all important business entities are captured in some way. We've seen many teams waste lots of time developing use cases for CRUD behavior and thus not have enough time to dig into the "real" behavior of the system. One project on which we consulted had spent nearly all the time in the first iteration writing the trivial use cases, all the while ignoring the use case they knew contained all the "hard" stuff. They used the simple use cases as an excuse to procrastinate on the ones that really required forethought. So in this case employing use cases to document CRUD rules actually increased the risk. Although it is technically appropriate to employ use cases to describe this kind of behavior, it's probably not a great use of time to describe this behavior in terms of use cases. We summarize this guideline as "use cases should contain more than CRUD."

Broadly considered, use cases are a great technique for managing certain types of risks, specifically risks such as failing to understand the sequential behavior of the system, the flow of events that a system must follow. Most administrative systems have lots of different kinds of information that must be entered and maintained. Most of this entry/maintenance is uninteresting from a behavioral standpoint: The system displays the fields into which data is entered, the user enters data, the system validates the data, the user commits the transaction, corrects errors, and so on. Except for the data validation rules and the specific fields entered, the pattern is repetitive. There is very little "flow of events" to these parts of the system. Elucidating use cases for this behavior is tedious—more than tedious, it is wasteful. Typically, it is faster to prototype the behavior using modern prototyping tools than it is to write the use cases. The important parts of the CRUD behavior—the data validation—can be captured in the domain model, along with the definition of the data itself, by specifying the cardinalities on relationships, constraints on the values of attributes, and other information that can be used to validate behavior. Often, the "prototypes" produced by these tools are more than adequate for production-quality work and can be easily evolved.

A better solution to this problem is to capture the data requirements in the domain model. Domain classes should be used to capture relationships among different types of information as well as required attributes. Validation rules can be captured as operations on the domain classes, especially if validation requires computations or comparisons of attributes. Simple validation rules can also be captured in the description of the attribute itself.

Don't Be Afraid of Capturing the Detail

By now it should be quite clear that we believe effective use-case models are unambiguous and contain the detail of what the system must do. To achieve this, you will have to buckle down and write detailed descriptions. Do not let fear of detail serve as an excuse for procrastination; the problem never gets simpler with the passage of time, and every day that passes without forward progress increases the likelihood that the project will fail. There's an old saying, "the long journey begins with a single step"; it's best to get started as soon as possible.

SUMMARY

The real value of a use case emerges from its description; everything that precedes the description—identifying actors and use cases, creating use-case diagrams, even writing the brief descriptions—is of little value without the details of the flows of events. Some teams have failed with use cases because they have not grasped this basic fact: It is the description of the flows of events of the use case that matters, for this is where the behavior of the system is described.

Because it is the use-case description that matters, writing clearly and concisely is important to being successful. Because of this, describing use cases is a different kind of activity than other development tasks and also sometimes suffers from neglect. While different techniques can be used to capture the behavior of the system (written text, storyboards, prototypes), what matters most is the thought process behind the descriptions. Have the needs of the various stakeholders been considered? Is the system easy to use? Does it accomplish important business goals? Does the system support providing value to its users and stakeholders? Beyond the specifics of how the use case is captured and presented, the greatest value of the use-case technique is that it forces us to consider these questions directly, and it allows the developers and stakeholders to discuss how the system provides value in a way that is independent of implementation.

This chapter has presented an overview of the goals and challenges of writing good descriptions. The next chapter will continue this discussion by focusing on the process of writing the descriptions and the practicalities of working with these descriptions on a daily basis.

Chapter 9

Writing Use-Case Descriptions: Revisited

By the time you are ready to write use-case descriptions, you will have completed the following tasks:

- Identified actors and use cases
- Created a use-case diagram showing the associations between actors and use cases
- Written a short description of the role the actor or use case plays in the context of the system
- Drafted a bulleted outline of the basic flow and identified the major alternatives for the significant use cases

Some, perhaps even many, use-case projects do not go beyond this point. If the flow of events is simple and team members agree on the required behavior of the system specified by the use case, it might be time to simply prototype and confirm the behavior and move on. But before you make a hasty decision, consider the needs of the following groups of people:

- Developers, who will have to analyze, design, and implement the system
- Testers, who will have to verify that the system meets its intended goals
- Technical writers and user-education staff, who will have to help the user understand how to use the system
- Support staff, who will have to maintain and keep the system running

If the use cases are not described, will these people have the information they need to do their jobs? If the answer is "no," you will have to describe the use cases in greater detail.

In this chapter, we provide strategies for evolving the description of the use case to meet the needs of these stakeholders, including how to capture and manage the details of a use-case description. This is done by evolving the *Withdraw Cash* example use case (last seen as an outline in Chapters 4 and 7) by progressively and systematically applying a variety of techniques to improve the quality of the use-case description.

HOW MUCH DETAIL IS ENOUGH?

If you stop after writing a brief description for the use case, you still do not have very much to work with. Brief descriptions are a useful starting point, and they help to clarify the meaning of what may be a somewhat cryptic name for the use case. However, the brief description still doesn't convey what specifically the system does for its actors. But how far do we need to do go in writing the description?

Broadly considered, a use case is a technique for mitigating risk—specifically the risk that someone might misunderstand what the system is required to do to produce value for its users. Sometimes, what the system must do is easy to understand and there is no possibility of mistaking it; other times, it is not so clear. In deciding whether to further document the use-case description, make sure you understand your options if you want to confirm that you understand the behavior required of the system. The discussion of the different forms a use case can take in Chapter 6, The Life Cycle of a Use Case, should help you reach the correct decision for your project.

Many times, perhaps most times, teams need more depth in their use-case descriptions. The reasons for this are many, the principal ones being

- The need to document requirements because of legal or contractual constraints
- The need to record information for team members who cannot attend every meeting with subject-matter experts
- The need to record decisions so that the team does not need to rely on memory and verbal communication to determine what has already been decided
- The need to specify the system to a level that will enable testing

The need for deeper and more-comprehensive description will also vary with the complexity and risk of the system. The people paying for a system whose budget may be millions of dollars may not feel comfortable with informal "stories" and undocumented requirements. Similarly, systems on which lives depend are too risky to build without rigor.

At minimum, the use case should be detailed enough to completely specify the inputs to the system (the events initiated by the actors of the system and the information the actors exchange with the system) and the outputs of the system. If the dialog between the actors and the system is complex, the description of the interaction will be complex as well. If the dialog between the actors and the system is simple, the use case may be simple.

What other factors will influence the complexity of the description? In addition to the complexity of the dialog with the actors, the complexity of the system's internal behavior will require more detailed description. As we have previously discussed, systems may have simple external interactions but very complex internal behavior. In order to ensure that the right system is built, this behavior needs to be described.

The final answer to the question "how much detail is enough?" is that the use case must contain enough detail so that all stakeholders are satisfied that the system is defined in sufficient detail to allow the *right* system to be built. In the ATM system, the *Withdraw Cash* use case is one of the most significant use cases; it is one of the highest-priority use cases for the users of the system as well as being one of the most architecturally significant. In this case, a full description will be required.

DESCRIBING PRECONDITIONS

As described in detail in Chapter 7, The Structure and Contents of a Use Case, a precondition defines the state that the system must be in or conditions that must be satisfied before the use case can be performed. The following sections will help you identify and write use-case preconditions.

Deciding Whether a Precondition Is Needed

The first thing you should realize is that it may not be necessary to define a precondition for the use case; it may be possible to perform the use case at any time. Preconditions only need to be defined in situations where the use case cannot be performed unless certain conditions are true. The preconditions define those conditions.

Describing Preconditions

If certain conditions must be satisfied before the use case can be performed, state them in a clear and easily verifiable way.

Example Preconditions (from the *Automated Teller Machine*)

Use Case—*Withdraw Cash*
- The network connection to the **banking system** must be active.
- The system must have at least some **currency** that can be dispensed
- The user must be **authorized** to perform the requested transaction.

You should think of the preconditions as *requirements* that must be satisfied before the use case can be performed. Preconditions should be written as simple statements of the state that the system must be in, this state should be expressed in terms of conditions that must be true before the use case can be performed.

As previously discussed, preconditions should *never* be stated in terms of some other use case having been performed. If you have a desire to do this, it probably means that you have broken the use cases into chunks that are too small to have value by themselves. To resolve the problem, you can do one of two things: combine use cases or state the precondition in terms of the state in which the preceding use case will leave the system. Combining the use cases is fairly obvious, but to determine the state in which a use case leaves the system, ask yourself "what is the result of the preceding use case?" This result or condition should be the precondition of the succeeding use case, not a statement of the fact that some other use case has been performed.

If you define multiple preconditions, be clear about how they should be combined; the default for preconditions is to AND them.

DESCRIBING POSTCONDITIONS

As described in detail in Chapter 7, The Structure and Contents of a Use Case, a postcondition defines the state that the system is in once the use case has been performed. The following sections will help you identify and write postconditions.

Deciding Whether Postconditions Are Needed

In many cases, it may be acceptable to simply omit the postcondition entirely when the result of the use case is obvious or when there is no significant state change in the system. In the event-reporting example we have previously used, the use case *Monitor Building* for a building security system, there is no need for a postcondition on the use case because monitoring does not change the state of the system (it detects and reports events and then returns to a monitoring mode). Postconditions are only needed when the state is important to one of the actors for the use case, such as when the end state of the use case helps a stakeholder achieve a goal.

To determine whether you should introduce a postcondition, ask yourself the following questions:

- Does the completion of this use case leave the system in a particular state that may need to be a precondition for other use cases? If so, record this as a postcondition.

- Are the possible outcomes of the use case obvious, so that it will be easy for developers, testers, or users to understand the result of performing a use case? If not, record the outcomes as postconditions on the use case.

Specifying all the postconditions for a use case can be helpful in cases where it is important to call attention to the different possible conditions that may exist when the use case completes. Enumerating the postconditions can assist the testers in verifying that all possible outcomes are accounted for in the test cases. It may also help developers to account for the different possible use-case outcomes.

Describing Postconditions

Postconditions are conditions that are fulfilled when the use case is terminated, no matter how the use case terminated. Look at *Withdraw Cash* again:

Example Preconditions (from the *Automated Teller Machine*)

Use Case—*Withdraw Cash*

For the use case *Withdraw Cash*, the following postconditions may exist:

1. The ATM has returned the card and cash to the Customer and the withdrawal is registered on the customer's account.

2. The ATM has returned the card to the Customer and no withdrawal is registered on the customer's account.

3. The ATM has returned the card, but neither cash nor receipt, to the Customer and the withdrawal is registered on the Customer's account; the failure to dispense is registered in the logs.

4. The ATM keeps the card and no withdrawal is registered on the Customer's account.

As with preconditions, stick to simple statements of the state or condition the system will be in when the use case completes. If the use case achieves some stakeholder goal, be sure to call that out. Express a use case's postcondition in terms of a state that the system is in, or a condition that is true, when the use case completes. If the system can be in different states depending on the path taken through the use case, these states should be enumerated.

If you define multiple postconditions, be clear about how they should be combined; the default for postconditions is to OR them.

WRITING THE FLOW OF EVENTS

Good writing typically proceeds from an outline; use cases are no different. Outlines of the flows of events help to clarify the purpose of the use case. The outline will help you to think through each step. The brief description tells us what happens, usually in terms of some end result, but with the outline we start to spell out how the system arrives at the end result.

We discussed a number of techniques for presenting "outline-level" descriptions of the use case in Chapter 6, including the "essential" and "conversational" descriptions. If you stop at the "outline" level of description, you will have a general idea of the flow of events and may even understand a few of the alternative flows of events. This may be sufficient if the team has a good understanding of the problem domain and has ready access to a subject-matter expert or business representative to fill in the gaps in its understanding.

As you evolve the use-case description from an outline to a potentially complete description of the desired behavior, focus first on the "basic" flow of events. The basic flow is what happens if everything goes "right"—no alternatives or exceptions, just the most likely things that should happen. Discussing all the alternative flows (the things that can go wrong) too early can be distracting and often prevents useful progress. Alternative flows and exceptions are complex, and they are easier to deal with when one already has the framework of the basic flow of events on which to build.

Writing the Basic Flow of Events

How much detail should you include in the basic flow? The use case should unambiguously describe the required behavior. If the system must respond in a certain way to a certain event, then you must say so in the use case. The trick is to express the behavior without dictating or constraining the design. For example, consider the following simple use case:

Example #1 (from the *Automated Teller System*)

Use Case—Withdraw Cash

Basic Flow

1. The use case starts when the Customer inserts the bank card.

2. The system reads the card and requests the Customer to enter the Personal Identification Number (PIN).

3. The system presents a menu of choices.

4. The Customer indicates a wish to withdraw cash.

5. The system requests the amount to be dispensed and the Customer enters the amount.

6. The system dispenses the desired amount of cash and ejects the card.

7. The Customer takes the cash and card.

8. The use case ends.

This is pretty much where we left off in Chapter 4—with a basic outline. The outline captures the essence of the use case, but it lacks all sorts of important details. First, what information does the system read from the banking card? What does the system do to verify that the correct PIN has been entered? How does the system know that the customer has sufficient funds in the account? What information gets recorded as part of the transaction?

Pay Attention to What's Behind the Screen

You must pay attention to what's behind the screen; a good use-case description does not stop at the "glass."

Some people think that a use case just describes the user's view of the system, that it is simply a description of the user interface. For them, the use case is simply a series of "the actor does this" and "the system responds with that." A use case is more than just the user interface ("the glass"); it encompasses the internal behavior of the system as well. A use case that focuses too much on just the user interaction might look like the following example:

Example #2

Use Case—Withdraw Cash

Basic Flow

1. The use case starts when the Customer inserts the bank card.

2. The system then requests the Customer to enter the PIN. The PIN can be up to 6 numbers in length and must not include any repeated digits.

3. The Customer enters the PIN.

4. If the PIN entered is valid, the system offers to the Customer the opportunity to withdraw cash.

5. The system requests the amount to be dispensed and the Customer enters the amount.

6. The system dispenses the desired amount of cash.

7. The system ejects the card.

8. The Customer takes the cash, card, and receipt.

9. The use case ends.

The "externally focused" description is typical of the initial result of evolving the outline of the use-case description from a bulleted list toward an essential outline, as we discussed in Chapter 6, The Life Cycle of a Use Case. This kind of outline has many uses, but ask yourself this: If you are a designer, do you have enough information to design the system at this point? If you are a customer would you trust the designer to design the system so that it works "correctly"? The answer in both cases is "no"; this use case only describes the most superficial aspects of the human-machine interaction. Unfortunately, this is often the point at which the use-case description stops. No wonder some people refer to them as *"useless cases."*

So what is missing? Well, specifics about the information exchanged for one. When the customer inserts the card, what information is read from the card? The customer's number, the financial institution's interbank identifier, and perhaps even the identification number (all encrypted, of course). We're also missing the information that the banking machine must record about the transaction for audit trail purposes. We're also missing how the banking machine determines how much money is available to dispense. We're also missing validation information. How does the system know if the amount entered is appropriate? The banking machine must communicate with some other system to see if the customer has sufficient funds on hand. Once the funds are dispensed, the banking machine must communicate the amount dispensed to the bank's accounting systems to make sure the transaction is recorded properly.

Some people will say that these things amount to going into "too much detail" or are things that should be left for later. But these details are important, and leaving them for later is at best procrastination, at worst a lost opportunity as the task is often never taken up again. The details are important components of the requirements of the system, and they need to be captured. Other people might say that these "details" are design issues (misunderstanding what design is really about). Should the rules on how the system validates whether customers are who they say they are be left up to the designer? Should the rules on how overdrafts are detected be left to the designer as a "detail" to be dealt with as the designer sees fit? No! This behavior is *the* behavior of the system, and ignoring it as a mere "detail" is failing to define the most important behavior of the system. Overlooking it is really just procrastination thinly veiled. The internal details matter, and use cases that go no deeper than the user interface are really "useless cases" that are hardly worth the bother of writing. If you're going to take the time to describe the behavior, do it right.

But look what happens if we start including this information:

Example #3

Use Case—*Withdraw Cash*

Basic Flow

1. The use case starts when the Customer inserts the bank card.

2. The system reads the bank card and obtains the bank number, the account number, and the Personal Information Number (PIN). The system then requests the Customer to enter the PIN. The PIN can be up to 6 numbers in length and must not include any repeated digits.

3. The system compares the entered PIN to the PIN read from the card to determine if the PIN entered is valid.

4. If the PIN entered is valid, the system offers to the Customer the opportunity to withdraw cash.

5. The system requests the amount to be dispensed and the Customer enters the amount.

6. The system checks to see if it has sufficient funds in its dispenser to satisfy the request.

7. The system ensures that the amount entered is a multiple of $5 and does not exceed $200.

8. The system contacts the Customer's bank to determine if the amount requested can be withdrawn from the Customer's bank account.

9. If the Customer has sufficient funds on hand, the system dispenses the desired amount of cash.

10. The system logs the transaction with the following information:

    - The date and time of the transaction
    - The location of the ATM
    - The Customer's bank number
    - The type of transaction
    - The amount of the transaction
    - The transaction identifier (for tracking within the interbank network)

11. The system ejects the card.

12. The Customer takes the cash, card, and receipt.

13. The use case ends.

Notice that the description of the basic flow becomes substantially longer after we add details about what the system does and what information is captured. Some of you are probably thinking that this is too much detail, but ask yourself this: If you were paying someone to develop the system, wouldn't you want to know exactly what the system was going to do?

In fact, this description is still lacking in detail—it has no description of alternative flows (the things that happen when things go wrong), and a lot of important information has yet to be defined. The way to find this detail is to keep asking "What does this mean?" until the ambiguities have been resolved. The author of the use case will continue to add detail until all the stakeholders (mentioned at the start of this chapter) are satisfied that the use case is "done" and all of the inputs to the system and outputs from the system have been defined.

Building on that description, we can add more detail as follows:

Example #4

Use Case—*Withdraw Cash*

1. The use case begins when the actor Customer inserts the automated bank card.

2. The system reads the bank card and obtains the bank number, the account number, and the Personal Information Number (PIN). The system then requests the Customer to enter the PIN. The PIN can be up to 6 numbers in length and must not include any repeated digits.[*]

3. The system queries the Customer's bank to ensure that the Customer's account is active at the financial institution identified by the interbank number.

4. The system prompts the Customer for the identification number, which the Customer enters.

5. The system validates the number entered by the Customer with the number read from the card. (Note: Alternative flows describing how to handle errors would be described below.)

6. The system prompts the customer to enter the amount of the withdrawal.

7. The system indicates that the amount entered must be a multiple of $5. (Assume for the moment that this system allows only withdrawals and that the Customer has only one account.)

8. The Customer enters the desired amount.

[*] Alternative flows, describing how exceptions and alternatives are handled, will be discussed in a later section.

9. The system then determines whether it has sufficient funds on hand to dispense the requested amount.

   - It first checks to see if the total amount requested is greater than the amount on hand. (Note: Insufficient funds would be handled in an alternative flow, not shown here for brevity.)
   - If sufficient funds exist, it then checks to see if the requested amount can be dispensed with the denominations on hand. (Note that it is possible to have sufficient funds in total and still be unable to dispense funds; consider the case where the Customer has requested $35 but the system only has $40 in the form of two $20 bills.)

10. The system contacts the financial institution to see if the Customer has sufficient funds in the account.

11. The system begins a transaction with the financial institution and requests to withdraw the amount requested plus the transaction fee from the Customer's account.

12. If the request is successful, the amount of the transaction fee is transferred to the organization owning the system.

13. The system then dispenses the requested amount to the Customer.

14. The system closes the transaction with the financial institution.

15. The system logs the transaction with the following information:

    - The date and time of the transaction
    - The location of the ATM
    - The Customer's bank number
    - The type of transaction
    - The amount of the transaction
    - The transaction identifier (for tracking within the interbank network)

16. The Customer's banking card is ejected.

17. The use case ends when the Customer takes the banking card from the machine.

Now, this use case is still pretty simple (we haven't shown all the alternative flows, the system supports only one kind of transaction from a single customer account, and only one transaction is allowed per session). But the level of detail is starting to get realistic, and if this is the behavior that the customer wanted, we could probably get a fairly good start on the design of the system from this information.

A common mistake when writing use-case descriptions is to fear adding detail. If the use case remains vague and imprecise, it is useful for little more than conveying a general sense of what the system will do. Faced with vague descriptions, teams will be forced to create other detailed descriptions of the behavior of the system. This is unnecessary—the use case can be employed to convey the necessary detail. The real concern with "too much detail" is that use cases can become unreadable if the detail is not presented and managed effectively. The topics in the next three sections are intended to help you manage the detail so that the use case can present a complete picture of the system's behavior while still remaining understandable.

USING THE GLOSSARY AND THE DOMAIN MODEL

Use cases often contain a lot of information that can be better presented in other ways. Using a glossary of terms is one way to present necessary information that can otherwise be distracting to the reader. In the *Withdraw Cash* use case, some terms need to be defined and information needs to be presented. If you look at the *Withdraw Cash* use case presented in Example 4, you will see terms such as *customer, customer's bank, account, bank card*, and *PIN*. These terms need to be defined if the use case is to provide an unambiguous description of the system's behavior. We could define these terms in the use case itself, but we choose not to for several reasons:

- It would be distracting and get in the way of the flow-of-events description.
- Other use cases for the system probably use the same terms, so we should define the terms once, in one place.

Start creating a glossary as soon as special terms start to appear. This often happens early in the process, when you are still discovering the use cases.

Example Glossary for ATM System (partial)

account: An obligation on the part of the financial institution to pay the customer, upon demand and adhering to the terms of the account agreement, a defined sum of money.

bank card: A physical identification device, imprinted with magnetic information pertaining to the issuing financial institution (**bank number**), the customer (the customer **number** with the issuing financial institution), and a **Personal Information Number (PIN)**, chosen by the customer at the time the card was issued.

customer: A person who holds accounts at a financial institution that is a member of the ATM interbank network.

customer's bank: The financial institution that issued the bank card and at which the customer has one or more accounts. The customer's bank is contacted via the financial institution network. The financial institution is identified via an institution interbank number.

log: A permanent record used to prevent against data loss in the event of a subsequent system failure. The log contains the following information for each transaction:

- The date and time of the transaction
- The location of the ATM
- The customer's bank number
- The type of transaction
- The amount of the transaction
- The transaction identifier (for tracking within the interbank network)

Personal Identification Number (PIN): An identification number, chosen by the **customer**, used in conjunction with the card for security purposes. The PIN can be up to 6 numbers in length and must not include any repeated digits. A PIN is used to verify the identity of the customer by asking the customer to reenter the PIN; when the customer enters the same number as the PIN stored on the card, the customer's identity is considered authenticated.

Armed now with an evolving glossary of terms, we can move some details from the use case to the glossary, as shown in the following example:

Example #5

Use Case—*Withdraw Cash* (refined, incorporating glossary terms)

1. The use case begins when the actor **Customer** inserts the **bank card**.

2. The system reads the **bank card** information from the card.

3. The system queries the **Customer's bank** to ensure that the Customer's **account** is active.

4. The system prompts the Customer for the **PIN**.

5. The Customer enters the **PIN**.

6. The system validates the entered **PIN** with the PIN read from the card.

7. The system prompts the Customer to enter the amount of the withdrawal.

8. The system indicates that the amount entered must be a multiple of $5. (Assume for the moment that this system allows only withdrawals and that the Customer has only one account.)

9. The **Customer** enters the desired amount.

(continued)

10. The system then determines whether it has sufficient funds on hand to dispense the requested amount.

   - The system checks to see if the total amount requested is greater than the amount on hand.[*]
   - The system checks to see if the requested amount can be dispensed with the denominations on hand. (Note that it is possible to have sufficient funds in total and still be unable to dispense funds; consider the case where the Customer has requested $35 but the system only has $40 in the form of two $20 bills.)

11. The system contacts the financial institution to see if the Customer has sufficient funds in the account.

12. The system begins a transaction with the Customer's bank and requests to withdraw the amount requested plus the transaction fee from the Customer's account.

13. The amount of the transaction fee is transferred to the organization owning the system.

14. The system then dispenses the requested amount to the Customer.

15. The system closes the transaction with the **Customer's bank**.

16. The system records a **log** entry for the transaction.

17. The Customer's **bank card** is ejected.

18. The use case ends when the Customer takes the bank card from the machine.

   [*] Insufficient funds on hand would be handled in an alternative flow, not shown here for brevity.

The good thing about the glossary is that we don't have to define these terms again when we write the next use case. If relationships emerge between concepts in the glossary, a domain model can be used, as discussed in Chapter 8. For the simple ATM example we have presented thus far, a domain model is not yet necessary.

If we were to consider the ATM in the context of a full banking system (as we no doubt would if we were actually developing the system), the domain model would include definitions of things like customers, accounts, account types, and so on as the use cases expanded to provide functionality that exercised these concepts. We have omitted this for simplicity and to emphasize that the domain model should never exist on its own, but rather should only be used to augment the use-case descriptions (at least in the context of use-case modeling).

As we have shown in the preceding examples, the use cases of even simple systems can become detailed. For a complex system, the detail can sometimes become overwhelming, obscuring the flow of events of the system and making the real behavior of the system hard to understand.

WRITING "NAMED" SUBFLOWS

In the course of writing the use-case descriptions, you will find sections that perform important behaviors but that are not essential to understanding the basic flow of events. An example of this occurs in our *Withdraw Cash* use case at the following steps:

---

4. The system prompts the Customer for the **PIN**.

5. The Customer enters the **PIN**.

6. The system validates the entered **PIN** with the PIN read from the card.

These steps perform an essential function—validating the identity of the customer—but the details start to get in the way, even in this simple example. In more complex systems, we will find many such groups of steps that can be isolated, given a name, and moved into sections of their own. These sections, called *named subflows*, are presented at the end of the Basic Flow, in a section of the use case called *Subflows*.

The subflows should be given an active name that communicates the objective of the flow of events, for example, *Authenticate Customer* not *Customer Authentication*. Named subflows are numbered as well as given names, for convenient reference. Numbers are arbitrary and are assigned as the named subflows are identified. The naming convention we recommend is to prefix the numbers with "S" (for subflow). Organized into a named subflow, the steps just presented appear as:

S1 *Authenticate Customer*

1. The system queries the **Customer's bank** to ensure that the Customer's **account** is active.

2. The system prompts the Customer for the **PIN**.

3. The Customer enters the **PIN**.

4. The system validates the entered **PIN** with the PIN read from the card.

5. Resume at the next step.

This named subflow is referenced as follows:

Example #6

> **Use Case—*Withdraw Cash***
>
> 1. The use case begins when the actor **Customer** inserts the **bank card**.
>
> 2. The system reads the **bank card** information from the card.
>
> 3. Perform ***Authenticate Customer***.
>
> 4. The system prompts the Customer to enter the amount of the withdrawal.
>
> (The remainder of the use case has been deleted for purposes of brevity.)

As you can see, this greatly simplifies the description of the use case. Further opportunities for extracting subsections of the use case are shown next:

> **S2 *Assess Funds on Hand***
>
> 1. The system determines whether it has sufficient funds on hand to dispense the requested amount.
>
>   a. The system checks to see if the total amount requested is greater than the amount on hand.
>
>   b. The system checks to see if the requested amount can be dispensed with the denominations on hand. (Note that it is possible to have sufficient funds in total and still be unable to dispense funds; consider the case where the Customer has requested $35 but the system only has $40 in the form of two $20 bills.)
>
> 2. Resume at the next step.
>
> **S3 *Conduct Withdrawal***
>
> 1. The system contacts the financial institution to see if the Customer has sufficient funds in the account.
>
> 2. The system begins a transaction with the Customer's bank and requests to withdraw the amount requested plus the transaction fee from the Customer's account.
>
> 3. The amount of the transaction fee is transferred to the organization owning the system.
>
> 4. The system closes the transaction with the **Customer's bank**.
>
> 5. Resume at the next step.

With these additional subflows, our use case now looks as follows:

Example #7

Use Case—*Withdraw Cash* (refined, incorporating glossary terms)

1. The use case begins when the actor **Customer** inserts the **bank card**.

2. The system reads the **bank card** information from the card.

3. Perform ***Authenticate Customer.***

4. The system prompts the Customer to enter the amount of the withdrawal. (Assume for the moment that this system allows only withdrawals and that the Customer has only one account.)

5. The system indicates that the amount entered must be a multiple of $5.

6. The Customer enters the desired amount.

7. Perform ***Assess Funds on Hand.***

8. Perform ***Conduct Withdrawal.***

9. The system then dispenses the requested amount to the Customer.

10. The system records a **log** entry for the transaction.

11. The Customer's **banking card** is ejected.

12. The use case ends when the Customer takes the bank card from the machine.

Notice that the creation of a few named subflows has done two things: It has simplified the description of the main flow of events, and it has given cohesive meaning to several groupings of steps, making them more understandable in the process. Notice also that the combination of the techniques we have presented so far has had the effect of making our use case simpler, more readable, and yet at the same time more detailed.

In our example, we have shown the evolution of named subflows by showing how the basic flow can be simplified by extracting fragments. In practice, named subflows also evolve simultaneously with the basic flow. Often, we will immediately recognize a step that will have several substeps and can be given a name and split out as a named subflow even before the substeps are written. For pedagogical purposes, we have spared you that scenario, but you should recognize that it will occur, especially as you gain experience.

One final use of named subflows is to handle repetitive description within the same use case. In cases where the same description might occur in several different places, named subflows can be employed to reduce the redundancy, improve the consistency, and improve the readability of the use case.

We have but one more step in our evolution of the description: handling the description of optional, alternative, and exception flows.

WRITING OPTIONAL, ALTERNATIVE, AND EXCEPTION FLOWS

Optional, alternative, and exception flows are flows of events that occur when something other than the normal course of events has occurred. They are really all the same thing by different names: *Optional flows* implies that the behavior is optional and doesn't always need to be performed, *alternative flows* implies some sort of alternative decision is taken, and *exception flows* implies that something other than the ordinary has occurred. In all cases, we need to describe what happens when something occurs at a particular point in the use case. For simplicity of explanation, we will simply refer to all of them as *alternative* flows, since the mechanics of writing their descriptions is the same.

Identifying Alternative Flows

Simple alternative flows can be handled in the description of the basic flow itself if the alternative steps are few and short and do not distract from the understanding of the main flow.

Example

. . .

The system reads the **bank card** information from the **card**.

*If the system cannot read all the **bank card** information, then the system informs the Customer that the card cannot be read, the card is returned to the Customer and the use case ends.*

Otherwise, the system queries the **Customer's bank** . . .

In this example, the failure to read the card is an exception flow of events (see the italicized text in the example), but because the action required is very simple—the card is returned, the customer informed, and the use case ended—it can easily be handled in-line. The possible distraction that might occur by presenting the alternative behavior in the description of the main flow of events is more than offset by the decreased complexity of not having alternative flows of only a few sentences scattered in other sections that makes their context harder to understand.

Representing Alternative Flows in Separate Sections

As the number of alternative steps grows, however, they begin to distract the reader from the main flow of events. Since the behavior of most systems tends to be dominated by handling alternative and exception behavior, describing this behavior in the main flow of events can obscure the real purpose of the use case. For this reason, we need a way to describe alternative and exception behavior in separate sections of the use case.

Consider the following expansion of our *Withdraw Cash* fragment:

Example

. . .

The system reads the **bank card** information from the **card**.

If the system cannot read all the **bank card** information, then the system informs the Customer that the card cannot be read, the card is returned to the Customer, and the use case ends.

The system queries the **Customer's bank** to verify that the **Customer information** is correct.

If the **Customer's bank** reports that the card has been stolen, it:

- Confiscates the card and reports the confiscation to the **Customer's bank**
- Records a video of the Customer for future reference
- Terminates the transaction
- Reports to the Customer that:
  - The card has been reported stolen
  - The card has been confiscated
  - The Customer should contact their bank if there are any questions

The use case then ends.

Otherwise . . . [the use case continues].

This addition of the behavior to handle stolen cards is important; we don't want to leave it out. At the same time, the addition of this behavior is very disruptive to the presentation of the basic flow of events. What we need to do is to set aside this exceptional behavior in an alternative flow, leaving the basic flow to stand alone.

Presenting complex alternative flows (consisting of behavior that requires more than a few sentences to describe) *in-line* makes the basic flow of events very hard to understand if there are more than a few alternatives, or if the alternative flows have more than a few steps. In such cases, organizing the information in separate sections makes the reading easier, as shown in the next example.

Example

Basic Flow (fragment)

. . .

{Read Card}

The system reads the **bank card** information from the **card**.

{Validate Card Information}

The system queries the **Customer's bank** to verify that the **Customer information** is correct.

Alternative Flows

A1 *Hand Unreadable Bank Card*

At **{Read Card}** if the system cannot read all the **bank card** information, then the system informs the Customer that the card cannot be read, the card is returned to the Customer, and the use case ends.

A2 *Handle Stolen Bank Card*

At **{Validate Card Information}** if the **Customer's bank** reports that the card has been stolen, it:

- Confiscates the card and reports the confiscation to the bank
- Records a video of the Customer for future reference
- Terminates the transaction
- Reports to the Customer that:
  - The card has been reported stolen
  - The card has been confiscated
  - The Customer should contact the bank if there are any questions

The use case then ends.

Let's spend some time examining what we have presented here.

Naming Alternative Flows

The alternative flow should be given a name, as we did with named subflows. The name should represent the goal the alternative flow achieves. In our example, the alternative flows are intended to handle problems reading data from the card and to handle the case where the card has been stolen. Naming the alternative flows with their purpose helps the reader to more easily understand the alternative flow.

We have also found it useful to number the alternative flows, as we did with named subflows. The numbers should be prefixed with an "A" (for Alternative) and should be numbered sequentially as they are identified. The numbering provides a shorthand reference mechanism that is useful when discussing a number of alternative flows or when presenting the alternative flows in documents or reports.

Using Extension Points to Target Alternative Behavior

First, notice that in the basic flow of events, we have two labels {**Read Card**} and {**Validate Card Information**}. As described in Chapter 7, these labels are called *extension points*, because they allow the flow of events to be extended at the point at which they occur. If we move optional, alternative, or exception behavior to a separate section, we need a way of referring to the point at which the behavior will either be inserted or supersede the behavior presented in the basic flow of events.

In the example, the {**Read Card**} extension point provides a target for the handling of unreadable card information, and {**Validate Card Information**} enables us to deal with events such as expired cards or stolen cards (shown in the example). The extension points allow us to refer to some section of behavior without resorting to using step numbers, which tend to change as the use case evolves. In the example, we specifically removed the step numbers to highlight the use of extension points as textual reference mechanisms.

Always make the extension points useful in the context of the flow of events in which they appear. In our example, the extension points also serve as useful labels that improve the readability of the description. Keeping the extension point names descriptive will help the reader. The extension point names should be unique within the use case to prevent confusion.

Describing Alternative Flows That Can Occur Anywhere in the Use Case

An alternative flow may be performed at one or more places in a use case, so there may in fact be more than one extension point at which the alternative flow can be performed. In some cases, the alternative flow has no specific extension point, as in the case of handling a general system failure:

Example

A3 *Handle Security Breaches*

At any point in the main flow or any alternative flow when an attempt to gain physical access to the currency dispenser is detected:

1. The system terminates the current transaction.

2. The system disables any subsequent transactions.

3. The system alerts the ATM network that an unauthorized access has occurred.

4. The use case in progress is ended.

This example illustrates several important concepts:

- An alternative flow can be performed at any time *when* a particular event occurs.
- The alternative flow can terminate the use case currently being performed.
- A security requirement can be described by using the use case to describe what happens when an attempted security breach is detected.

Alternative flows can also begin at a specific point, when a specific condition occurs, as shown in our earlier example of the A1 alternative flow. For the full details of the syntax used to define alternative flows, see Chapter 7, The Structure and Contents of a Use Case.

Resuming the Use Case After the Alternative Flow Completes

When the alternative flow completes, it resumes at the place where the flow of the use case was interrupted, unless otherwise specified. For clarity, it is good practice to be explicit about what happens when the alternative flow ends. If the alternative flow does not resume at the extension point where it started, you will need to insert an additional extension point at the point at which the flow of events should resume. As with all extension points, use a descriptive name for the point.

Examples

Poor names for extension points

{Resume Processing}

{Continue Transaction}

The reason these names are poor is that they indicate that the transaction or processing has been interrupted by some alternative flow. Extension points should not reveal that an alternative flow exists. Try using the extension point name as a section heading that describes what happens in the next set of steps. This will improve readability and will render the use case more maintainable.

If an alternative flow can be performed at more than one place in the use case, it will need to resume at the next step after the initial extension point or terminate the use case. Resuming at different steps depending on where the use case was interrupted will make the alternative behavior very hard to understand.

Alternative Flows for Alternative Flows and Named Subflows

In the preceding sections, we simplified reality a bit by discussing alternative flows that apply only to the basic flow of events. In reality, an alternative flow or a named subflow can also have alternative flows. The mechanics of this are identical: An alternative flow can occur at any place in the use case, even in alternative flows themselves. When an alternative flow extends an alternative flow, be very clear about how each alternative flow ends. Let's assume that we have two alternative flows, A1 and A2, with A2 providing alternative behavior for A1. When A2 ends, does A1 resume, or does the basic flow resume? Either is possible and either may be correct; you will need to be explicit about what happens.

WRITING SPECIAL AND SUPPLEMENTARY SPECIFICATIONS

Special requirements are requirements (typically, nonfunctional) that apply to one or more use cases; *supplementary requirements* are requirements (also typically nonfunctional) that apply to the system as a whole. Both types of requirements represent things that the system must do that are difficult to capture in the context of the use-case description. Examples of special requirements include requirements related to performance of a particular use case or a particular part of a use case. If the performance requirement applies to only part of the use case, extension points can be used to limit the scope of the requirement. For example: All processing between {**Extension Point A**} and {**Extension Point B**} will be completed in under 1 second.

Special requirements can be captured in a number of ways:

- The special requirements can be added as a section of the use-case description. This is simple and practical when the special requirements apply to one or a few use cases. This approach is also useful when the special requirements apply only to a particular section of the use case, since they can easily refer to the extension points in the use-case description.

Presenting the special requirements as a section in the use-case description itself becomes impractical when they apply to several or many use cases, because of the additional effort required to maintain the special requirements when the use cases change.

- The special requirements can be captured in a requirements-management tool[1] and traced to the use cases to which they apply. This makes reporting and impact analysis easy and eliminates the overhead of maintaining requirements in the documents themselves. The disadvantage is that it is more difficult to refer to specific sections of the use case using extension points.

Supplementary requirements, because they typically apply to many or all use cases, are best handled in a requirements-management tool where they can be associated with use cases when necessary. Alternatively, supplementary requirements can be presented in a *Supplementary Requirements* document.

CAPTURING USE-CASE SCENARIOS

Capturing scenarios (a specific instance of a use case consisting of the basic flow plus none or other alternative flows) is useful for a number of reasons:

- The scenarios will match the test cases one for one, providing an important source of information for testing the system.
- Scenarios are what actually gets performed, so they are useful when discussing how the system will work in practice. This makes them useful for producing documentation, since the scenarios reflect how the system will be used.
- Scenarios are useful for analysis and design, since they help the developers think about how the system will be used.

To document a scenario, give it a descriptive name and simply enumerate the flows that comprise the scenario.

---

[1] Such as Rational RequisitePro™.

Example (for the *Withdraw Cash* use case)

> Scenario "Attempt to Use Stolen Card" : flows "Basic Flow," "Handle Stolen Bank Card"
>
> Scenario "Out of Cash": flows "Basic Flow", "Dispenser Empty"[*]
>
> Scenario "Withdrawal Successful": flow "Basic Flow"

[*] The alternative flow Dispenser Empty was not presented in the examples but would handle the case in which the ATM is out of cash.

When enumerating the scenarios, it is not necessary to describe the inputs and outputs, those will have to be documented in the test cases anyway, so there is no need to document the test data in the scenarios. The scenarios should be documented either as a separate section of the use-case description or as part of the associated test cases.

SUMMARY

In this chapter, we have learned more about how to write use-case descriptions using an extended example,[2] and in so doing have revisited the internal structure of the use case (the basic and alternative flows). We have also looked more closely at related concepts such as the glossary and how to use it in conjunction with the use cases as a way of managing detail and capturing common descriptions across use cases.

Use-case descriptions should be detailed; without the details, use cases fail to describe what the system will do and thereby become "useless cases." But sometimes detail can get in the way of understanding and prevent us from seeing what the system *really* does. The techniques summarized in Chapter 8 and applied here provide a number of ways to manage the detail without losing it entirely.

The glossary provides a way to define simple concepts that have limited interrelationships with other concepts. If the concepts are interrelated, a domain model can be used in conjunction with the glossary to represent the structural relationships among the concepts. Business rules and special requirements can provide additional detail to the use cases, allowing the use cases to focus on the "big picture" while still providing the details in supporting documentation. As with any art, the right approach blends a variety of techniques in proportions guided by experience.

---

[2] The full *Withdraw Cash* use-case description can be found in Appendix C.

We looked at ways of handling alternative and exception behavior, showing how simple alternative behavior can be represented in the basic flow itself and how more complex alternative behavior should be separated into a separate *alternative flow*.

We also discussed how *nonfunctional* (or nonbehavioral) requirements are handled in conjunction with use cases. Nonfunctional requirements define nonbehavioral qualities of the system that may need to be satisfied by various use cases (for example, performance, security, scalability, maintainability, reliability).

Armed with this information, you should be ready to try your hand at defining and developing basic use cases. Before you move on to more advanced topics, such as structuring the use-case model, it is important that you get some real experience with writing use cases. We have intentionally avoided discussing structuring the use-case model until after discussing how to write descriptions, having found disaster resulting almost universally when people try to impose a structure on the use-case model before they even know what they are structuring. Once you have written some use cases and worked with the techniques discussed in this chapter, you may find a need to introduce additional structure in the use-case model. At this point, you will be ready for the topics of Chapter 10, Here There Be Dragons.

Chapter 10

Here There Be Dragons

Those of you with some prior exposure to use-case modeling may have wondered why we have waited ten chapters to describe relationships in the use-case model other than simple communication between actors and use cases. There are several reasons, the most compelling of which is that the behavior of most systems can be described by collections of simple use cases that interact with their actors but otherwise have no other relationships. A more subtle reason is implied by the title of this chapter (taken from the warnings on old maps that dangers lie beyond). If there is one thing that sets teams down the wrong path, it is the misuse of the use-case relationships *include, extend,* and *generalization.*

It's uncertain why teams have such difficulty with these relationships. Perhaps we can blame it on a long tradition in Western culture of breaking big problems into smaller problems to make their solution easier. This approach works well when working with problems, but a use case is not a problem statement, it is the description of a solution to some problem. Breaking a solution description into component parts can sometimes help, but mostly it makes the solution harder to understand. If we break big use cases down into smaller and smaller use cases, we end up with a situation where we can no longer *see* the solution—it is too fragmented to understand. When this happens, we lose the value of use cases. They can no longer to be used to confirm our understanding of the solution, and they can no longer serve as a common language for all the stakeholders. The goal of the use case is to create shared understanding; in order to do so it must be understandable.

We have seen teams spend lots of time structuring the use-case model under the mistaken assumption that the structure of the model will have some significant effect on the architecture of the system. It won't, except to the extent that a system that has confusing and poorly understood requirements will probably also have a confusing and poorly understood architecture. Good systems have a purpose that is easy to understand and, more important, one that is understood by all members of the team. The structure of the use-case model bears no relationship to the architecture of the system under development. An overly structured use-case model obscures, rather than reveals, the real purpose of the system.

So, if the relationships between use cases are not meant to help us design the system, what is their intent? If they are to be useful at all, they must help us to better understand what the system is supposed to do. The focus of this chapter is to present the conditions under which creating relationships between use cases will aid understanding and to discuss the situations in which their careless use can lead to significant problems.

USING NAMED SUBFLOWS AND ALTERNATIVE FLOWS TO STRUCTURE TEXT

As discussed in Chapter 8, named subflows and alternative flows provide powerful techniques for structuring a use case's flow of events *without* resorting to creating relationships between the use cases. Named subflows allow reuse of common behavior within a single use case and often foreshadow the introduction of included behavior when the same behavior occurs in more than one use case. Similarly, alternative flows allow the introduction of optional or alternative behavior within a use case. These techniques should be used to their fullest before additional relationships between use cases are introduced. Many systems can be fully described using these techniques without the need to resort to any additional structuring of the use-case model.

DEFINING RELATIONSHIPS BETWEEN USE CASES

If most systems can be fully described using only use cases with relationships only to their actors, what would force us to add relationships between use cases, especially when we have already noted that most teams get into trouble when they try to use them? The simple answer is that two forces draw us toward using relationships. One force is commonality in behavior between two or more use cases, and the other is reducing complexity by isolating portions of use cases that may apply only in specific circumstances. When common behavior occurs, gathering it into a use case of its own *can* lead to improved readability and consistency of description. Similarly, if some behavior applies only in very specific contexts, separating that behavior into a use case of its own *can* make the rest of the use case easier to understand. The trick is knowing when to separate behavior into its own use case and when to leave well enough alone.

No matter what—and we cannot emphasize this enough—*do not introduce relationships between use cases until you have at least a draft of the flow of events of the use cases.* Outlining may seem sufficient, but it often lacks the detail necessary to see commonality (in the case of inclusion) or variation (in the case of extension). The only reason for introducing relationships is to deal with commonality and variations in the flows of events of the use cases; if you introduce them earlier, you are doing so without any real knowledge. Once you have at least drafted the use-case descriptions, commonality and variations will become obvious and you may safely proceed, *provided that introducing the relationships will increase the understandability of the use-case descriptions.*[1]

Using the Include *Relationship*

The *include* relationship provides the ability to extract common *sections* from two or more use-case descriptions and place them in a separate use case from which they can be referenced. The key point about this is that in order to use the *include* relationship, you must have the same descriptive text in at least two different use-case descriptions. This requires you to have actually written something. There are two critical mistakes that teams make that cause them to go awry with the *include* relationship. The first is that they introduce *included* use cases before they have written any descriptive text (working only with diagrams). The second is that they introduce use cases that are only included by one use case.

To understand how the *include* relationship can be used effectively, let's consider two different use cases that share repeated sections.

Example

Use Case—*Answer Customer Inquiries*
Basic Flow

1. The use case begins when the actor Customer calls the Customer Service Center Support Number.

2. The system opens a **customer service request (CSR)** and logs the date and time of the **call**.

3. The system then obtains the number of the phone from which the incoming **call** was placed.

(continued)

---

[1] Extension and Generalization were originally introduced by Ivar Jacobson. Inclusion came later, with the definition of UML 1.0.

4. The system records this in the **CSR** log entry.

5. The system then uses the **phone number** to determine whether there have been any prior **calls** placed from this number; if prior calls have been made, the system records references to the prior call information in the **CSR** and then routes the call to the next available Customer Service Representative and displays the **CSR** to them.

6. The Customer Service Representative enters the Customer's **identification number**.

7. The system determines whether the Customer's **personal information** is already on file.

8. If it is, the system then uses the **customer identification number** to determine whether there have been any prior **calls** placed by this Customer; if prior calls have been made, the system records references to the prior call information in the **CSR**.

9. If it is not, *the system asks the Customer Service Representative to capture*

   a. *the Customer's name (last name, first name, and middle initial)*

   b. *the mailing address (street address or post office box number, city, state or province, postal code, and the country)*

   c. *the phone number*

   d. *the hours during which the Customer can be contacted at that number*

   e. *an alternate contact phone number*

   f. *and the e-mail address*

10. *When the state or province is entered, the system checks to see if the state or province is valid for country entered.*

11. *The system also checks the postal code to see if it is valid for the country and province indicated.*

12. *The system stores the customer information and allocates the Customer the next available **customer identification number**.*

13. *The Customer Service Representative captures information about the preferred method of contact.*

14. The system adds the **customer identification number** to the **CSR**.

15. The Customer Service Representative then captures the product number of the **product** the customer is using.

16. The Customer Service Representative then captures, in textual form, the customer's question.

17. The system creates a new *inquiry* and stores the **question**.

[The remainder of use case is omitted for brevity and clarity.]

Use Case—*Order Products*

Basic Flow

1. The use case begins when the actor Sales Representative selects to place an **order**.

2. The system asks the Sales Representative to enter the customer's **customer identification number**.

3. If the customer is a new customer, *the Sales Representative records*

   a. *the customer's name (last name, first name, and middle initial)*

   b. *the mailing address (street address or post office box number, city, state or province, postal code, and the country)*

   c. *the phone number, the hours during which the customer can be contacted at that number*

   d. *an alternate contact phone number and the e-mail address*

   e. *When the state or province is entered, the system checks to see if the state or province is valid for country entered.*

   f. *The system also checks the postal code to see if it is valid for the country and province indicated.*

   g. *The Sales Representative records information about the preferred method of contact.* The Sales Representative then records the "ship-to" information, if it is different from the customer's billing address.

[The remainder of use case is omitted for brevity and clarity.]

From these two short use-case extracts, it is easy to see that there are some similarities in the text marked in *italics*. Perhaps there is an opportunity to record some of this information in a way that makes it easier to reuse. There are a couple of ways that we could do this.

First, we could define *customer information* in our glossary, recording the information that we need to capture about the customer. That will take away a lot of the common information, but we are still left with some common behavior that must be described. The *include* relationship enables us to separate this common text into a use case of its own, with references from the description in the *including* use cases to the *included* use case. A diagram showing the new use case and its relationships is presented in Figure 10-1.

In addition to being represented in the diagram, the *include relationship* manifests itself in the use-case descriptions. The following example shows the descriptions for all three use cases after we have extracted the common text into an included use case.

Figure 10-1 Updated use cases and their relationships

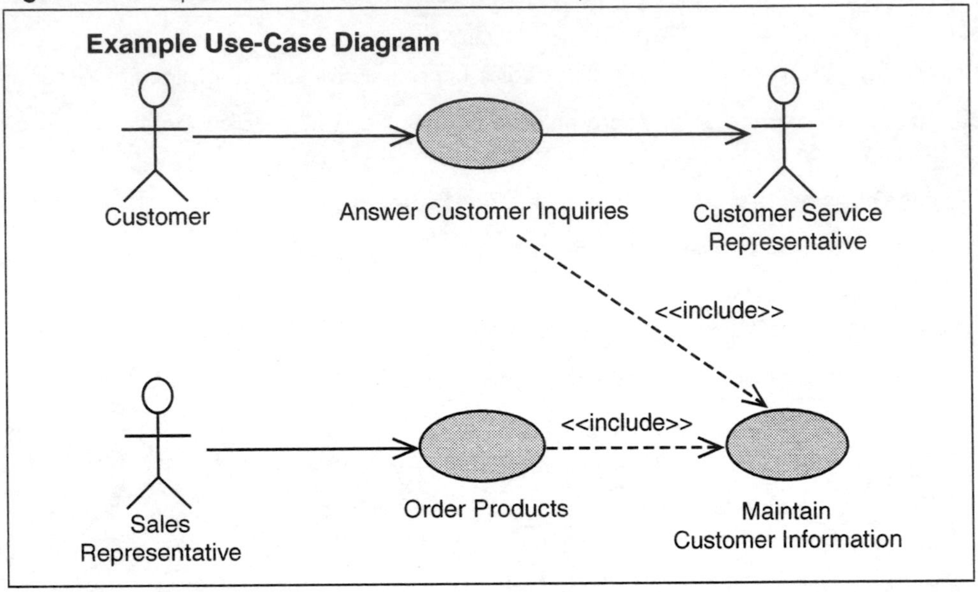

Example Use-Case Diagram

Customer — Answer Customer Inquiries — Customer Service Representative

<<include>>

Sales Representative — Order Products — <<include>> — Maintain Customer Information

Example

Use Case—*Answer Customer Inquiries*

Basic Flow

1. The use case begins when the actor Customer calls the Customer Service Center Support Number.

2. The system opens a **customer service request (CSR)** and logs the date and time of the **call**.

3. The system then obtains the number of the phone from which the incoming **call** was placed.

4. The system records this in the **CSR** log entry.

5. The system then uses the **phone number** to determine whether there have been any prior **calls** placed from this number.

6. If prior calls have been made, the system records references to the prior **call information** in the **CSR** and then routes the call to the next available Customer Service Representative and displays the **CSR** to them.

7. The Customer Service Representative enters the Customer's **identification number**.

8. The system determines whether the Customer's **personal information** is already on file.

9. If it is, the system then uses the **customer identification number** to determine whether there have been any prior **calls** placed by this Customer; if prior calls have been made, the system records references to the prior call information in the **CSR**.

10. If it is not, **include use case *Add Customer Information* so the Customer Service Representative can record information for this customer.** [*]

11. The system adds the **customer identification number** to the **CSR**.

12. The Customer Service Representative then captures the product number of the **product** the customer is using.

[The remainder of use case is omitted for brevity and clarity.]

Use Case—*Order Products*
Basic Flow

1. The use case begins when the actor Sales Representative selects to place an **order**.

2. The system asks the Sales Representative to enter the customer's **customer identification number.**

3. If the customer is a new customer, **include use case *Add Customer Information* so the Sales Representative can record information for this Customer.**

4. The Sales Representative then records the "ship-to" information, if it is different from the customer's billing address.

[The remainder of use case is omitted for brevity and clarity.]

Use Case—*Maintain Customer Information*
Brief Description

This use case is included by other use cases. It is used to add **customer information** for new Customers (see glossary for full definition). **Customer information** may be entered or modified in any order.

Basic Flow

1. The system prompts the user to enter the customer information.

2. When adding or modifying customer information:

   a. When the **state or province** is entered or changed, the system checks to see if the state or province is valid for the country entered.
   b. When the **postal code** is entered or changed, the system checks to see if it is valid for the **country** and **state or province** indicated.

3. The use case ends when the additions or changes to the customer information are saved, or the additions or changes are aborted.

---

[*] Note that in addition to the use-case name, we have added a brief explanation for the inclusion. This helps the reader to understand why the use case is being included.

Notice that by using an included use case, we have simplified the original use cases. We have also used the glossary to good effect, locating the definition of *customer information* there instead of cluttering our use cases with the information. Notice also that in creating the new included use case, we had to rewrite some of the descriptions in both the original use cases as well as in the new included use cases. In the original use cases, we removed the redundant description and inserted a reference to the included use case. In the included use case, we generalized the description so that it would be useable anywhere there is a need to add customer information.

An included use case should never be included by only one use case. If that happens, then it means that we have simply started to break down use cases into smaller use cases, with the result that we start to lose the thread of the use case. *Do* use techniques like the glossary or the domain model, or even appendices and reference documents to manage details, but *do not* use the include relationship to start breaking your use cases down into smaller use cases. Inclusion should only be used to manage common behavior.

One characteristic of an included use case is worth noting: It *never* has specific knowledge of the use cases that include it. The result is that included use cases are reuseable because they are not constrained by a particular context—they may be included by any use case without modification.

Common Errors Using the Include Relationship

The most common error is using the *include* relationship to perform a functional decomposition of the system. An example of this approach is treating the included use case as some sort of option in a menu, or a function. The error with using inclusion in this way is that the use case doing the including tends to become an empty shell—it often will have no real behavior of its own but becomes merely a dispatcher, calling other included use cases to do the real work. The included use cases, in turn, contain no common behavior and tend to be included by only one use case. The result is that none of the use cases, taken by themselves, provide any real value for a stakeholder of the system; they must be combined in some way to provide value. Since providing value is one of the key attributes of a use case, these *fragments of use cases* fail in at least one significant respect. A fragmented use-case model makes it very hard to see what the system does, and therefore it is very hard to tell if the system provides any value. The use cases, while perhaps technically correct, no longer convey a clear picture of what the system does and who it does it for. The more *structured* the model, the worse the problem.

Another common error is that behavior is added to the included use case outside the context of the use cases that include it. In the preceding example, it is very tempting to start to add behavior to cater to the update of existing customer information, the deletion of existing customers, or alternative and exceptional circumstances that could never occur within the context of the including use cases. Soon, the included use case takes on a life of its own as people continue to expand on its functionality without paying attention to the requirements of the original use cases where the need for the behavior was first identified. As well as causing uncontrolled and unintended scope creep, this often makes it impossible to identify the threads through the original use cases. When an include is used, it means that the whole of the included use case is part of the including use case and, therefore, that the entire included use case must be in place before any of the flows that include it.

Inclusion, when it is used at all, should clarify understanding, not impede it. If you find that use cases have been created for each function the system can perform, reorganize your use cases so that the value provided to the customer is evident in the names of the use case. Take each "functional" use case and turn it into a major subflow in the use-case description of the larger, value-oriented use case. This will reduce the total number of use cases, making the use-case model easier to understand at a glance, while still providing structure to the definition of the behavior of the system.

Using the Extend Relationship

The *extend* relationship is used in cases where *optional* or *exceptional* behavior is *inserted into* an existing use case. The original purpose of extension was to provide a mechanism for specifying options that could be added to an existing product, such as adding a feature for voice mail to an existing telephony switch. It is helpful to think of the *extend* relationship as being an *add to* relationship, since it always adds behavior to an existing use case. The defining characteristic of the *extending* use case is that it requires no changes in the use cases it extends. This means that the *extended* use case must be able to stand alone; it must be complete, without any need for extension in order to provide value.

Circumstances that may warrant *extension* include

- Descriptions of features that are optional to the basic behavior of the system. Examples of this include behavior that may be optionally purchased, either from the original provider of the system or from third parties.
- Descriptions of complex error- or exception-handling behavior that would otherwise obscure the primary behavior of the system. Examples of this are alternative flows that are of significant length, especially those that are longer than the main flow of the use case.
- Customization of the requirements model for specific customer needs. Examples of this include alternative flows that specify how specific

customers handle different conditions that occur within the same standard use case.

- Scope and release management. Examples of this include behavior that will not be introduced until later releases.

Unlike the *included* use case, the *extending* use case is by necessity aware of the use case that it extends (henceforth called the *base* use case). It always extends a base use case at one or more extension points or under particular conditions. As a result, it is very unusual for a use case to extend more than one use case, since it is unlikely that more than one use case could have sufficiently common flows of events to enable effective extension.[2]

Conceptually, the mechanics of how an extending use case works is identical to that of an alternative flow. An extending use case explicitly inserts itself into the flows of the use case it is extending, just like an alternative flow, only the extending use case knows where in the base use case the behavior will be inserted. As a result, an extending use case will often begin life as an alternative flow.

Not every alternative flow can be turned into an extending use case. The rules for alternative flows are looser than those for extending use cases. Because alternative flows are part of the use case, they can exploit their knowledge of the use case's state, preconditions, and other flow of events to end the use case or to resume the flow of the use case at extension points other than the one from which they assumed control. *All extending use cases know about is the extension point at which they insert themselves into the flow of events of the use case that they extend.* This enables the extended use case to be evolved without the need to worry about or consider the extending use cases.

The easiest way to understand extension is with a simple banking transaction processing example (see also Figure 10-2):

Figure 10-2 Basic *Process Transactions* use case diagram

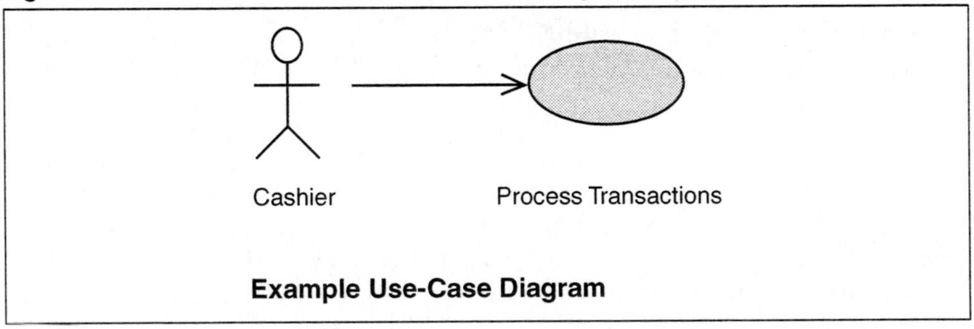

Cashier   Process Transactions

Example Use-Case Diagram

---

[2] It is possible for a use case to extend a use case that is included by other use cases. One must be careful in doing this, lest the use cases become hard to understand because they are split into so many parts.

Example

Use Case—*Process Transactions**

Brief Description

Processes **transactions** against the **customer**'s bank **account**.

Basic Flow

1. The use case begins when the actor Cashier initiates transaction processing for a set of **unprocessed transactions**.

2. The system orders the **transactions** so that all **transactions** for a particular **account** are grouped together, and within this grouping the **deposit transactions** are processed first to avoid unnecessary **overdraft** processing.

3. For each **account**:

   {Determine Customer Account}

   a. The system determines the **customer account** to which the **transaction** is applied.

   b. For each **transaction**:

      {Apply Transaction}

      i. The system applies the **transaction** to the **customer account**. **Deposit transactions** increase the balance of the **account**; **withdrawal transactions** decrease the balance of the **account**.

      {Record Transaction}

      ii. The system records the **transaction information** to a log to ensure a permanent record of the **transaction**.

      iii. The system marks the **transaction** as **completed**.

      {Summarize Transactions}

      iv. When all **transactions** for a particular **account** have been processed, the system creates a **transaction summary** for the **account**.

4. When all **transactions** have been processed, the use case ends.

A1 *Alternate Flow: Account Not Found*

At **{Determine Customer Account}**, if the **customer account** is not found:

The system marks all **transactions** for the **account** as **suspended transactions**.

Processing continues for the next account at **{Determine Customer Account}**.

(continued)

---

* This is also an example of how use cases can be used to describe batch processing.

A2 *Handle Account Overdrawn Without Overdraft Protection*

At {**Apply Transaction**}, if the **transaction** causes an overdraft (the **account** balance goes negative) and the **account** has no **overdraft protection**:

The system applies the **transaction** and marks the **transaction** as "overdraft."

The system applies an **overdraft fee** against the **account**.

Processing continues at {**Record Transaction**}.

A3 *Handle Account Overdrawn with Overdraft Protection*

At {**Apply Transaction**}, if the **transaction** causes an overdraft (the **account** balance goes negative) and the **account** has **overdraft protection**:

If the transaction does not cause the account to exceed the **maximum overdraft allowance** specified for the **customer**, the system apples the **transaction** to the **customer account**.

Processing continues at {**Record Transaction**}.

[Other alternative flows, including the one to handle exceeding the **maximum overdraft allowance**, are omitted for the sake of brevity and clarity.]

This sort of system has been around for years, since the days when nearly all applications were *batch processing* applications. Let's assume that the company that provides this application has decided to update the application to use the latest technology, allowing the bank customer to be notified of the overdraft through a variety of electronic means, including e-mail, voice mail, or instant messages, according to preference. Because the *Process Transactions* use case is already complete in itself, the best way to describe this new behavior is to write a new use case that *extends* the existing use case (see also Figure 10-3).

Example

Use Case—*Notify of Overdraft*

Brief Description

This use case notifies the customer that the account has become overdrawn. This service is only available if the customer has purchased the overdraft notification service.

Extension

Extensions use case *Process Transactions* at {**Summarize Transactions**} if the **customer** has purchased the **overdraft notification** service and the set of **completed transactions** has caused the **account** to become **overdrawn**.

Basic Flow

1. The system determines the **customer**'s preferred **notification mechanism**, as recorded in the **customer profile**.

2. The system composes the **overdraft notification**, providing the **transaction information**, the date and time the **transaction** was processed, the **account information**,* the balance prior to the **transaction**, the balance subsequent to the **transaction**, and the amount of the **overdraft fee**, if any.

3. The **system** transmits the overdraft notification message to the customer using the **customer**'s preferred **notification mechanism**.

4. The use case ends.†

[For the sake of brevity and clarity the alternative flows, including the ones to handle there being no completed customer profile and communications failure, are omitted.]

---

* For the sake of simplifying the example, we won't worry about the wisdom of transmitting account information over potentially unsecured media, although a real solution would have to contend with this issue.

† This indicates that the extending use case does **not** end the use case being extended. Extending use cases cannot end the use cases they extend. Remember that extending use cases **must** return to the extension point from which they took control.

Figure 10-3   A base use case, *Process Transactions*, being extended

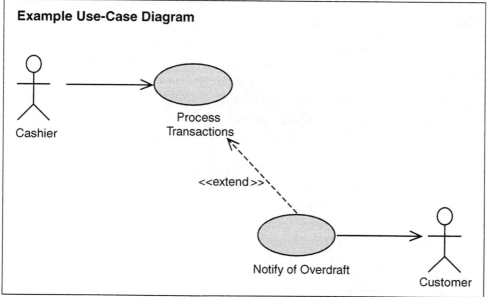

Example Use-Case Diagram

Cashier

Process Transactions

<<extend>>

Notify of Overdraft

Customer

This simple example illustrates the appropriate usage and benefits of *extension*: By enabling us to describe *add-on* features of the system in a simple way, separate from the base system itself, it simplifies the description of the system and makes it easier to understand. If an alternative flow is primarily providing behavior that is optional, meaning that the system could be delivered without it, it could be considered a candidate for becoming an extending use case. The decision to make it an extending use case should be based on these considerations:

- Making it a separate use case makes it easier to manage from a versioning and configuration perspective.
- The use cases will actually be owned and maintained by different people, perhaps because different expertise is required for the extension.
- Separating it from the original use case makes both use cases easier to understand.

Extension could also be used to describe complex exception processing that would otherwise make the basic behavior system hard to understand.

The key thing to keep in mind about extension is that it *always adds* behavior to a use case. Because the base use case must remain intact and valuable on its own, the extension cannot modify the base use case. The basic behavior of the use case always remains intact.

Extension Points, Revisited

As introduced in Chapter 7, The Structure and Contents of a Use Case, **extension points** are named places in the flow of events where additional behavior can be inserted or attached. We introduced the notion in Chapter 7 that there are *private* extension points, visible only within the use case in which they occur, and *public* extension points, which are visible to extending use cases. Now that we have introduced extension, we should explore this statement further.

Extension points provide an easily readable way to refer to a particular location in the use-case description. This is useful because it removes the need to refer to step numbers (which tend to change) or to describe a synopsis of the use case to establish location (such as "the point after which the card has been validated but before the transaction proceeds"). The reason for introducing private and public scope to extension points is to reduce complexity. Since both alternative flows and extending use cases need to be inserted at a particular location within a use case, it is logical to have a single location reference mechanism to define this "insertion" or "extension" point. Within the flow of events extension points are shown in bold, enclosed in curly brackets.[3]

The difference between alternative flows and extending use cases is that alternative flows are contained within the same use case to which they refer. In addition, alternative flows are more numerous than extending use cases, and so it is typical for the extension points they use to be more numerous. Since most of these extension points are only meaningful for the alternative flows and not for extending use cases, we have made the distinction between these extension points, which are "private" in scope, and the extension points that may be referred to by extending use cases, which are "public" in scope.

Since public extension points represent a kind of "protocol" for the use case, special attention is paid to them when documenting the use case. Public extension points are enumerated in a separate section of the use-case description, as shown in the following example:

Example

Use Case—*Browse Products and Place Orders*
Public Extension Points

{Display Product Catalogue}

{Out of Stock}

{Process the Order}

{Order Processed}

Public extension points can be shown as part of the use case on use-case diagrams in a compartment named extension points, as shown in Figure 10-4. Declaring an extension point to be public indicates that it can be used by any extending use case to add behavior to the base use case. Not all extensions will be

Figure 10-4 Showing public extension points on a use-case diagram

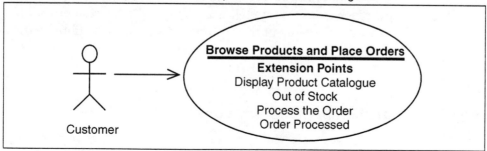

---

[3] There are other ways of showing extension points, but this is the one we prefer and is therefore the one that we have used throughout this book.

made public, nor should they be made public. Only the extension points that represent locations at which the use case can be extended should be made public.

In most cases, the public extension points section will simply enumerate the extension points that appear in the use-case description that should be made public. It is also possible for the public extension points section to declare extension points that do not appear in the use-case description. The reason for doing this is to prevent the use-case description from having to be modified in order for behavior to be added to it. This is essential in cases where use-case descriptions may be under strict configuration control and cannot be modified by the team adding the extending behavior. The format of the extension point declaration is

```
{extension-point name}
    at <some location in the use-case description>, or
    before <some location in the use-case description>, or
    after <some location in the use-case description>
```

The location description is informally described, such as "after the card is validated," or "before currency is dispensed."

Evaluating the Resulting Use-Case Model

The basic use cases of the system should reflect the essential value provided by the system. It should be possible to look at these use cases, excluding any included or extending use cases, and be able to understand what the system principally does for its stakeholders. Included and extending use cases should fill in more of the details, but they do not fundamentally change the principal value provided by the system. If you choose to use included or extending use cases, examine the model to make sure that their introduction has not changed the use-case model for the worse. If you remove all of the included and extending use cases from the model, the purpose of the system should still be clear. If the principle value of the system is still understandable without reference to any of the included or extending use cases, then you are probably on the right track.

Using Generalization Between Use Cases

The *included* use case gives us a way to share significant sections of common description among use cases, and the *extending* use case gives us the ability to add significant new behavior to an existing use case. Although these are powerful techniques, neither allows us to describe those situations where we wish to generalize or specialize a use case. The generalization relationship allows us to create generalized behavior descriptions that we can then specialize to meet particular needs.

So why would we want to do this?

The impetus to generalize use cases arises from the need to describe *families of systems*. Suppose we are developing a telecommunications service billing system that we would like to market to companies large and small. In order to meet the needs of these varied firms, we need a system that is very flexible. How can we express the variability of this kind of system without the flexibility of the system becoming so complex that the use cases become impossible to understand? The solution is *generalization* combined with *extension* to describe the optional features of the system. As before, it's easier to understand this from an example.

Let's consider our now-familiar ATM and assume that we work for a firm that produces software for ATMs. Let's assume that we would like to expand our business into new areas, since the market for ATMs is growing more slowly than we would like. One morning, while on the way to work, we need some fuel in our automobile. While standing at the pump at the gas station, it occurs to us that the sequence of steps one goes through to purchase gas using a bank card is very similar to the sequence of steps that one goes through to withdraw cash from an ATM. The diagram of the use cases and actors is presented in Figure 10-5. Perhaps we can exploit this similarity to expand our ATM software business into new areas.

Figure 10-5   Use cases for *Withdraw Cash* and *Fuel Vehicle*

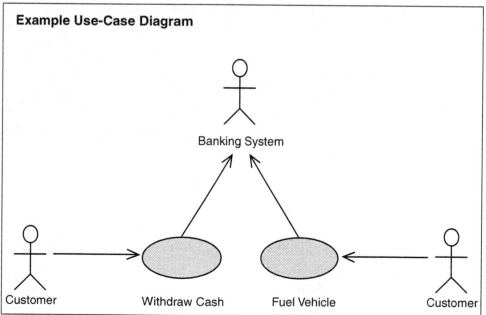

Example Use-Case Diagram

Banking System

Customer   Withdraw Cash   Fuel Vehicle   Customer

Once at the office, we start outlining the basic flow of events for the ATM *Withdraw Cash* use case and the gas pump *Fuel Vehicle* use case:

Withdraw Cash (ATM)	Fuel Vehicle (Fuel Pump)
Brief Description	**Brief Description**
Provides the customer with the ability to withdraw cash from a bank account using an automated teller machine.	Provides customers with the ability to fuel their vehicle, paying for the fuel directly from their bank account.
Basic Flow	**Basic Flow**
1. The Customer inserts a **bank card** into the ATM.	1. The Customer inserts a **bank card** into the pump.
2. The system reads the **customer account information** from the **bank card**.	2. The system reads the **customer account information** from the **bank card**.
3. The system requests the Customer to enter the **PIN**.	3. The system requests the Customer to enter the **PIN**.
4. The Customer enters a **PIN**.	4. The Customer enters a **PIN**.
5. The system verifies that the **PIN** entered is correct by comparing it to the **PIN** that was read from the **bank card**.	5. The system verifies that the **PIN** entered is correct by comparing it to the **PIN** that was read from the **bank card**.
6. The system contacts the Banking System to verify that the **customer account information** is valid.	6. The system contacts the Banking System to verify that the **customer account information** is valid.
7. The system asks for an amount to withdraw. The Customer enters an amount.	7. The system asks for the amount of fuel to be dispensed. The Customer enters an amount.
8. The system contacts the Banking System to verify that the Customer has sufficient funds to cover the withdrawal.	8. The system contacts the Banking System to verify that the Customer has sufficient funds to cover the withdrawal.
9. The system checks to see if it has sufficient funds on hand to dispense the requested amount.	9. The system asks the Customer to lift the **pump handle** and begin dispensing **fuel**.
10. The system dispenses the requested amount and records the amount dispensed.	10. The Customer dispenses the desired amount of **fuel**, or until the vehicle is full. When done, the Customer replaces the pump handle.
11. The Customer takes the cash.	11. The system records the amount dispensed.
12. The system communicates that the **transaction** has been completed to the Banking System.	12. The system communicates that the **transaction** has been completed to the Banking System.

Withdraw Cash (ATM)	Fuel Vehicle (Fuel Pump)
13. The system logs the transaction, capturing the date and time of the transaction, the amount dispensed, and the **account** from which the funds were withdrawn.	13. The system logs the transaction, capturing the date and time of the **transaction**, the amount dispensed, and the **account** from which the funds were withdrawn.
14. The use case ends.	14. The use case ends.

If we look carefully at this example, the first six steps of the two use cases are virtually identical and steps 7–9 are very similar. The final steps in each use case are also very similar.

What if we wanted to define a framework for a general-purpose dispenser device, one that could dispense cash, or fuel, or theatre tickets, or even train tickets with only a few small changes? If we wanted to build such a system, we would want to have a set of use cases for the general-purpose dispenser, with specialized use cases for the specific customizations of this device. We can see from the example that neither extension nor inclusion could provide us with a good way to describe the general behavior. Inclusion of the various common parts of the use cases would leave us with very fragmented use cases. Extension does not provide a good way to express the variability in the framework, to expose the specific points at which the common behavior is specialized.

The solution is to create an abstract use case, *Conduct Financial Transaction*, that represents the dispenser framework, with specialized use cases *Withdraw Cash* and *Fuel Vehicle*. This is represented visually in Figure 10-6. The important parts of the use cases, however, are the use-case descriptions. These look as follows:

Examples

Conduct Transaction *(abstract use case)*

Brief Description

Provides the customer with the ability to receive goods from an automated dispenser, paying for them by an automated withdrawal from a bank account.

Basic Flow

1. The actor Customer inserts a bank card into the dispenser machine.

2. The system reads the **customer account information** from the bank card.

3. The system requests the Customer to enter the **PIN**.

4. The Customer enters a **PIN**.

5. The system verifies that the **PIN** entered is correct by comparing it to the **PIN** that was read from the **bank card**.

(continued)

6. The system contacts the Banking System to verify that the **customer account information** is valid.

7. The system asks for an amount of the **transaction**. The Customer enters an amount.

8. The system contacts the Banking System to verify that the Customer has sufficient funds to cover the **transaction**.

{The Customer Conducts the transaction}

9. The system records the amount of the **transaction**.

10. The system communicates that the **transaction** has been completed to the Banking System.

11. The system logs the **transaction**, capturing the date and time of the **transaction**, the amount of the **transaction**, and the **account** from which the funds were withdrawn.

12. The use case ends.

Withdraw Cash *(concrete use case)*

Brief Description

Specializes *Conduct Transaction* to enable a customer to withdraw cash from an Automated Teller Machine (ATM).

Basic Flow

At {The Customer Conducts the Transaction}:

1. The system checks to see if it has sufficient funds on hand to dispense the requested amount.

2. The system dispenses the requested amount of cash.

3. The system asks the Customer to take the cash.

4. The Customer takes the cash.

5. The behavior described in use case *Conduct Transaction* resumes.

Fuel Vehicle *(concrete use case)*

Brief Description

Specializes *Conduct Transaction* to enable a customer to obtain fuel from a fuel pump by paying directly from a bank account.

Basic Flow

At {The Customer Conducts the Transaction}:

1. The system asks the Customer to lift the pump handle and begin dispensing fuel.

2. The Customer dispenses fuel up to the value of the amount entered, or until the tank is full.

3. The Customer replaces the pump handle.

4. The behavior described in use case *Conduct Transaction* resumes.

Figure 10-6 Use-case generalization and specialization represented visually

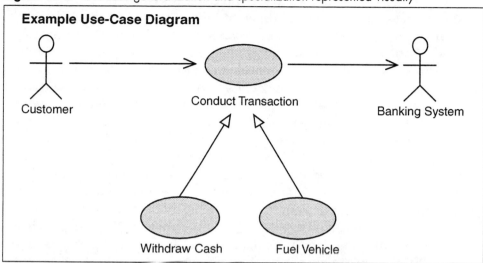

In cases where specialization is used, it is important to recognize that it is the specialized use cases that are actually performed. They reuse parts of the generalized use case. In a sense, specialization has the mechanics of an include, since it reuses description in another use case (in this case, the generalized use case), but the semantics of an extend, since it is the specialized use case that provides the additional behavior. When the specialized use case is performed, behavior from both the generalized and specialized use case is performed, as visualized in Figure 10-7.

Figure 10-7 Behavioral "flow of control" in specialized and generalized use cases

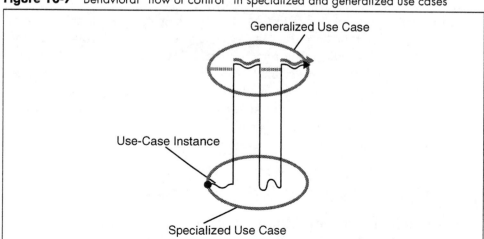

Specialization makes it easy to see the common behavior and how and where it is specialized to provide different kinds of similar behavior. In addition, the resulting use cases become easier to read and understand. Specialization is a powerful technique for simplifying the description of similar behavior. Specialization, like extension, always adds behavior or overrides existing behavior. It utilizes the same *extension point* mechanism as extension. Unlike extension, specialization is used to refine the description of behavior. A generalized use case may be useable in its own right, but more probably it is abstract, meaning that it cannot be performed without being specialized. The value of specialization is that it simplifies complex descriptions.

A use case may be specialized at any number of extension points. The example shown shows specialization at only a single extension point to simplify the presentation. If we were to refine our example, we would find that further specialization would be required at a number of other points, such as printing the receipt, handling the card, and a number of other areas. As with extension, specialization only occurs at public extension points. At this point, it may sound like specialization and extension are the same things, since both *add* behavior to some existing use case. Although that much is true, they serve different purposes and work in different ways.

A single use case can be extended by more than one extending use case. The extended use case is the one that the actor starts and it must be "complete and meaningful" on its own, as there is a possibility that none of the extensions will be performed. When the extended use case is performed, the extending behavior is *inserted* into the flow of events when certain conditions occur. As a result, extensions affect the instances of the use case. Because multiple extensions can occur, the behavior of the use-case instance derives it behaviors from not only the base use-case but also some set of extending use cases.

Contrast this with specialization. In this case, it is the specialized use case that is started and not the base use case. The base use case, therefore, does not need to be "complete and meaningful"—in fact, it will have blanks in it that are to be completed by the specializations. When the specialized use case is performed, it follows only itself (some of which derives from its parent or parents). If more than one use case specializes a base use case, an instance of the use case follows only one of the specialized use cases. So, as you can see, extension and generalization are quite different.

DEFINING RELATIONSHIPS BETWEEN ACTORS

The only relationship *between* actors is *generalization*. Generalization is used to show similarity between actors. The main value in this is to show that some group of actors share common responsibilities or common characteristics. It is never used to reflect security permissions; security needs to be enforced by the system and therefore needs to be described in the use cases. Actors, by definition, are outside the system.

Useful characteristics to attach to actors include things that the testers will need to know about the actors, such as their expertise, the things that they need from the system, and the useability and response requirements the actors impose on the system. The actor generalization shown in Figure 10-8 illustrates that the Field Sales Representative and the Telesales Representative inherit the characteristics of the Sales Representative. This also means that they inherit the Sales Representative's *communicates* relationships, with the use cases with which it interacts, and the set of user types it is associated with.

Sometimes, the use of actor generalization can simplify the use-case model by reducing the number of communicates relationships required, but usually it is of little or no use. The use of actor generalization is typically a symptom of the modelers confusing the actors with organizational roles and job titles (as discussed in Chapter 3, Establishing the Vision, and Chapter 4, Finding Actors and Use Cases). It is often a misguided attempt to model the organization's communications, authority levels, and reporting hierarchies using actors. Remember that the actors only define roles with respect to the system that the users can take on, and nothing more.

Figure 10-8 Actor generalization and specialization represented visually

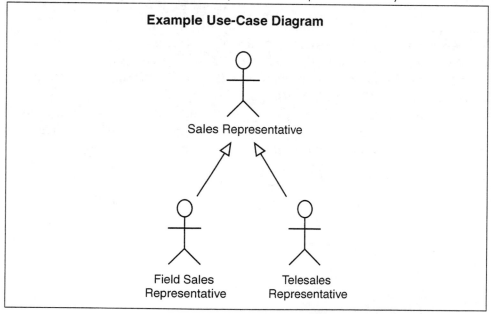

Example Use-Case Diagram

Sales Representative

Field Sales
Representative

Telesales
Representative

There is no need for any other relationships between actors, as they do not communicate with one another. Some people find this strange—people who will play the actors will of course interact with one another in the organization in which the system exists. The point is that since these interactions do not directly involve the system, they are outside the scope of the system. Athough it is tempting to try to turn the *system* use-case model into a model of the business, that will only confuse everyone. As discussed in an earlier chapter, a *system* use-case model is completely different from a use-case model of the business, so in the system use-case model we ignore things that happen outside the system. This enables us to focus on understanding what the system does for its actors.

SUMMARY

The relationships between use cases are problematic. Although powerful, they typically lead the inexperienced use-case modeler into dangerous terrain. Inappropriately applied, the *include, extend,* and *generalization* relationships lead to fragmented, overly structured models that resemble more complex designs than the simple descriptions of behavior that use-case models should be. When used correctly, the use-case relationships should simplify the use-case descriptions, not complicate them. The use-case relationships are summarized in Table 10-1.

It is not by accident that the examples we have presented have focused on use-case descriptions and not diagrams. The real value of the relationships comes not from their representation in use-case diagrams, but their effect on the use-case descriptions. As a result, use-case relationships should *never, ever* be introduced before fairly detailed descriptions have been written. Until descriptions have been written, there is not enough information present to justify the introduction of relationships. As we have stressed throughout this book, the use-case model is primarily a vehicle for facilitating communication and agreement among the stakeholders. Extending the communication metaphor, the use of use-case relationships can be compared to swearing: If used in moderation, and at the appropriate time, they can be very effective in communicating your message, but if overused, or used inappropriately, they will distract from the message, often putting people off so much that they ignore your message entirely.[4]

---

[4] As they say to children who swear in the UK, "It's not big or clever."

Table 10-1 Summary of Use-Case Relationships

Relationship	Graphical Representation	Meaning
include	`- - - - - - - ->` `<< include >>`	Specifies that the source (including) use case explicitly incorporates the behavior of the target (included) use case at a location specified by the source use case. Used to share behavior between use cases.
extend	`- - - - - - - ->` `<< extend >>`	Specifies that the source (extending) use case extends the behavior of the target (extended) use case at a given extension point. Used to add optional behavior to use cases without their knowledge.
generalization	`————————▷`	Specifies that the source (specialized) use case specializes the target (generalized) use case. Used to create general-purpose framework use cases that can be specialized to provide variations of the general behavior to cater to specific customizations of the system.

Chapter 11

Reviewing Use Cases

Reviews are often neglected. In the course of the project, effort is typically focused on producing artifacts—requirements, use cases, test cases, code itself—but often little time is given to reviewing these artifacts. This is a grave error; reviews are an excellent and inexpensive way of spotting errors early enough to do something about them.

The typical error with use cases is that they tend to be written and more or less forgotten; they are often never really reviewed with the stakeholders to ensure that the team has the right understanding of the required behavior. This is not entirely the fault of the development team; it is often difficult to get stakeholders to take an active interest in reviewing use cases. Nevertheless, if you can't get the stakeholders to review the use cases, you'll never know whether they are correct. Similarly, use cases cannot be just "thrown over the wall" to developers. Time must be spent to ensure that the entire team understands the use cases. Furthermore, developers often discover important omissions in the use cases. If they can't understand the use cases sufficiently well to design and develop the system, there is often something missing.

The time taken to review the use cases is well spent: It helps to improve the quality of the use cases, but more important, it helps to improve communication among team members. Remember, the purpose of reviews is to gather feedback and to ascertain correctness. Reviews are not intended to share information. Too often, review meetings will become large and unfocused because of too many attendees who are in the meeting to gather information, not to participate. To avoid this problem, separate review and communication meetings, so that reviews can focus on improving and approving the use case. Hold separate meetings to present the results from the reviews to the broader set of stakeholders. Include only those people in reviews who are empowered to make decisions.

WHY FOCUS ON PRESENTING AND REVIEWING USE CASES?

Use cases can be strange to people who have not seem them before. Taking time to explain the purpose and presentation of the use case can make the task faced by reviewers much easier. Explaining what use cases and actors are need not take long; presenting a few slides and working through a simple example can be an immense help to the reviewer and offers a good return on an investment of an hour or so of time. Without providing background to the reviewers, there is a strong risk of confusion as to the goals and objectives of the review session.

Example

A development team had worked for some time on a number of use cases and was ready for review by the subject-matter experts from the business area. The development team presented use cases to the subject-matter experts (several technical users) for the first time without any kind of explanation of the purpose of the use cases, their format and organization, or the anticipated roles of the review-meeting participants. The result was a meeting lasting many hours and producing a great deal of frustration for all parties concerned.

Regrouping from this disaster, the team briefly explained the use-case approach, explaining the purpose of use cases and their format. They also explained the roles people would play in the review—the development team would present the use cases, soliciting feedback on whether the use cases correctly captured the desired behavior of the system. Once the users understood the role they were expected to play and how to understand what was being presented to them, the next review meeting took less than 30 minutes and was called "the most effective meeting we have ever had with development" by the users.

As a final observation, keep in mind that many people won't read more than a few pages of text, and even when they do, they may be unaccustomed to reading with a critical eye and providing constructive feedback. In these cases, it can be useful to conduct *walk-through* sessions using storyboards, essentially stepping through the use case using visualizations of the user interface and discussing the things that the users do to interact with the system and the things that the system does in response. This is not to say that the use cases are not useful—they are valuable tools for examining the behavior of the system—it's just that the written documents may not be the most effective facilitation technique.

Keep this in mind: The goal in a review session is not to validate or approve the use cases, it is to uncover flaws in the understanding represented by the use cases. Much in the same way that the goal of testing is not to verify that the system is free from defects but rather to uncover defects that would otherwise go undetected, the goal of use-case review sessions is to uncover misunderstandings so that they can be corrected before additional work is undertaken. As a result, facilitation techniques should be used to maximize the amount of interactive discussion directed at making sure the use cases describe the way that the system should work. Don't just circulate documents for review.

TYPES OF REVIEWS

Reviews can be either formal or informal. Informal reviews tend to be held frequently, on an ad hoc basis, to gather feedback on the evolving use cases. Formal reviews tend to occur at major milestones, to confirm that the project is ready to proceed to the next phase. Informal reviews are low-cost and light-weight and are valuable for their immediacy. Formal reviews are more expensive and are therefore used infrequently, primarily to make major decisions about the status of the project.

The most common mistake made with respect to reviews is that teams do not have enough informal reviews and too many formal reviews. The result is that the use cases have not been adequately discussed by the time the formal review is conducted, and so the formal reviews tend to be too long and poorly focused.

Informal Reviews

Informal reviews often take the form of walk-throughs, in which the author of the use case steps through some or all of the use-case descriptions for the purpose of getting feedback. A useful technique is to use a *use-case storyboard,* usually composed of a series of screen shots of a user interface prototype, to step through some part of the use case. Use-case storyboards are an effective way of presenting and gathering feedback on the flow of events of a use case. Use-case descriptions, while important for capturing the details, are sometimes difficult for busy people to read and understand. If the main purpose of the review is to confirm your understanding of the flow of events (and not necessarily the details), use-case storyboards are a useful tool.

Use-case storyboards are powerful tools for bringing the use cases to life. The screen shots used in the storyboards are typically provided by prototypes of the user interface. Development of the user interface prototype and the use cases occurs in parallel, so it is natural to use the user interface prototype to *enact* the use case in informal reviews. Doing so provides feedback on both the user interface and the use-case flow of events.

Informal reviews can also consist of circulating the use-case descriptions for comment. We have found this to be less effective than using walk-throughs with use-case storyboards. The reasons for this are various, but the common theme is that reading detailed descriptions is hard work and most people do not have the time or attention span to be effective reviewers. We emphasize *most*, so if you have found it to be effective, count yourself among the fortunate.

Formal Reviews

Formal reviews should be reserved for approval and sign-off, not for gathering feedback. A typical but unproductive scenario is to schedule one large review with many attendees who have not yet seen the use cases and then try to review the use cases with the purpose of "approving" them by the close of the meeting.

A more effective formal review approach is to use a number of informal reviews to obtain agreement that the details of the use cases are correct, and then use the formal review to review the results of the informal reviews, communicating to the attendees the results from the informal reviews. The formal review is, in a sense, a review of the informal reviews and not a review in itself. At the end of the formal review, a decision is made either that the use case is *complete enough to move ahead*[1] or that it needs more work.

WHAT TO REVIEW, AND WHEN TO REVIEW IT

The following kinds of reviews are needed:

- **Reviewing the use-case model, following identification of actors and use cases.** The focus of this review is to ensure that the use cases and actors have been identified, gaining agreement that the names, brief descriptions, and associations are correct. Early in the project, this

---

[1] It is important in an iterative project lifecycle that we not unwittingly impose restrictions that the use case must be wholly complete before any design, development or testing work can begin. Frequently, a use case will be completed in parts, a flow at a time. The main flow may be completed in one iteration, while several alternative flows may be completed in subsequent iterations. The main benefit to use-case modeling from an iterative approach is that it may be impossible to fully assess the quality or completeness of a use case until one tries to develop from it or test it. This is especially true of use cases written by teams new to the technique.

review will be limited to the most important use cases. Once the project is underway, the team needs to also ensure that *all* use cases have been identified.

- **Reviewing the outlines of sets of conceptually related use cases.** The focus of this review is to ensure that the behavior of similar use cases has been partitioned effectively and that each use case identified provides observable value to the actors and stakeholders. Undertaken early in the project, this review will be limited to sets of use cases that address similar areas of behavior (say, all of the sales-related use cases in an order-management system).[2]

- **Reviewing each use case, once descriptions are written.** The focus of this review is to ensure that the use-case description is accurate, gaining agreement that the use case describes *all* relevant behavior needed to achieve the intended result. If the use case is being developed iteratively, the review team must be clear on what parts of the use case are intended to be complete at the time of the review. If the use case description being reviewed relies upon an *included* use case, the included use case must be reviewed at the same time. If the use case being reviewed *extends* another use case, the extended use case must be available to the participants of the review and have been previously reviewed, if it is not to be reviewed at the same time.

In the context of the Rational Unified Process, reviewing the use-case model will occur toward the end of the Inception Phase,[3] and at any subsequent time when new use cases are identified. Reviewing use-case descriptions tends to occur in every iteration in the Elaboration and Construction phases. It is often useful to attempt some analysis of the use cases before they are reviewed; the process of having to allocate use-case behavior to analysis elements forces a deep consideration of the use-case description that often uncovers errors. Similarly, it is a useful exercise to try to develop test cases from the use case because that forces a deep examination of the use case. For this reason, it is always a good idea to include developers and testers as participants in use-case reviews.

---

[2] During this review we are not considering the use of include and extend (that would come later if required), but addressing the number of use cases required to address the key areas of functionality. In the ATM machine case, it is one use case called *Undertake Financial Transaction* or a multiple use case, one for each type of transaction: *Withdraw Cash, Deposit Funds, and so on.*

[3] If you are not familiar with the four phases of the Rational Unified Process (Inception, Elaboration, Construction, and Transition), we explain these in more detail in the Use Cases Across the Life cycle section of Chapter 12, Wrapping Up.

Who Should Review the Use Cases

Use cases need to be reviewed from a number of different perspectives, including

- **The affected business areas.** Use cases should be reviewed by subject-matter experts and representatives of the business areas affected to confirm that they describe the desired behavior and accurately reflect the target domain.
- **Software development.** Developers should review the use cases to ensure that they are sufficiently detailed to enable the design and implementation of the system.
- **Testing.** Testers should review the use cases to ensure it will be possible to objectively determine that the completed system meets the objectives that they set forth.

We will look at the other roles required to undertake an effective and productive review in the Running the Review Meeting section later in this chapter.

UNDERSTANDING THE AUDIENCE

The audience for the use cases will determine a number of things:

- The amount of detail needed in the use case descriptions
- The areas that will require the greatest focus
- The approach to reviewing the use cases and the most appropriate way to communicate feedback

Different audiences will respond to use cases differently. Failure to understand this often causes projects to fail because they cannot get high-quality participation from reviewers.

The key principle in reviews is to respect the time of others, understanding that people are busy and that reviewing your use cases is probably not the most important thing they have to do. The easier you can make the reviewer's job, the better feedback you will get.

Setting Expectations

Using an iterative approach, use cases may be reviewed before they are 100 percent complete. In fact, in order to obtain the essential feedback that is needed to improve the content and quality of the use cases, they *must* be reviewed before they are complete. Accustomed to reviewing only completed work, some reviewers will find this discomforting. To overcome this, make sure to set the reviewers' expectations appropriately.

Reviewers need to understand

- **The intended state of the use cases, and the expected next steps.** If you know that only the main flow is complete and that alternative flows must still be written, tell the reviewers this; it will help them to understand where to focus.
- **What you expect from them.** If you need them to confirm your understanding of a business process but are not yet ready to have them focus on the behavior of the entire use case, tell them.
- **When you need their response.** If you need the information by a particular date, tell them. Do not simply say "as soon as possible"; this makes you look poorly prepared and conveys a lack of respect for their other priorities. Saying "as soon as possible" implies a state of emergency that is probably unwarranted if you plan your project appropriately. Giving them clear but realistic deadlines will help them plan their schedules accordingly.
- **Why you need their participation.** People are much more willing to participate if they know why they are being asked to participate. If you specifically need their expertise, they need to know this so that they can set their priorities appropriately.
- **What's in it for them.** People who feel that they will benefit in some way from providing the feedback are more likely to provide good feedback. The most direct way that they might benefit is that they will be able to use the system being developed. In cases where the reviewer will not be a user, other rewards can be compelling, such as recognition for their contribution.

In other words, don't just assume that because you send them the use cases for review that the reviewers will take the time to provide feedback. In order to get good participation, you must *sell* them on why they should participate.

Preparing for the Review

Make sure that review materials are well organized and free from defects, except where noted. Call out specific sections that need specific attention, and provide review questions to direct the reviewers' efforts. Review materials should be circulated to reviewers so as to allow sufficient review time. For most people, this means several days ahead of time. In any event, reviewers should be contacted in advance of this to solicit their participation and schedule time for the review.

RUNNING THE REVIEW MEETING

The first principles of meeting organization are to have an agenda and to make sure that participants are prepared for the meeting. Setting an agenda communicates the meeting objectives to the participants. Distributing the agenda to participants beforehand, along with the use cases to review and the review instructions, will ensure that review meeting time is used to its best advantage.

Review instructions are guidelines provided to reviewers that ask them to focus on specific aspects of the use cases when reviewing. In an iterative project, use cases may be partially complete for a number of iterations; communicating to reviewers the parts of the use case on which to focus and the specific feedback desired is essential to making the best use of the reviewers' time.

During the review meeting, assign roles to participants. The following roles are typical:

- **Moderator.** The moderator ensures that the meeting runs smoothly and stays within the agenda established for the meeting. The moderator is not an active reviewer but rather acts as a facilitator, eliciting participation and ensuring that all participants have an opportunity to provide comments. The moderator also is empowered to table any discussions that go beyond the intended scope of the meeting.
- **Author.** The author of the use case provides additional information about the use case. The author is not present to defend the use case, however, and it is up to the moderator to ensure that the discussion remains focused on identifying issues that need to be resolved (but not solving them).
- **Recorder.** The recorder captures any issues that need to be resolved. To ensure that the focus remains on this task, the recorder should not be an active participant in the review.
- **Participants.** The participants provide feedback and identify issues that need to be resolved with the use case.

The review meetings need to be kept relatively small to be manageable. They should always include a moderator, recorder, and author, and should consist of 4–7 people, depending on the specialization of roles. Don't allow the meeting to grow larger than this; it will increase the complexity of the meeting and reduce the quality of feedback. This restriction can lead to the need for multiple review meetings to cater to all of the different perspectives required on the use cases (including at least the business, development, and test teams).

During the meeting, the moderator should lead the team, section by section, through the document to be reviewed. Well-prepared participants should not need to read the use case, so the meeting should focus strictly on identifying issues. This approach keeps review meetings short and value-packed and respects everyone's time.

Remember, the point of the review meeting is to identify issues and, if no issues are identified, to approve the use cases for further development. Hold separate meetings to communicate the results of the reviews.

Handling Issues

In any type of review (and we mean design and code reviews as well), issues should be recorded and assigned an owner, but not resolved. Many an unproductive meeting has sprung from giving in to the temptation to resolve the issue on the spot. Issues frequently need to be researched and alternative solutions considered, and this research is best undertaken by an individual or a small team. Gaining the discipline to identify issues, then assigning priority and ownership, rather than trying to resolve or even discuss the issues is a difficult but valuable accomplishment. The hallmark of great meeting leaders is that they can identify the point at which the discussion should be cut short and an issue should be identified and tabled until the end of the meeting.

WHAT TO LOOK FOR WHEN REVIEWING

There are two main things to review in the use-case model: diagrams and use-case descriptions. It would be impractical and illogical to enumerate all the things to consider (that's what the rest of the book is about), but we will present here the most common errors that are likely to be present.

Reviewing Diagrams

Use-case diagrams present the structure of the use-case model. Diagrams should be reviewed first to ensure that they express the desired behavior of the system. The most common problems you will see in diagrams result from a misunderstanding of the purpose and scope of a use case. Use-case diagrams that look too complex probably are.

The first thing to look at is the names of the use cases: Do the names convey the value provided by the use case? Use cases that do not provide value by themselves are not use cases. The exception to this are included use cases, which become part of some other use case's value proposition, and extending use cases that add value to some other use case. Use cases that do not pass the *value test* must be reconsidered and reformulated, perhaps by eliminating them or combing them with other *fragmentary* use cases to form new, whole use cases.

Next, look for actors without use cases and use cases without actors. Use cases exist to provide value to their actors, so a use case without an actor (included and extending use cases excepted) is an error. Actors without use cases are not so much wrong as pointless—if the actors do not use the system there is no point in documenting them.

Communication between actors should be eliminated, as it is outside the system. Do not use communication between actors to document the business process; use business models to document the business process.[4]

Make sure that all use cases and actors have brief descriptions; names are not enough. The brief description of actors should convey the role they play *with respect to the system*, and the brief description of the use case should portray the value the use case provides to its actors.

Included use cases should be part of two or more use cases. Inclusion is used to represent portions of the flow of events that are common to two or more use cases. An included use case that is only used in one use case can be a sign of functional decomposition in the use-case model and should be eliminated. If the inclusion is legitimate, it may be a sign that some use case or relationship is missing. In no event should inclusion be present in a diagram before the flows of events for the use cases are written (at least in draft form).

Abuse of extension is rarer, but extension is more often misapplied when it is used. Examine all extending use cases to make sure that they only *add* value to the extended use case. Because extension requires knowledge of the flow of events of the extended use case, it is rare for one use case to extend more than one other use case. Examine all extensions to make sure they are appropriate. In no event should extension be present in a diagram before the flows of events for the use cases are written (at least in outline form). Extending use cases should extend the base use cases only at public extension points.

Use of generalization is rare and typically restricted to descriptions of application frameworks. Examine all generalizations to ensure that they are not hiding functional decompositions. In no event should generalization be present in a diagram before the flows of events for the use cases are written (at least in draft form).

Finally, review the model as a whole to ensure that it is easy to grasp the value provided by the system by examining the diagrams, the actor and use case names, their relationships, and brief descriptions.

---

[4] Jacobson, et al., *The Object Advantage*, is an excellent reference for this purpose.

Reviewing Brief Descriptions

Brief descriptions for actors should clearly convey the role played by the actor in the context of the system. Brief descriptions for use cases should clearly convey the value provided by the use case. The brief description should indicate what goals of the actors are accomplished by performing the use case. Look especially for brief descriptions that do not significantly add to the meaning provided by the name of the use case.

Reviewing Use-Case Descriptions

The biggest problem with use-case descriptions is insufficient or vague descriptions. Teams fail more often because of lack of detail than too much detail. The use-case description should not be a summary of the flow of events; it should capture the details of the flows of events. Of course, as already discussed, details can be presented in the glossary, in the domain model, or in appendices, but the details must be presented somewhere. If the use-case descriptions are ambiguous, they still need work.

Use-case descriptions should omit user-interface details; these details are best presented in use-case storyboards or in prototypes.

Use-case descriptions should not constrain the design. Any discussion of how the system is structured internally should be removed. At the same time, the use case must be sufficiently detailed to enable the design, implementation, and testing of the system.

References between use cases should only occur in two contexts:

- References in the description of a *base* use case, referring to an included use case
- References in the description of an *extending* use case, referring to a particular public extension point in the description of a *base* use case

The use-case descriptions should be reviewed for conformity to the adopted style guide.

Reviewing Preconditions and Postconditions

Preconditions and postconditions should describe the state that the system is in before the use case can begin or after the use case ends successfully. Preconditions and postconditions should not refer to other use cases under any circumstances. When preconditions refer to another use case, the precondition should be rewritten to match the postconditions of the preceding use case.

Reviewing the Glossary and Domain Model

The subject-matter experts should review the glossary and domain model for completeness, redundancy, and ambiguity. Look for terms that are not used within the use-case model; these either are irrelevant or indicate that the use-case model itself is not complete. The definitions should be available to the participants involved in the reviews of the use-case descriptions. It is imperative that terminology be used consistently throughout the use-case model.

THE ROLE OF PROTOTYPES AND STORYBOARDS IN USE-CASE REVIEWS

Prototypes are executable models of part of a system, often constructed to evaluate technical risk or to provide mock-ups of system behavior. Storyboards are sequences of screen shots that depict some set of behaviors of the system. Both prototypes and storyboards can be used to illustrate the behavior described in a use case. They have the advantage of making the use case more tangible and therefore easier to understand. Their principal disadvantage is that they take time and resources to produce. Furthermore, if their development is not well managed and integrated with the development of the use cases, they can be a distraction, or may even detract attention from the use cases themselves. Used judiciously, prototypes and storyboards can help bring the use cases to life.

The best uses for storyboards and prototypes is to illustrate the behavior of use cases, and by doing so make them understandable to people who may be too busy to read and visualize the behavior of a use case. Typically, they will be used in the context of a presentation to aid in walking through or enacting some part of the use case.

When using prototypes, take special care that the goal does not become developing the system. Prototypes are used only to explore behavior and to gain consensus on the appropriate direction for further development. Once these issues are resolved, proper development can proceed.

SUMMARY

In this chapter, we have discussed the importance of reviewing use cases. Reviews provide an opportunity to gather feedback to improve the use cases. Informal reviews play the greatest role in improving use cases, while formal reviews are critical milestones for the project.

Selecting the right people to involve in reviews is important if reviews are to be valuable. Make sure to involve a cross section of stakeholders—domain experts, developers, testers all play a role in determining if the use case is "complete." Once you have selected the reviewers, make sure to gain their support and participation. Prepare for the review ahead of time, considering the needs of reviewers, the best way to present the use cases, and the best way to gather feedback.

Finally, pay attention to the guidelines presented throughout this book, especially those describing common problems and pitfalls.

Chapter 12

Wrapping Up

In the preceding chapters, we have focused principally on use-case modeling as a technique for capturing and communicating requirements. Before we conclude, a few issues remain to be resolved: a quick overview on how use cases are used in the broader life cycle and a brief discussion of how use cases are developed across the project life cycle, especially in the context of an iterative software development life cycle. Finally, we conclude with a look toward the future, toward new ways of using use cases to develop solutions.

USE CASES AND THE PROJECT TEAM

As we have shown in the previous chapters, use cases are a simple but powerful technique for capturing and communicating requirements. This is certainly important, but there is more. Use cases can be used as a unifying principle that unites the activities of the project and gives the project a consistent, solution-oriented focus that always keeps the customer solution in mind.[1]

In the Introduction, we mentioned that the following kinds of people are interested in use cases:

- **Customers**, who need to be sure that the system that is getting built is the one that they want

---

[1] The use of use cases to unify software development activities was introduced by Ivar Jacobson and explained in *Object-Oriented Software Engineering*.

- **Managers**, who need to have an overall understanding of what the system will do in order to effectively plan and monitor the project
- **Analysts**, who need to describe and document what the system is going to do
- **Developers**, who need to understand what the system needs to do in order to develop it
- **Testers**, who need to know what the system is supposed to do so that they can verify that it does it
- **Technical writers**, who need to know what the system is supposed to do so that they can describe it
- **User-Experience designers**, who need to understand the users' goals and how they will use the system to achieve these goals

By this point, it should be obvious how customers and users would be interested in use cases—they are, in fact, some of the major stakeholders with whom one will work when establishing the vision (for a review of this, see Chapter 3, Establishing the Vision). It should also be obvious that most of this book is for analysts, the people who elicit the requirements from stakeholders, capture the requirements in an understandable form, and communicate the requirements to the rest of the development team. But what about the other stakeholders presented here? How do they use use cases? This was touched on in Chapter 6, The Life cycle of a Use Case, but it is worth another, more detailed examination.

Developers *and Use Cases*

Developers are responsible for realizing the requirements in software, translating descriptions of what the system must do into actual code. In this process, they will analyze the use cases, perhaps describing how the system works as a series of collaborations of objects. These collaborations are first done at a high level, from an "ideal" perspective that omits details of the implementation environment to ensure a focus on supporting the behavior of the use case. These ideal descriptions are later refined by considering the details of the implementation environment.[2]

The value of using use cases is that the same description that is used to gain agreement with the stakeholders can also be used to drive the analysis,

---

[2] The details of this process are the subjects of a number of excellent books, among which are Ivar Jacobson's *Object-Oriented Software Engineering: A Use Case Driven Approach*, Doug Rosenberg and Kendall Scott's *Use Case Driven Object Modeling With UML : A Practical Approach* and Craig Larman's *Applying UML and Patterns: An Introduction to Object-Oriented Analysis and Design and the Unified Process*.

design, and implementation efforts. This greatly reduces the chance that the requirements will be ignored, forgotten, or overlooked by the development team. In addition, and perhaps more important, it gives the development team a place to start and an easy way to understand what it is supposed to build.

Testers *and Use Cases*

Requirements have always had a central role in testing. In order to determine whether the system does what it is supposed to do, it's necessary to know just what the system is supposed to do. Testers often suffer from a lack of adequate information about what the system is supposed to do. We have seen many projects on which testers expended great effort reconstructing the requirements from inadequate documentation. The existence of use cases solves this problem, allowing testers to focus on testing the system, not trying to figure out what the system is supposed to do.

As we have discussed at length, use cases are excellent vehicles for describing the behavior of the system and so provide an excellent source for defining test cases. Since use cases describe what the users want from the system, they are an excellent source for defining user-acceptance test cases. In addition, because the use cases drive the development of the system, they provide important inputs for the definition of performance, system, and integration tests.[3]

Use Cases and the User Experience

It stands to reason that use cases and usability will be intimately intertwined. Use cases describe how the system is used, and understanding how the system is used is essential to ensuring that the system is useable.

As we discussed earlier, details of the user interface should not be included in use cases. Doing so renders the use cases difficult to understand because it obscures the objectives of the system behind a mass of user-interface details and difficult to maintain because the user interface will continue to evolve long after the use-case descriptions have stabilized. User-interface designs will evolve in parallel with the use cases in the form of use-case storyboards and user-interface prototypes, which in turn give rise to the actual user interfaces.

---

[3] An excellent reference for defining test cases (as well as the rest of the testing process) is *Lessons Learned in Software Testing* by Cem Kaner, James Bach, and Bret Pettichord.

Even though the details of the user interface are omitted from the use cases, the use-case descriptions provide essential context for the user-interface design. In addition, development of use-case storyboards and user-interface prototypes, coupled with walk-throughs of the use cases using the storyboards and prototypes, provides an excellent way of reviewing the use cases with key stakeholders. The storyboards and prototypes bring the use cases to life, while the use cases provide a coherent thread through the storyboards and prototypes.[4]

Use Cases and Documentation

Typical software documentation tends to be organized around features, which tend to be rather arbitrary and only loosely related to the things of value the users want from the system, or around functions, which are capabilities of the system but are also only loosely related to the things of value the system does for its users. As a result, documentation is often not very useful in helping users to accomplish their goals when using the system. Even when the documentation is task oriented, a great deal of effort has to be expended by technical writers to determine the system's intended uses and the users' desired results.

Because use cases describe how the users will use the system, they provide a natural way of organizing the documentation. Documentation that mirrors the use cases, and which helps users understand how to use the system to achieve their goals, will immediately be of greater value to users than functionally organized documentation. Documentation can be organized by using the use cases as major sections in the documentation, with the help topics mirroring the basic flow, the named subflows, and the alternative flows. By doing this, the documentation leverages the work already done to understand what the system does for its users and how the users use the system.

Managers, Use Cases, and Planning

Since use cases can define a very large subset of the system, they will drive a substantial amount of the overall work on the system. The relationship of the use cases to the other software development activities, as described in the preceding sections and Chapter 6, The Life Cycle of a Use Case, makes them ideal

---

[4] A number of excellent references provide the full story on how this happens, notably Constantine and Lockwood, *Software for Use: A Practical Guide to the Models and Methods of Usage-Centered Design.*

for structuring the work breakdown structure and planning the development activities.

The structure of the use-case model and the use-case descriptions is also ideal for scope managing the project, as their additive nature allows the impact of removing flows and use cases from the project scope to be particularly visible and understood in terms of the value to the user of the sets of functionality.

They are also very useful for tracking the progress of the project and how much value the project has earned to date. They are particularly powerful when used in conjunction with an iterative and incremental development process, as the defining of the results of iterations in terms of use cases and flows of events allows the system to demonstrably deliver additional value to the users with each iteration.

The nature of, and the role played by, the structure of the use-case model and the use-case descriptions was discussed in detail in Chapter 7, The Structure and Contents of a Use Case. To fully understand the role that use cases can play in the planning and execution of a project, you need to understand the role that the use cases play as the project progresses. This is discussed in the next section.

USE CASES ACROSS THE LIFE CYCLE

In the preceding chapters, it is easy to get the idea that one develops use cases all at once, then hands them off to other people to develop, test, and document. While it is possible to take this approach (sometimes called the *waterfall* approach, since each discipline tends to cascade into the next[5]), it tends to ignore the synergy achieved by having all team members participating in the evolution of the use cases. The reality is that each team member brings a different and valuable perspective to the process, and engaging all members in the evolution leads to an overall improvement in the end result.

The truth is that finding the right level of detail in the use-case description is a collaborative effort. Developers need a certain amount of detail to build the system, testers need a certain amount of detail to test the system, and so on. Working on requirements, development, testing, documentation, and other project activities in a more concurrent manner enables the team to identify knowledge gaps sooner, resulting in a better system. This is not to

---

[5] For a discussion of project life cycles and how to manage project iteratively, see Walker Royce's *Software Project Management: A Unified Framework.*

say that things happen randomly—in fact, to be successful at a more "parallel" approach, some strategies are needed to get the team fully engaged and working on the right things at the right time.

Use Cases and Iterative Development

A modern software development project is conducted as a series of *iterations*, each of which consists of a little requirements definition, analysis, design, implementation, and testing. Each iteration results in something executable, possibly just a prototype, but increasingly a larger and larger portion of the complete system as the project nears completion. A widely used process framework that embodies the principles of iterative software development is the Rational Unified Process (RUP).[6] In describing how use cases are used to develop a system in a series of iterations, we will use the project phases it defines.

The RUP divides the process into four sequentially arranged phases, each of which may contain one or more iterations:

- **Inception:** dealing with business risks (the vision for the project, the funding for the project, and issues dealing with the financial viability of the project)
- **Elaboration:** dealing with technical and architectural risks
- **Construction:** dealing with "project execution" risk (building the project on time and within budget), and finally
- **Transition:** Dealing with risks related to rolling the project out to its users

Use Cases in the Inception Phase

As noted, the purpose of the Inception phase is to define the vision for the system and by doing so to assess the business viability of the project. In addition to defining the vision as described in Chapter 3, actors and use cases will be identified as described in Chapters 4 and 5. Finding actors and use cases helps us to understand the value that the system provides to its stakeholders, which is an important part of determining whether the system is worth building. In addition to identifying actors and use cases, use-case storyboards and user-interface prototypes are often created in the Inception phase to help visualize and illustrate the use cases. Planning for the user documentation is also begun, based on the identified use cases. Use cases may be outlined, to help give a better understanding of the behavior of the system, but the work

---

[6] For an introduction to the Rational Unified Process, see *The Rational Unified Process: An Introduction* by Philippe Kruchten.

is bounded by the goal of determining whether the system has a viable business case.

Use Cases in the Elaboration Phase

In the Elaboration phase, a subset of the use cases is selected for detailing, analysis, design, implementation, and testing, for the purpose of exploring the architecture of the system. Not all use cases are architecturally significant, and in fact it is often only part of a use case that significantly exposes architectural issues. The art of planning the Elaboration phase involves selecting the scenarios that will expose architectural issues that, when addressed, will define the architecture of the system.

Once a set of architectural scenarios is selected, the portions of the use cases that define the scenarios are detailed, as described in Chapters 8 and 9. Following this, the use cases are analyzed, designed, and implemented to a degree sufficient to allow the validation of the architecture. This means that some of the functionality of the system will be implemented as *stubs*, in which the real behavior of the system is only simulated. Behavior is stubbed when it is determined to be architecturally insignificant.

During Elaboration, test cases are also written to assess the architectural viability of the system, based on the use cases that are determined to be architecturally significant. The test cases are evaluated against the architectural prototypes, resulting in either identification of new architectural risks or retirement of existing architectural risks. Also, work on the user documentation continues.

At the end of the Elaboration phase, the requirements should be stable and understood. This does not mean that all of them have been captured and documented, but that there should be no major surprises as the requirements specification is incrementally completed. The additive structure of the use-case model, and the use cases' flows of events, is again very important here as it provides a high-level framework for assessing the stability of the system's requirements. If it is felt that a use case contains areas of instability, risk, or complexity, then these unstable flows of events can be detailed to a level that removes the uncertainty. If a use case or a flow of events is considered to be low risk and well understood, its detailed authoring can be left until a later iteration. This allows the use cases to be completed in a "just-in-time" fashion as part of the iteration that implements them.

Use Cases in the Construction and Transition Phases

Not all use cases are completely detailed by the end of the Elaboration phase. Typically, some of the use cases have a number of flows detailed, but many use cases may still be only briefly described. In the Construction phase, the remaining use cases are detailed (if detailed descriptions are determined to be needed), analyzed, designed, and implemented. The resulting system is progressively tested until, by the end of the Construction phase, the system is ready to be delivered for beta testing. User documentation needed for beta testing is completed based on the use cases completed.

No use-case work is done in the Transition phase, except indirectly; testing is completed using test cases that are derived from use cases. Work on the user documentation concludes, final defects are fixed, and the product is prepared for final release.

Use Cases After Product Release

And what happens to use cases once the product is released? Use cases continue to provide value to the people who maintain and support the system—they provide a way to understand what the system was supposed to do. The use cases also provide a basis for future development of the system when it requires enhancements, which begins a new project and a new round of evolution of the use cases.

Effort Across the Life Cycle

Another interesting perspective on the role of use cases across the life cycle is that of the relative amounts of effort expended on requirements work in general and use cases in particular across the phases of a typical project. This is shown in Figure 12-1. As you can see from the figure, if the approach recommended by this book is adopted, then the majority of the requirements work is typically related to the development and detailing of the use-case model. This is not the only requirements effort necessary, as we would also recommend developing a vision document and a Supplementary Specification. (Note: The glossary is so tightly coupled to the use-case model that it is considered to be part of the use-case model when assessing the effort expended.) You can also see that requirements work, and use-case modeling in particular, continues throughout all of the phases of the project. The amount of effort expended in these areas typically peaks during the Elaboration phase when the majority of the requirements are discovered and the overall requirements definition stabilizes.

TRACEABILITY, COMPLETENESS, AND COVERAGE

The preceding sections described a number of artifacts that are derived from use cases (principally use-case realizations—that is, collaborations—and test cases), and the preceding chapters of the book described a number of types of requirements that are related in some way to use cases (needs, features, special requirements, and supplementary requirements). These artifacts are related by traceability relationships (a kind of dependency in UML). Trace-

Figure 12-1   Requirements effort across the lifecycle*

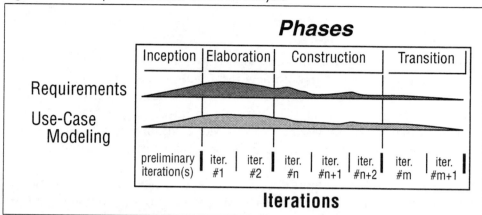

* The source for the requirements effort is the Rational Unified Process, version 2002.05.

ability relationships indicate that one thing is derived from or dependent on another thing.

While knowing about what a thing was derived from is interesting, the main benefit of traceability comes from its role in assessing the completeness of a system with respect to its requirements and from determining the coverage of testing. Traceability's role in assessing completeness and coverage arises from being able to use the relationships to determine the following:

- Whether every requirement is handled by at least one use case
- Whether every user type has at least one actor whose role it can play
- Whether every actor is involved in at least one use case
- Whether every use case has at least one use-case realization
- Whether the use-case realizations have participating classes that are fully designed and implemented
- Whether all use cases have associated test cases and, more specifically, whether all scenarios are covered
- And finally whether all test cases have been successfully executed

Traceability is also useful in managing change on the project, by allowing the team to determine what things need to be updated when something changes. By following the traceability relationships, the team can find the use-case realizations and test cases that need to be updated when a use case changes or find the use cases that need to be updated when a stakeholder need changes (due to a change in the business environment, for example).

Traceability is, in effect, the glue that holds the artifacts together and makes iterative software development possible.

WHAT'S NEXT?

Our journey into the world of use cases has drawn to a close, and yet in many respects it has just begun. First, no new technique is mastered without practice. We have tried to share with you the many years of experience of a great number of people. As hard as we have tried to impart this experience, only practice will hone this knowledge to a keen edge. You must try, struggle, fall short, and then succeed on your own, building your own knowledge with experience.

In addition, we have intentionally kept our examples simple as an aid to understanding. The real world is considerably more varied, and while our lessons still apply, there are subtle nuances of technique to be applied to different kinds of systems. There are, in effect, patterns of description to use cases that can be identified and shared among teams working on similar kinds of systems. We hope that future authors (perhaps even ourselves) can focus on these areas to continue to expand the usefulness of use-case modeling.

We have provided what we hope is a strong foundation for these efforts. Use cases are a simple but powerful technique, one that is easily applied to a wide range of projects and problem domains. We wish you good luck in your efforts to apply them to your projects.

Appendix

Examples

This appendix contains excerpts from a completed use-case model intended to complement the smaller examples embedded throughout the book.

It does not include the complete set of artifacts discussed in the book. In fact it does not contain

- A complete use-case model as these often run to hundreds of pages
- A complete Vision document as these are typically 10 to 20 pages in length
- A complete Supplementary Specification
- A glossary and domain model
- Templates for the documents
- A style guide based on the guidance contained in the book

The examples in this section are based on the *Automated Teller Machine* model that was fleshed out in Chapter 9, Writing Use-Case Descriptions: Revisited. The examples show the final form of the completed use cases and may differ slightly from the evolutionary fragments found in Chapter 9.

THE ATM EXAMPLE

In this example we provide edited highlights of the use-case model for an Automated Teller Machine (ATM). We only include the following elements of the model to prevent this appendix from running to literally hundreds of pages and taking up a disproportionate amount of the book:

1. A cut down use-case model survey to provide an overview of the entire ATM model.

2. The full *Withdraw Cash* use case to provide an example of what a completed use case would look like and demonstrate the level of detail required for a fully described use case.[1]

3. The full *Authenticate Customer* use case to provide an example of an included use case. This use case is included by 4 of the use cases in the model.

4. An extract from the project's glossary to support the use-case descriptions.

This set of suggested solutions to the classic ATM problem is inspired by Swedish, American, Australian, Canadian, and British ATM systems. The authors of this example have never built a real ATM system. They have just used their knowledge as ATM Customers and use-case authors. The point of this set of solutions is to show what a solution may look like and the level detail that should be used when describing use cases.

A lot of the ideas in this example come from training courses run in Australia and England that involved developers who actually built bank applications. BEWARE: THIS IS NOT A REAL SYSTEM! The supporting definitions and descriptions of ATM and Bank System dialogues are all fictitious. The purpose of the examples is not to provide an accurate use-case model for an ATM but to provide examples of fully complete use-case descriptions.

THE *ACME SUPER ATM* USE-CASE MODEL SURVEY

Brief Description

For	Current Account-Holding Customers
Who	Require instant access to their account details and the funds they contain
The	**Super ATM** is an automated teller machine
That	Provides the ability to perform simple bank transactions (such as withdrawing or depositing funds, or transferring funds between accounts)
Unlike	Accessing funds and details over the branch counter
Our product	Is available 24 hours a day and does not require the assistance of a bank teller

---

[1] See Chapter 6, *The Life Cycle of a Use Case*, for definitions of the other states that use case could be in.

Actor Catalogue

Figure A-1 shows all the actors in the *ACME Super ATM* use-case model. The brief descriptions of the actors are given in the subsections that follow the figure.

Customer

The Customer conducts transactions at the ATM. He or she may withdraw funds, check account balances, deposit funds, and transfer amounts between accounts. A Customer is created when a person opens an account at an affiliated financial institution.

Burglar

The Burglar represents any individual who tries to break into or vandalize the ATM.

Bank System

The Bank System provides services to the ATM. It is responsible for verifying Customers, authorizing transactions, and supplying the ATM with information about the Customers' accounts. The Bank System acts as a gateway to the Customer's bank.

Figure A-1   The actors of the *ACME Super ATM*

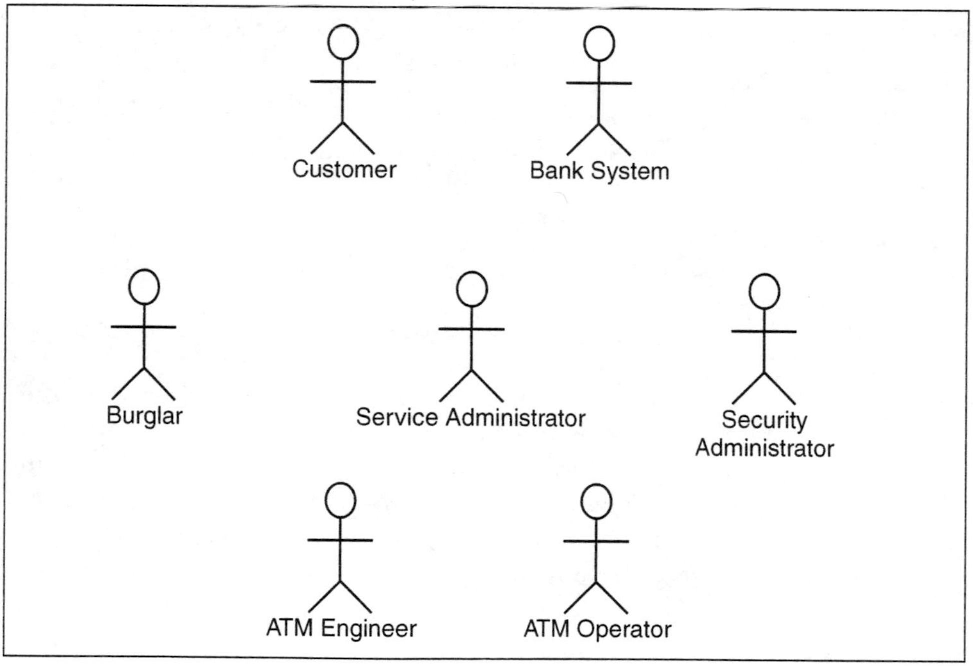

Service Administrator

The Service Administrator is responsible for ensuring that a set of ATMs meets required service levels and for installing and running advertising campaigns.

Security Administrator

The Security Administrator monitors the ATM for security breaches such as the fraudulent use of cards and any attempts to physically break into the ATM.

ATM Engineer

The ATM Engineer is responsible for the physical maintenance of the ATM, refilling the machine with cash and paper, clearing any mechanical problems, and undertaking the on-site configuration of the machine.

ATM Operator

The ATM Operator is responsible for the operation of the ATM, analyzing the performance of the system, reconciling the accounts between the ATM and the Bank System, and updating the system configuration. The ATM Operator may be accessing the machine by directly connecting to the machine or remotely over a networked communications link.

Use-Case Catalogue

Primary Use Cases

Figure A-2 shows the primary use cases from the *ACME Super ATM* use-case model. The brief descriptions of the use cases are given in the subsections that follow.

WITHDRAW CASH

This use case describes how a Customer uses an ATM to withdraw money from a bank account.

DEPOSIT FUNDS

The use case describes how a Customer uses the ATM to deposit money into an account. The Customer places the money or checks into an envelope and inserts the envelope into the ATM. The envelopes are securely stored within the machine until the ATM engineer picks them up at a later date as part of the machine's daily maintenance. Note: The ATM does not actually credit the amount deposited to the Customer's account.

Figure A-2 The primary use cases for the *ACME Super ATM**

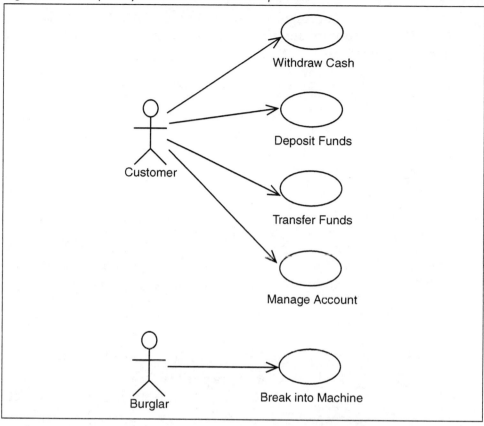

> * The secondary actors and any related use cases are suppressed from the diagram to aid readability and allow the diagram to illustrate the purpose of the ACME Super ATM.

TRANSFER FUNDS
This use case describes how a Customer uses the ATM to transfer money to and from an account.

MANAGE ACCOUNT
This use case describes how a Customer uses the ATM to manage his or her account: viewing balances and mini-statements, requesting full statements, and ordering account-related products such as check books and paying-in books.

BREAK INTO MACHINE
This use case describes how the system responds when someone attempts to break into or vandalize the machine.[2]

---

[2] This use case is more of an abuse case than a typical use case, but it does represent one of the stakeholders' indirect goals for the system: that it should be secure.

Supporting Use Cases

Figure A-3 shows the supporting use cases from the *ACME Super ATM* use-case model. The brief descriptions of the use cases are given in the subsections that follow the figure.

Figure A-3 The supporting use cases for the *ACME Super ATM**

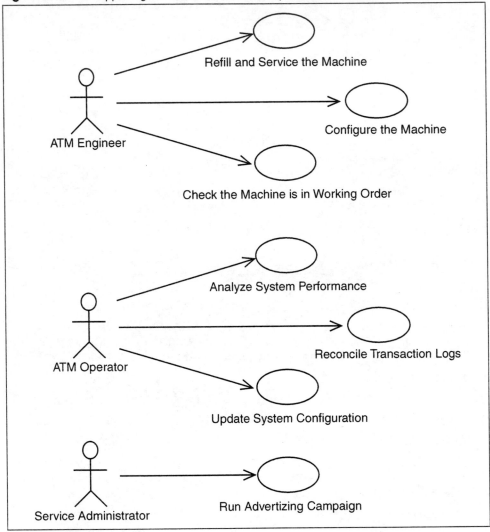

* Again the secondary actors and any related use cases are suppressed from the diagram to aid readability.

REFILL AND SERVICE THE MACHINE

This use case describes how an ATM Engineer keeps the ATM running on a day-to-day basis by refilling the machine with cash, emptying the machine of any deposits, refilling the machine with receipt paper, and generally servicing the hardware.

CONFIGURE THE MACHINE

This use case describes how an ATM Engineer sets up or reconfigures the ATM for use at a specific location, with a specific Bank System, and with a set of financial institutions.

CHECK THE MACHINE IS IN WORKING ORDER

This use case describes how an ATM Engineer uses the ATM to run a set of diagnostic routines to ensure that it is functioning correctly.

ANALYZE SYSTEM PERFORMANCE

This use case describes how an ATM Operator can interrogate the ATM's internal records to analyze performance and diagnose problems.

RECONCILE TRANSACTION LOGS

This use case describes how an ATM Operator uses the ATM to reconcile any differences between its transaction history and that of the Bank System. Errors can cause the ATM and the Bank System to have different understandings of how much money has been dispensed or collected.

UPDATE SYSTEM CONFIGURATION

This use case describes how an ATM Operator can update the tunable parameters of the system's configuration without taking the ATM out of service. Tunable parameters include, among others, the set of Banks supported, the maximum withdrawal amount, the maximum deposit amount, and the set of services available.

RUN ADVERTISING CAMPAIGN

This use case describes how a Service Administrator can use the ATM to run an advertising campaign that displays advertisements when the machine is idle and during the performance of the other use cases. This use case is provided on behalf of the Marketing Department, one of the major stakeholders in the Super ATM project.

USE-CASE DESCRIPTION—*WITHDRAW CASH*

1. Brief Description

This use case describes how a Bank Customer uses an ATM to withdraw money from a bank account.

2. Use-Case Diagram

See Figure A-4.

Figure A-4 Use-case diagram for the *Withdraw Cash* use case

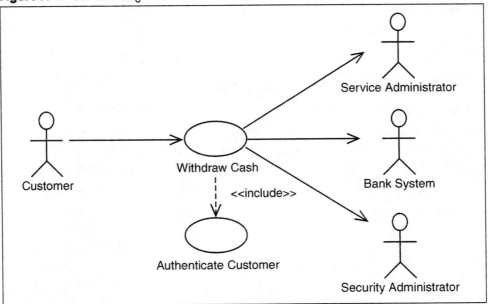

3. Preconditions

- The bank Customer must possess a **bank card**.
- The network connection to the **Bank System** must be active.
- The system must have at least some cash that can be dispensed.
- The cash withdrawal **service option** must be available.

4. Basic Flow

{Insert Card}

  1. The use case begins when the actor **Customer** inserts a **bank card** into the card reader on the ATM.

2. The system allocates an **ATM session identifier** to enable errors to be tracked and synchronized between the ATM and the Bank System.

{Read Card}

3. The system reads the **bank card information** from the card.

{Authenticate Customer}

4. Include use case *Authenticate Customer* to authenticate the use of the **bank card** by the individual using the machine.

{Select Withdrawal}

5. The system displays the different **service options** that are currently available on the machine.
6. The Customer selects to withdraw cash.

{Select Amount}

7. The system prompts for the amount to be withdrawn by displaying the list of **standard withdrawal amounts**.
8. The Customer selects an amount to be withdrawn.

{Confirm Withdrawal}

9. Perform *Assess Funds on Hand*.
10. Perform *Conduct Transaction*.

{Eject Card}

11. The system ejects the Customer's **bank card**.
12. The Customer takes the **bank card** from the machine.

{Dispense Cash}

13. The system dispenses the requested amount to the Customer.
14. The system records a **transaction log** entry for the withdrawal.

{Use Case Ends}

15. The use case ends.

5. Alternative Flows

5.1 Specialist Withdrawal Facilities

5.1.1 Handle the Withdrawal of a Non-Standard Amount

At **{Select Amount}** if the Customer requires a non-standard amount,

1. The system asks the Customer for the required amount indicating that the amount entered must be a multiple of the **smallest denomination note held** and must be below the amount of the

ATM's **withdrawal limit** and the amount of currency held by the machine.

2. The Customer enters the desired amount.
3. Resume the basic flow at {**Confirm Withdrawal**}.

5.2 Card Handling

5.2.1 Handle Card Jam

At {**Insert Card**}, {**Eject Card**}, or {**Retrieve Card**}, if the **bank card** jams in the card reader,

{Emergency Eject Card}

1. The system attempts to eject the card.
2. If the card ejection is successful, the system informs the Customer
   a. That the card may be faulty
   b. That he or she should contact the Bank to get a replacement card
   c. That the Customer should take the **bank card** from the machine
3. The use case resumes the basic flow at {**Use Case Ends**}.

{Emergency Confiscation}

4. If the emergency ejection fails, the system attempts to retrieve the card and add it to the **confiscated cards**.
5. If the card retrieval is successful, the system
   a. Captures a 10-second video image of the Customer.
   b. Creates an **event log** entry to record the fact that a card has been retained because it became stuck in the card reader. The **event log** entry includes the video image and the current **bank card information** (excluding the **PIN**) if it is available.
   c. Sends the **event log** entry to the Bank System and the Service Administrator to inform them that a card has been retained because it became stuck in the card reader.
   d. Informs the Customer that the card cannot be returned because of a technical error and that he or she should contact the **Service Organization** for the return of the card.

{Card Jammed}

6. If the card could not be ejected or retrieved, the system,
   a. Captures a 10-second video image of the Customer.
   b. Creates an **event log** entry to record the fact that a card is jammed in the card reader. The **event log** entry includes the video image and the current **bank card information** (excluding the **PIN**) if it is available.

    c. Sends the **event log** entry to the Bank System and the Service Administrator to inform them that a card has become jammed in this ATM.

    d. Informs the Customer that the card cannot be returned because of a technical error and that he or she should contact the **Service Organization** for the return of the card.

  7. If the card is still jammed, the system Performs Service Shutdown to shutdown all **service options** and end the use case.

5.2.2 *Handle Unreadable Bank Card*

At {**Read Card**} if the system cannot read all the **bank card** information,

1. The system captures a 10-second video image of the Customer.
2. The system creates an **event log** entry to record the fact that the card could not be read. The **event log** entry includes the video image and any **bank card information** (excluding the **PIN**) that it managed to read.
3. The system informs the Customer that the card cannot be read and that he or she should contact the bank to have the card checked.

{Eject Card}

4. The system ejects the Customer's **bank card**.
5. The Customer takes the **bank card** from the machine.
6. The use case resumes the basic flow at {**Use Case Ends**}.

5.2.3 *Handle Invalid Card*

At {**Read Card**} if the system does not support the **financial institution** associated with the card or cannot identify the **financial institution** associated with card,

1. The system captures a 10-second video image of the Customer.
2. The system creates an **event log** entry to record the fact that an attempt was made to use the ATM using an invalid card. The **event log** entry includes the video image and the **bank card information** (excluding the **PIN**).
3. The system informs the Customer that the card cannot be used in this ATM.

{Eject Card}

4. The system ejects the Customer's **bank card**.
5. The Customer takes the **bank card** from the machine.
6. The use case resumes the basic flow at {**Use Case Ends**}.

5.2.4 *Handle Card Left Behind By Customer*

At {**Eject Card**} or {**Emergency Eject Card**} if the **bank card** is not removed from the ATM within 30 seconds,

1. The system beeps to alert the Customer.
2. If the card has still not been removed within a minute of the alert being sounded, then the system

{**Retrieve Card**}

a. Retrieves the card and adds it to the **confiscated cards**.

{**Adjust the Account Balances**}

b. If there are funds still to be dispensed, then the system Performs **Handle Transaction Adjustments** to put the money back into the **account** as it will not now be dispensed.

{**Record the Event**}

c. The system creates an **event log** entry to record the fact that the card was left behind in the ATM. The **event log** entry includes the **bank card information** (excluding the **PIN**).
d. The system sends the **event log** entry to the Bank System to inform it that the card has been left in the ATM.
e. The system turns off the alert.
3. The use case resumes the basic flow at {**Use Case Ends**}.

5.3 *Receipt Handling*

5.3.1 *Offer Receipt Handling to the Customer*

At {**Select Withdrawal**} if the ATM is not out of paper,

1. The system offers the Customer the facility to have a receipt printed for the transaction.
2. The Customer indicates whether a receipt is required.
3. The use case resumes from the place where it was interrupted.

5.3.2 *Withdraw the Receipt Facility*

At {**Select Withdrawal**} if the ATM is out of paper or the paper is jammed,

1. The system informs the Customer that the facility to have a receipt printed for the transaction is currently unavailable.
2. The use case resumes from the place where it was interrupted.

5.3.3 *Handle the Printing of Receipts*

At {**Dispense Cash**} if a receipt was requested,

1. The system prints a **withdrawal receipt**.

2. If the ATM does not have sufficient paper to print the receipt or the printer jams, the system
   a. Creates an **event log** entry to record the fact that the receipt printing is out of order. The **event log** entry includes the **bank card information** (excluding the **PIN**).
   b. Sends the **event log** to the Bank System and the Service Administrator to inform them of the failure and its reason (out of paper or paper jam).
   c. Informs the Customer that the receipt cannot be printed.
   d. Displays the **withdrawal receipt** information to enable the Customer to take a manual record of the transaction.
   e. Asks the Customer to ackowledge the receipt information has been displayed.
   f. Displays the receipt information for 2 minutes or until it is acknowledged by the Customer.
3. The system beeps to alert the Customer that the receipt information is available.
4. The use case resumes from the place where it was interrupted.

5.4 Error Handling

5.4.1 Handle Authentication Failures

At {**Authenticate Customer**} if the **bank card** is not authenticated, then

1. Unless the card has been deliberately retained the card is returned to the Customer:

   {**Eject Card**}
   a. The system ejects the Customer's **bank card**.
   b. The Customer takes the **bank card** from the machine.
2. The use case resumes the basic flow at {**Use Case Ends**}.

5.4.2 Handle the Bank Not Approving the Withdrawal

At {**Validate the Withdrawal**} if the Bank System responds with a **withdrawal rejection**, then

1. If the Bank System rejected the withdrawal because there are not enough funds in the **account** the system, the system
   a. Informs the Customer that the withdrawal has been rejected because the **account** does not have sufficient funds
2. If the Bank System rejects the withdrawal for any other reason, the system
   a. Informs the Customer that the withdrawal has been rejected by the **Customer's Bank**

b. Advises the Customer to contact the Bank for further details

3. The system records a **transaction log** entry for the transaction including the reason given for the transaction's rejection.

4. Resume the use case from {**Select Withdrawal**}

5.4.3 Handle Cash Dispensing Errors

At {**Dispense Cash**} if the full amount cannot be dispensed (notes might be rejected by, or get stuck in, the counting and dispensing device), then

1. The system records an **event log** entry to record the fact that there has been a dispensing error. The **event log** entry includes the **bank card information** (excluding the **PIN**) and the details of the cause of the dispensing error.

2. The system sends the **event log** entry to the Service Administrator and the Bank System to inform them that the ATM is no longer able to dispense cash.

3. The system disables the cash withdraw **service option**.

4. The system records a **transaction log** entry for the transaction including both the amount that should have been dispensed and the amount that was actually dispensed.

5. Perform Handle Transaction Adjustments to balance the ATM and the Bank System.

6. The use case resumes the basic flow at {**Use Case Ends**}.

5.4.4 Handle Money Left Behind By Customer

At {**Dispense Cash**} if the cash is not removed from the ATM within 30 seconds,

1. The system beeps to alert the Customer.

2. If the cash has still not been removed within a minute of the alert being sounded, then the system

   a. Retrieves the cash, checking the amount that has been left behind.

   b. Creates an **event log** entry to record the fact that cash has been left uncollected. The **event log** entry includes the **bank card information** (excluding the **PIN**), the amount of cash retrieved, and the amount of cash dispensed.

   c. Records a **transaction log** entry for the transaction including both the amount that should have been taken and the amount that was actually taken.

   d. Performs Handle Transaction Adjustments to balance the ATM and the Bank System.

   e. Turns off the alert.

3. The use case resumes the basic flow at {**Use Case Ends**}.

5.4.5 *Handle Running Out of Critical Resources*

At {**Use Case Ends**} if the system does not have the capacity to log any more events or log any more transactions, then the system

1. Performs Service Shutdown to shutdown all **service options** and end the use case

5.4.6 *Handle Running Out of Cash*

At {**Use Case Ends**} if the system has no more funds to dispense,

1. The system removes Withdraw Cash from the list of available **service options**.
2. The system creates an **event log** entry to record the fact that the ATM has run out of cash.
3. The system sends the **event log** entry to the Service Administrator and the Bank System to inform them that the ATM is no longer able to dispense cash.
4. The use case resumes from the place where it was interrupted.

5.4.7 *Handle Security Breaches*

At any time when an attempt to gain physical access to the currency dispenser is detected,

1. The system starts to video the Customer.
2. The system creates an **event log** entry to record the fact that the ATM has detected an attack.
3. The system sends the **event log** entry to the Security Administrator, the Service Administrator, and the Bank System to inform them that the ATM is being attacked.
4. If the card has not yet been ejected, the card is confiscated.
5. If a withdrawal has been approved but the cash has not yet been dispensed, the transaction is canceled.
6. The system creates an **event log** entry to record the actions taken. The **event log** entry includes the **bank card information** (excluding the **PIN**).
7. The system sends the **event log** entry to the Security Administrator, the Service Administrator, and the Bank System to inform them what action has been taken.
8. If a transaction was canceled, the system
   a. Records a **transaction log** entry for the transaction including both the amount that should have been dispensed and the amount that was actually dispensed

    b. Performs Handle Transaction Adjustments to balance the ATM and the Bank System

9. The Customer is informed that the card has been confiscated and the transaction ended.
10. The system saves the video recording with the **session ID**.
11. The use case resumes the basic flow at {**Use Case Ends**}.

5.4.8 Handle the Customer Quitting the Session

At any time if the Customer elects to quit the session,

{Tidy Up the Session}

1. The system stops the current transaction.
2. If the Customer quits after a withdrawal has been authorized but before the cash has been dispensed, then the system
    a. Records a **transaction log** entry for the transaction including both the amount that should have been dispensed and the amount that was actually dispensed
    b. Performs Handle Transaction Adjustments to balance the ATM and the Bank System

{Eject Card}

3. The system ejects the Customer's **bank card**.
4. The Customer takes the **bank card** from the machine.
5. The use case resumes the basic flow at {**Use Case Ends**}.

5.4.9 Handle the Customer Stopping Responding

At any time where a response from the Customer is requested, if no response is made within 30 seconds (this does not include removing the card or the cash when it is dispensed as each is explicitly handled by its own flows),

1. The system beeps to alert the Customer.
2. If there is still no reply within a minute of the alert being sounded, then the system
    a. Confiscates the card.
    b. Creates an **event log** entry to record that the card has been confiscated. The **event log** entry includes the **bank card information** (excluding the **PIN**).
    c. Sends the **event log** entry to the Bank System to inform the Customer's bank that the card has been confiscated.
    d. If the event happens after a withdrawal has been authorized but before the cash has been dispensed, then the system

      I. Records a **transaction log** entry for the transaction including both the amount that should have been dispensed and the amount that was actually dispensed

      II. Performs Handle Transaction Adjustments to balance the ATM and the Bank System

      III. Turns off the alert

   3. The use case resumes the basic flow at {**Use Case Ends**}.

5.4.10 *Handle Video Recording Failure*

At any point in the flow of events where video is being recorded, if the video capture device fails or there is insufficient storage for the video images,

1. The system creates an **event log** entry to record the failure of the video system. The **event log** entry includes the type of failure (video storage full or video device failure).

2. The system sends the **event log** entry to the Service Administrator and the Bank System to inform them that the video system has failed.

3. The system turns off the video device to await the maintenance engineer. There is no need to disable the ATM as all functions can continue without the video being active.

4. The use case resumes from the point that the failure was detected.

5.4.11 *Handle Transaction Log Failure*

At any point in the flow of events where a **transaction log** is being recorded, if the log cannot be stored,

1. The system creates an **event log** entry to record the fact that **transaction log** has failed. The **event log** entry includes the current **bank card information** (excluding the **PIN**).

2. The system sends the **event log** entry to the Bank System and the Service Administrator to inform them that the transaction log is out of order.

3. If the event happens after a withdrawal has been authorized but before the cash has been dispensed, then the system

    a. Sends the **transaction log** entry to the Bank System to cancel the withdrawal.

    b. Creates an **event log** entry to record the fact that the transaction has been canceled. The **event log** entry includes the current **bank card information** (excluding the **PIN**), the fact that the transaction was a withdrawal, and the amount of the withdrawal.

4. The system informs the Customer that because of a technical problem the request could not currently be fulfilled.

{Eject Card}

5. The system ejects the Customer's **bank card**.
6. The Customer takes the **bank card** from the machine.

{Shutdown All Customer Services}

7. Perform Service Shutdown to shutdown all Customer services and end the use case.

5.4.12 *Handle Event Log Failure*

If at any point in the use case the **event log** fails, the use case will continue to completion without logging any events. At the end of the use case, the customer services will be shutdown (see Handle Running Out of Critical Resources). For the details of how event log failures are handled by the system, see the Supplementary Specification.

5.5 *Handle the Bank System Stopping Responding*

At **{Validate the Withdrawal}** if the Bank System cannot be contacted or does not reply within the set **communication time out period**,

{Attempt to Reestablish Communications}

1. If the communications link has not failed, during this use case, more times than the **communication retry number**, then the system will attempt to contact the Bank System until it has completed the number of retry attempts indicated by the **communication retry number**.
2. If communication is reestablished, the flow is resumed at {**Validate the Withdrawal**}.

{Cancel the Withdrawal}

3. If there is still no response from the Bank System, the system creates an **event log** entry to record the failure of the communication link to the Bank System. The **event log** entry includes the type of failure.
4. The system sends the **event log** to the Service Administrator to inform it that communication with Bank System has been lost.
5. The system records a **transaction log** entry for the transaction including the fact that the withdrawal was not authorized because of loss of communications with the Bank System.

6. The system informs the Customer that the withdrawal has been rejected because the Bank System cannot be contacted.

{Eject Card}

7. The system ejects the Customer's **bank card**.
8. The Customer takes the **bank card** from the machine.

{Resume the Basic Flow}

9. The use case resumes the basic flow at **{Use Case Ends}**.

5.5.1 Handle Loss of Connection to the Security Administrator or the Service Administrator

If at any time the system attempts to contact the Security Administrator or the Service Administrator and fails, the use case will still continue to completion. For the details of how these generic communications failures are handled by the system, see the Supplementary Specification.

6. Subflows

6.1 Assess Funds on Hand

1. The system determines whether it has sufficient funds on hand to dispense the requested amount.
   a. The system checks to see if the total amount requested is greater than the amount on hand.
   b. The system checks to see if the requested amount can be dispensed with the denominations on hand. Note that it is possible to have sufficient funds in total and still be unable to dispense funds. Consider the case in which the Customer has requested $35 but the system only has $40 in the form of two $20 bills.
2. If there are not sufficient funds on hand, the system
   a. Informs the Customer that the amount requested is not available from the ATM.
   b. Offers the Customer a choice of the nearest available amount(s). If the amount requested was rejected because the correct denomination notes were not available, then both the nearest amounts below and above that requested are offered. If the amount requested was rejected because it was higher than the amount of funds available, then the nearest amount below that requested is offered.
3. The Customer selects an amount to be withdrawn.
4. The flow of events resumes at the next step.

6.2 Conduct Withdrawal

{Validate the Withdrawal}

1. The system supplies the Bank System with the **bank card** information, the amount of the requested withdrawal, the **ATM Session Identifier**, and the **transaction fee** and asks the Bank System to approve the withdrawal.
2. The Bank System responds with a **withdrawal acceptance** to approve the withdrawal.

{Log the Authorization}

3. The system records a **transaction log** entry for the authorized withdrawal including the information that the cash is still to be dispensed.

{Return to Performing Flow}

4. Resume at the next step.

6.3 Service Shutdown

1. The ATM displays the fact that it is out of order and that no **service options** are available.
2. The system turns off the card reader to prevent the insertion of any more cards.
3. The system creates an **event log** entry to record the fact that the system has switched off all customer services. The **event log** entry includes the time of the of service shutdown. If the recording of the event log fails, the system just ignores it.
4. If they are still contactable, the system sends the **event log** entry to the Service Administrator and the Bank System to inform them that the ATM is out of order. If they are not available, the system continues to attempt to inform them of the current state of the system.
5. The use case ends.

6.4 Handle Transaction Adjustments

1. The system calculates the adjustment required by the Banking System for this withdrawal by subtracting the amount of cash dispensed from the amount approved for withdrawal.
2. The system informs the Bank System of the amount of the adjustment also specifying the **bank card information** and the **ATM Session Identifier**.
3. The Bank System accepts or rejects the adjustment.

4. The system records a **transaction log entry** for the adjustment indicating whether the transaction was accepted or rejected and including the Bank System's response.
5. Resume at the next step.

7. Postconditions

- The ATM has returned the card and dispensed the cash to the Customer, and the withdrawal is registered on the Customer's account.
- The ATM has returned the card to the Customer, and no withdrawal is registered on the Customer's account.
- The ATM has returned the card, but has not supplied the amount of cash registered as withdrawn from the Customer's account; the discrepancy is registered on the ATM's logs.
- The ATM has kept the card, no withdrawal has registered on the Customer's account, and the Customer has been notified where to contact for more information.

8. Public Extension Points

None

9. Special Requirements

9.1 Reliable Cash Dispensing

The ATM shall dispense the correct amount of cash in at least 99 percent of cash withdrawals.

USE-CASE DESCRIPTION—*AUTHENTICATE CUSTOMER*

1. Brief Description

This use case is included by other use cases.[3] It is used to authenticate that the individual using the ATM (the Customer) is authorized to use the inserted **bank card** and that the **account** associated with the **bank card** is active.

---

[3] In the *ACME Super ATM* use-case model, the *Authenticate Customer* use case is included in 4 of the other use cases: *Withdraw Cash, Deposit Funds, Transfer Funds,* and *Manage Account.* As shown in Chapter 9, it started out as a subflow in the *Withdraw Cash* use case but was turned into an included use case as the other use cases were written.

2. Use-Case Diagram

See Figure A-5.

Figure A-5 Use-case diagram for customer authentication

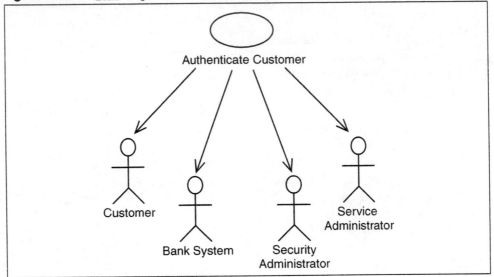

2. Preconditions

- The **bank card** has been inserted into the ATM.
- The **bank card** information has been read successfully.
- A **Customer** is in dialogue with the including use case.
- The **ATM Session ID** has been created.

3. Basic Flow

{Validate Card Information}

1. The system sends the **bank card information** to the **Bank System** to confirm that the **bank card** and its associated **account** are active, that the card has not been reported stolen, and that the **bank card** information (including the **PIN**) read from the **bank card** is valid.
2. The system also sends the **ATM ID** and the **ATM session identifier** to the Bank System along with the **bank card** information.
3. The Bank System acknowledges that the **bank card** information is valid and that the card can be used.

{Validate User Identity}

4. The system prompts the Customer for the **PIN**.
5. The Customer enters the **PIN**.

6. The system checks that the entered **PIN** is identical to the PIN read from the **bank card**.
{**PIN Validated**}

{**Use Case Ends**}

7. Resume the including use case at the next step.

5. Alternative Flows

5.1 Handle No Communications With the Bank System

At {**Validate Card Information**} if the Bank System cannot be contacted or does not reply within the set **communication time-out period**,

1. And if the communications link has failed more times than the **communication retry number,** then the authentication attempt is abandoned and basic flow is resumed at {**Use Case Ends**}.

2. The system will attempt to contact the Bank System until it has completed the number of retry attempts indicated by the **communication retry number**.

3. If communications are reestablished, the basic flow is resumed at {**Validate Card Information**}.

4. If there is still no response from the Bank System, the system creates an **event log** entry to record the failure of the communications link to the Bank System. The **event log** entry includes the type of failure.

5. The system sends the **event log** to the **Service Administrator** to inform it that communication with Bank System has been lost.

6. Resume the basic flow at {**Use Case Ends**}.

5.2 Handle No Communications With the Customer's Bank

At {**Validate Card Information**} if the Bank System reports that the **Customer's Bank** cannot be contacted,

1. The system creates an **event log** entry to record the fact that the **Customer's Bank** was unavailable. The **event log** entry includes the **bank card information** (excluding the **PIN**).

2. The system informs the Customer that communication with the Bank is not possible and that he or she should try again later.

3. Resume the basic flow at {**Use Case Ends**}.

5.3 Handle Inactive Card or Account

At {**Validate Card Information**} if the **Customer's Bank** reports that the card or its associated **account** are inactive,

1. The system creates an **event log** entry to record the fact that the Customer's account was inactive. The **event log** entry includes the **bank card information** (excluding the **PIN**).
2. The system informs the Customer that the account associated with the card is not active and that he or she should contact the Bank for more information.
3. Resume the basic flow at {**Use Case Ends**}.

5.4 Handle Stolen Bank Card

At {**Validate Card Information**} if the Bank System reports that the card has been stolen:

1. The system
   a. Confiscates the card.
   b. Captures a 10-second video image of the Customer.
   c. Creates an **event log** entry to record the fact that a stolen card has been used. The **event log** entry includes the video image and the current **bank card information** (excluding the **PIN**).
   d. Sends the **event log** entry to the Security Administrator, the Bank System, and the Service Administrator to inform them that a stolen card is being used.
   e. Continues to video the Customer.
2. The system delays for 5 minutes indicating that the system is busy (the system should try to keep the Customer at the machine for as long as possible).
3. After the delay the system reports to the Customer that
   a. The card has been confiscated.
   b. He or she should contact the bank with any questions.
4. The system stops the video and creates an **event log** entry to store the captured images. The **event log** entry includes the video image and the current **bank card information** (excluding the **PIN**).
5. Resume the basic flow at {**Use Case Ends**}.

5.5 Handle Invalid Bank Card Information

At {**Validate Card Information**} if the Bank System reports that the **bank card information** is not valid,

1. The system
   a. Captures a 10-second video image of the Customer.
   b. Creates an **event log** entry to record the fact that the card information was invalid. The **event log** entry includes the video image and the current **bank card information** (excluding the **PIN**).

    c. Sends the **event log** entry to the Security Administrator, the Bank System, and the Service Administrator to inform them that a card with invalid **bank card information** is being used.

2. The system reports to the Customer that

    a. The card could not be read.

    b. He or she should contact the bank with any questions.

3. Resume the basic flow at {**Use Case Ends**}.

5.6 Handle Correct PIN Not Entered

At {**PIN Validated**} if the **PIN** has not been entered correctly,

1. The system informs the Customer that the **PIN** has been entered incorrectly.

2. If the Customer has had fewer than 3 attempts at entering the **PIN**, the system informs the Customer that he or she should have another attempt.

3. If this is the Customer's third attempt, the system

    a. Confiscates the card.

    b. Captures a 10-second video image of the Customer.

    c. Creates an **event log** entry to record the fact that the Customer failed to get the PIN number correct in 3 attempts. The **event log** entry includes the video image and the current **bank card information** (excluding the **PIN**).

    d. Sends the **event log** entry to the Bank System and the Service Administrator to inform them that a Customer's **bank card** was confiscated because of the Customer's failure to enter the **PIN** correctly.

4. The system reports to the Customer that

    a. The card has been confiscated because the **PIN** number was not entered correctly.

    b. He or she should contact the **Service Organization** to retrieve the card.

    c. He or she should contact the bank with any questions.

5. Resume the basic flow at {**Use Case Ends**}.

6. Postconditions

- The Customer has been authorized to use the card.
- The Customer has been barred from using the card, and the card has been confiscated.
- The Customer has been barred from using the card, and the card has not been confiscated.

7. Public Extension Points

None.

8. Special Requirements

None.

SUPPORTING GLOSSARY TERMS

This section presents a condensed extract from the glossary that supports the *ACME Super ATM* use-case model. The definitions are summarized from the full glossary and domain model that support the *ACME Super ATM* use-case model, focusing just on those elements of the definitions required to understand the two examples presented.

Term	Description	Additional Information
Account	An obligation on the part of the financial institution to pay the Customer, on demand and adhering to the terms of the account agreement, a defined sum of money.	Accounts can be either • Active—available to support transactions • Inactive—unavailable for transactions
ATM ID/ATM Identifier	Each ATM machine has a unique identification code. This is the machine's serial number.	This allows the ATM to be uniquely identified within the ATM network.
ATM Session Identifier	A unique identifier for the current Customer session—includes the ATM Identifier.	This is used to identify the ATM and the ATM session in all dialogues with external systems. This allows Bank Systems and others to track the conversations with the ATM and compare the various logs and audits.

Term	Description	Additional Information
Bank Card	A physical identification device imprinted with magnetic information pertaining to the issuing financial institution (**institution interbank number**), the Customer (their **Customer number** with the issuing financial institution), a **Personal Information Number (PIN)** chosen by the Customer at the time the card was issued, and a **card number**.	
Bank Card Information	The standard information held on a **bank card**.	
Card Number	The unique 20-character code associated with the card that allows the Bank System to identify the account.	
Communication Retry Number	The number of times that the system will attempt to contact the Bank System after a failure.	One of the system's configurable parameters.
Communication Time-out Period	The period of time that the system will wait for a response from the Bank System.	One of the system's configurable parameters.
Confiscated Cards	The set of **bank cards** the system has retained either deliberately or because of errors.	
Customer	A person who holds accounts at a financial institution that is a member of the ATM interbank network and who possesses a **bank card**.	
Customer Number	The bank system's 20-character, alpha numeric Customer identification number. Unique within the bank.	ACME Super ATM handles Customer numbers up to 20 characters in length, although most banks only use 16 character numbers.

(continued)

Term	Description	Additional Information
Customer's Bank	The **financial institution** that issued the **bank card** and at which the **Customer** has an **account**. The Customer's bank is contacted by way of the Bank System. The **financial institution** is identified via by **institution interbank number**.	Setting which banks are supported is one of the Super ATM's configuration options.
Event Log	A permanent record used to record any noteworthy events within the ATM. The log contains at least the following information for each event: • The **ATM Session ID** • The date and time of the event • The nature of the event If the event occurs during a Customer session: • The current **bank card** information (excluding the **PIN**) • An optional video clip of the Customer	
Financial Institution	An issuer of **bank cards** and maintainer of **accounts**.	
Institution Interbank Number	A standard code number that uniquely identifies a financial institution. Eight-character, alpha numeric string.	Used to identify the owning bank on a **bank card**.
Personal Identification Number (PIN)	An identification number chosen by the **Customer** used in conjunction with the **bank card** for security purposes. The PIN can be up to 6 digits in length and must not include any repeated digits. A PIN is used to verify the identity of the Customer by asking the Customer to reenter the PIN; when the Customer enters the same number as the PIN stored on the card, the Customer's identity is considered authenticated.	

Term	Description	Additional Information
Service Option	A customer service available from the ATM. Services available from the Super ATM include • Cash Withdrawal • Deposit Funds • Transfer Funds • Manage Account	The current list of services available is configurable and reflects the state of the ATM (i.e., if there is no cash available in the machine, the Cash Withdrawal service will be unavailable).
Service Organization	The organization that services the ATM, refilling it with cash and keeping it in working order.	
Smallest Denomination Note Held	The smallest denomination of note the ATM currently contains.	
Standard Withdrawal Amount	Standard amounts offered for Customers to withdraw.	One of the system's configurable parameters.
Transaction Fee	The amount charged by the owner of the ATM for undertaking the transaction.	
Transaction Log	A permanent record used to guard against data loss in the event of a subsequent system failure. The log contains the following information for each transaction: • The date and time of the transaction • The **ATM Session ID** • The bank card details (excluding the **PIN**) • The type of transaction • The amount of the transaction • Whether the transaction was accepted or rejected • The bank system's response For a withdrawal, the log also shows • The amount dispensed • Whether the amount has been dispensed yet	

(continued)

Term	Description	Additional Information
Withdrawal Acceptance	The message sent by the Bank System to accept a request for the withdrawal of funds from an account.	
Withdrawal Limit	The maximum amount of cash that can be withdrawn in one transaction.	One of the system's configurable parameters.
Withdrawal Receipt	Customer facing record of a withdrawal typically printed on request. It contains • The date and time of the withdrawal • The bank **card number** • The location of the ATM • The Customer's bank's **Institution Interbank Number**. • The amount of the withdrawal • The transaction fee charged • The **ATM Session ID** (for tracking within the interbank network)	
Withdrawal Rejection	The message sent by the Bank System to reject a request for the withdrawal of funds from an account. It indicates why the withdrawal was rejected particularly if it was because of a lack of funds.	

Glossary

activity diagram A diagram that shows the flow from activity to activity; activity diagrams can be used to illustrate a use case's flow of events.

actor An actor defines a role that a user can play when interacting with the system. A user can either be an individual or another system. Actors have a name and a brief description, and they are associated to the use cases with which they interact.

alternative flow Description of variant or optional behavior as part of a flow of events. Alternative flows are defined relative to the use case's basic flow.

ambassador user A user seconded to a project who is responsible for bringing knowledge of the user community into the project team and disseminating information from the team back to the rest of the users. The ambassador users act as the major source of requirements to the project.

basic flow The description of the normal, expected path through the use case (sometimes referred to as the "happy day" scenario). This is the path taken by most of the users most of the time; it is the most important part of the flow of events.

business actor An actor defined as part of a business use-case model. A business actor defines a role that something outside the business (for example an individual, a system, or another business) can play when interacting with the business.

business-object model An object model describing the workings of a business. Typically it will describe the realization of business use cases. The business object model acts as a formal type of domain model.

business use case A business use case describes how a business actor uses a business to achieve a goal and what the business does for the business actor to achieve that goal. It tells the story of how the business and its actors collaborate to deliver something of value for at least one of the actors.

business use-case model A model of a business (defined in terms of business use cases, business actors, and the associations between them) that describes the requirements of a business. A use-case model describing the functions of a business.

communicates relationship A relationship representing communication between actors and use cases.

constraint A restriction on the degree of freedom the developers have in providing a solution.

construction phase The third phase of the Unified Process dealing with "project execution" risk (building the project on time and within budget).

conversational use cases A tabular style of use-case description in which the interaction is limited to a single actor and the system.

customers The stakeholders who are paying for the development of the system or who are expected to purchase the system once it is complete.

declarative requirements A style of requirements-capture in which the requirements are captured as individual statements rather than in the narrative format of a use-case description.

device A mechanism that an actor uses to communicate with the system, such as a printer, keyboard, or microphone. These devices should not be confused with the actors that use them.

discipline A collection of related activities that are related to a software development process's major areas of concern. The disciplines in Rational Unified Process include Business Modeling, Requirements, Analysis & Design, Implementation, Test, Deployment, Configuration & Change Management, Project Management, and Environment.

domain An area of knowledge or activity characterized by a set of concepts and terminology understood by practitioners in that area. The domain in which a system executes can be documented using a glossary, domain model, or business-object model.

domain model A model that captures the most important types of objects in the context of the domain. The domain objects represent the entities that exist or events that transpire in the environment in which the system works. The domain model is a subset of the business-object model and a formalization of the glossary.

elaboration phase The second phase of the Unified Process dealing with technical and architectural risks.

essential use cases A style of use-case description focusing on the usability of the system. Essential use cases provide a pure external "black box" view of the system.

exceptional flow An alternative flow dealing with error conditions.

extend relationship A relationship indicating that the flow of events in one use case (the extending use case) is inserted into the flow of events of another use case (the extended use case). The extending use case adds behavior to the extended use case, typically under specific conditions. Extension is most frequently used to describe additional, optional behavior (such as that provided by an optional purchase).

extension point A labeled point within a flow of events. Typically these are used to indicate where additional extending or alternative behavior can be inserted.

feature A high-level statement of the services or qualities that the system must provide. A feature is a kind of shorthand for a whole set of behaviors, but it doesn't describe those behaviors.

flow A description of some full or partial path through a use-case description. There is always at least a basic flow, and there may be *alternative* flows.

flow of events The entire set of a use case's flows. The major property of a use-case description.

formal review A review conducted with the intent of approving a use case.

functional requirements Requirements that define the required behavior of a system.

generalize relationship (between actors) A relationship used to show that one or more actors are derived from a more general, typically more abstract actor. The main value in this is to show that some groups of actors share common responsibilities or common characteristics.

generalize relationship (between use cases) A relationship used to show that one or more use cases are derived from a more general, typically more abstract use case. Generalized use cases are typically used to describe the behavior of an application framework.

glossary A description of common terms used in the use-case descriptions. A simplified form of domain model.

inception phase The first phase of the Unified Process dealing with business risks (the vision for the project, the funding for the project, and issues dealing with the financial viability of the project).

include relationship A relationship indicating that the flow of events in one use case (the *included* use case) is included in the flow of events of another use case (the *including* use case). The include relationship is used to show that two or more use cases share some common flow of events.

informal review A review conducted with the intent of gathering feedback on the use case.

model A semantically closed abstraction of a subject system.

need A reflection of the business, personal, or operational problem (or opportunity) that must be addressed to justify consideration, purchase, or use of a new system.

nonfunctional requirements General qualities of the system or constraints to which the system must conform. Examples of nonfunctional requirements are requirements related to the usability, reliability, performance, and supportability of the system.

operating requirement A requirement the product places on the operating environment in which it will be deployed.

package A general-purpose mechanism for organizing model elements into groups.

postcondition A statement describing the state of the system when the use case ends. A use case may have zero or more postconditions.

precondition A statement of a condition that must exist in order for the use case to be performed. A use case may have zero or more preconditions.

primary actors The actors that represent the roles adopted by the key users and the sub-set of the users for whom the system provides value. The primary actors are those for whom the system is built; they are those to whom the system provides sufficient economic value to warrant its construction.

problem statement A solution-neutral summary of the stakeholders' shared understanding of the problem to be solved.

product position statement The "mission statement" for the system to be built. The product position statement is a vehicle for communicating a brief definition of the system to all stakeholders.

prototype An executable model of part of the system, often constructed to evaluate technical risk or to provide mock-ups of system behavior.

Rational Unified Process A software engineering process framework. An instance of the unified process.

requirement A condition or capability that a system must provide; it is either derived directly from user needs or stated in a contract, standard, specification, or other formally imposed document.

requirements management A systematic approach to eliciting, organizing, documenting, and managing the changing requirements of a software application.

RUP An acronym for the Rational Unified Process.

scenario An instance or specific occurrence of a use case or use cases.

secondary actors These are the actors that support the use cases provided by the system and those that support the system itself.

software architecture The set of significant decisions about the organization of a software system.

software development process A well-defined systematic process that turns requirements into software.

software requirement A specification of an externally observable behavior of the system; for example, inputs to the system, outputs from the system, functions of the system, attributes of the system, or attributes of the system environment.

special requirements Additional requirements that complement, and only make sense in the context of, individual use cases.

stakeholder An individual who is materially affected by the outcome of the system or the project(s) producing the system.

stakeholder need Synonym for need.

stakeholder representative A member of the stakeholder community directly involved in the steering, shaping, and scoping of the project. A stakeholder representative represents one or more stakeholder types.

stakeholder request Any request for the change, creation, update, or maintenance of a system received from a stakeholder.

stakeholder role The classification of a set of stakeholder representatives who share the same roles and responsibilities in relation to the project.

stakeholder type The classification of a set of stakeholders sharing the same characteristics and relationships with the system and/or the project that produces the system.

subflow A self-contained, labeled section of a flow. Subflows can be reused in many places within the flow of events where they are defined.

supplementary requirements Functional or nonfunctional requirements that are traceable to a particular use case are said to *supplement* the use-case description.

supplementary specification An artifact used to capture supplementary requirements and any other requirements that are not captured in the use-case model.

system A group of things or parts working together or connected in some way to form a whole. Typically used to refer to the subject of the use-case model: the product to be built.

traceability Traceability indicates that one thing is derived from or dependent on another thing. While knowing about what a thing was derived from is interesting, the main benefit of traceability comes from its role in assessing the completeness of a system in relation to its requirements and in determining the coverage of testing.

transition phase The fourth and final phase of the Unified Process dealing with risks related to rolling the product produced by the project out to its users.

Unified Process A software development process based on the Unified Modeling Language that is risk-driven, iterative, architecture-centric, and use-case driven.

use case Describes how an actor uses a system to achieve a goal and what the system does for the actor to achieve that goal. It tells the story of how the system and its actors collaborate to deliver something of value for at least one of the actors.

use-case description The textual description of a use case's properties; primarily the flow of events.

use-case diagram A visual depiction of one or more actors and use cases and their relationships. The diagram is intended to summarize but not fully describe the behavior of the system.

use-case model A model of a system (defined in terms of use cases, actors, and the associations between them) that describes the requirements of a system. The set of all actors and use cases describing a system.

use-case realization A description of how a system carries out a use case. Typically used to describe how the behavior of a use case is performed by a collaboration of elements within the system's design.

use-case storyboard A sequence of mock-up "screen shots" used to illustrate what the system does as the use case is performed.

user The set of people and other systems that will use the system, playing the roles defined by the actors. The users are one particular kind of stakeholder.

user type The classification of a set of users with similar skill sets and other characteristics who share the same roles and responsibilities within the system's environment.

vision A description of the essential purpose of a system.

Bibliography

Grady Booch, James Rumbaugh, and Ivar Jacobson, *The Unified Modeling Language User Guide*, 1999, Addison-Wesley.

Alistair Cockburn, "Goals and Use Cases," *Journal of Object-Oriented Programming*, 10(5), Sept., 1997.

Larry Constantine, "The Case for Essential Use Cases," *Object Magazine*, May 1997, SIGS Publications.

Larry L. Constantine and Lucy A. D. Lockwood, *Software for Use: A Practical Guide to the Models and Methods of Usage-Centered Design*, 1999, Addison-Wesley.

Steve Cooke and John Daniels, *Designing Object Systems: Object-Oriented Modeling with Syntropy*, 1994, Prentice Hall.

Alan M. Davis, *Software Requirements: Objects, Functions, and State*, 1993, Prentice Hall.

Donald C. Gause and Gerald M. Weinberg, *Exploring Requirements: Quality Before Design*, 1989, Dorset House Publishing.

Robert B. Grady, *Practical Software Metrics for Project Management and Process Improvement*, 1992, Prentice Hall.

Ivar Jacobson, Grady Booch, and James Rumbaugh, *The Unified Software Development Process*, 1999, Addison-Wesley Longman.

Ivar Jacobson, Magnus Christerson, Patrik Jonsson, and Gunnar Overgaard, *Object-Oriented Software Engineering: A Use-Case Driven Approach*, 1992, ACM Press.

Ivar Jacobson, Maria Ericsson, and Agneta Jacobson, *The Object Advantage*, 1995, ACM Press.

Cem Kaner, James Bach, and Bret Pettichord, *Lessons Learned in Software Testing*, 2001, John Wiley & Sons.

Philippe Kruchten, *The Rational Unified Process: An Introduction,* 2nd Edition, 2000, Addison-Wesley.

Craig Larman, *Applying UML Patterns: An Introduction to Object-Oriented Analysis and Design and the Unified Process,* 2nd Edition, 2001, Prentice Hall.

Dean Leffingwell and Don Widrig, *Managing Software Requirements: A Unified Approach,* 2000, Addison-Wesley.

Geoffrey A. Moore, *Crossing the Chasm: Marketing and Selling Technology Products to Mainstream Customers,* 1991, Harper Collins.

Donald Norman, *The Design of Everyday Things,* 1990, Reissue Edition March 1990, Currency/Doubleday.

Object Management Group, *Unified Modeling Language,* accessed 2002, www.omg.org/uml.

Rational Software, *Rational Unified Process Version 2002.05.00,* 2002, Rational Software.

Doug Rosenberg and Kendall Scott, *Use Case Driven Object Modeling with UML: A Practical Approach,* 1999, Addison-Wesley.

Walker Royce, *Software Project Management: A Unified Framework,* 1998, Addison-Wesley Longman.

James Rumbaugh, Ivar Jacobson, and Grady Booch, *The Unified Modeling Language Reference Manual,* 1999, Addison-Wesley.

Antoine De Saint-Exupery, *Wind, Sand and Stars,* 1968, Harcourt Brace Jovanovich.

Software Engineering Institute, http://www.sei.cmu.edu/domain-engineering/context_diag.html.

Jennifer Stapleton, *Dynamic Systems Development Methodology,* 1997, Addison-Wesley Longman.

William Strunk Jr & E.B. White, *The Elements of Style,* 4th Edition, 2000, Allyn & Bacon Professional.

William Collins Sons & Co. Ltd, *Collins Modern English Dictionary,* 1984.

Rebecca Wirfs-Brock, "Designing Scenarios: Making the Case for a Use Case Framework," *Smalltalk Report,* Nov.-Dec., 1993, SIGS Publications.

Index

Rational Minds and Addison-Wesley Authors—
What a Combination!

DEVELOPING ENTERPRISE JAVA APPLICATIONS WITH J2EE AND UML

0-201-73829-5

USE CASE MODELING

0-201-70913-9

OBJECT-ORIENTED ANALYSIS AND DESIGN WITH APPLICATIONS

0-8053-5340-2

OBJECT SOLUTIONS MANAGING THE OBJECT-ORIENTED PROJECT

0-8053-0594-7

THE UNIFIED MODELING LANGUAGE USER GUIDE

0-201-57168-4

Software Leadership

0-201-70044-1

BUILDING WEB APPLICATIONS WITH UML SECOND EDITION

0-201-73038-3

BUILDING J2EE APPLICATIONS WITH THE RATIONAL UNIFIED PROCESS

0-201-79166-8

THE OBJECT ADVANTAGE

0-201-42289-1

Object-Oriented Software Engineering A Use Case Driven Approach

0-201-54435-0

SOFTWARE REUSE Architecture, Process and Organization for Business Success

0-201-92476-5

THE UNIFIED SOFTWARE DEVELOPMENT PROCESS

0-201-57169-2

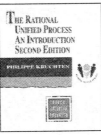
THE RATIONAL UNIFIED PROCESS AN INTRODUCTION SECOND EDITION

0-201-70710-1

MANAGING SOFTWARE REQUIREMENTS A UNIFIED APPROACH

0-201-61593-2

UML FOR DATABASE DESIGN

0-201-72163-5

VISUAL MODELING WITH RATIONAL ROSE 2002 AND UML

0-201-72932-6

SOFTWARE PROJECT MANAGEMENT A UNIFIED FRAMEWORK

0-201-30958-0

THE UNIFIED MODELING LANGUAGE REFERENCE MANUAL

0-201-30998-X

SOFTWARE CONFIGURATION MANAGEMENT STRATEGIES AND RATIONAL CLEARCASE® A PRACTICAL INTRODUCTION

0-201-60478-7

For more information on these books by Rational Software Corporation employees, please go to **www.awprofessional.com**